The Puppet Masters

The Puppet Masters

How the Corrupt Use Legal
Structures to Hide Stolen Assets
and What to Do About It

Emile van der Does de Willebois
Emily M. Halter
Robert A. Harrison
Ji Won Park
J. C. Sharman

Stolen Asset Recovery Initiative

The World Bank • UNODC

© 2011 The International Bank for Reconstruction and Development / The World Bank
1818 H Street NW
Washington DC 20433
Telephone: 202-473-1000
Internet: www.worldbank.org

1 2 3 4 14 13 12 11

This volume is a product of the staff of the International Bank for Reconstruction and Development / The World Bank. The findings, interpretations, and conclusions expressed in this volume do not necessarily reflect the views of the Executive Directors of The World Bank or the governments they represent.

The World Bank does not guarantee the accuracy of the data included in this work. The boundaries, colors, denominations, and other information shown on any map in this work do not imply any judgement on the part of The World Bank concerning the legal status of any territory or the endorsement or acceptance of such boundaries.

ISBN: 978-0-8213-8894-5
eISBN: 978-0-8213-8896-7
DOI: 10.1596/978-0-8213-8894-5

Cover design: 1127 Graphic Design

Library of Congress Cataloging-in-Publication Data has been requested

Contents

Boxes

Figures

Tables

Foreword

Corruption is estimated to be at least a $40 billion dollar a year business. Every day, funds destined for schools, healthcare, and infrastructure in the world's most fragile economies are siphoned off and stashed away in the world's financial centers and tax havens.

Corruption, like a disease, is eating away at the foundation of people's faith in government. It undermines the stability and security of nations. So it is a development challenge in more ways than one: it directly affects development assistance, but it also undermines the preconditions for growth and equity.

We need mobilization at the highest level so that corruption is tackled effectively.

This report, *The Puppet Masters*, deals with the corporate and financial structures that form the building blocks of hidden money trails. In particular, it focuses on the ease with which corrupt actors hide their interests behind a corporate veil and the difficulties investigators face in trying to lift that veil.

It serves as a powerful reminder that recovering the proceeds of corruption is a collective responsibility that involves both the public and private sector. Law enforcement and prosecution cannot go after stolen assets, confiscate and then return them if they are hidden behind the corporate veil. All financial centers and developed countries have committed, through the UN Convention against Corruption and international anti-money laundering and countering the financing of terrorism standards, to improving the transparency of legal entities and other arrangements.

This StAR report provides evidence of how far we still have to go to make these commitments a reality. Narrowing the gap between stated commitments and practice on the ground has a direct impact on actual recovery of assets.

As recent history shows, these issues are not hypothetical, they are real. Under the leadership of President Obasanjo, I initiated Nigeria's efforts to recover stolen assets. I know firsthand from that experience how corrupt officials hid their assets behind innocent sounding corporations and trusts.

Similarly, this report is firmly rooted in reality. It is based on documentary research, interviews with corporate registries, bankers, investigators, and other experts who confront this issue every day in the course of their work, and a "mystery shopping" exercise with relevant corporate service providers in multiple jurisdictions. The study highlights the weaknesses in the system that leave these structures open to manipulation and abuse. It provides a series of practical and balanced recommendations on how these weaknesses can be addressed.

At a time when the international community is stepping up its efforts to fight corruption and underlining the need for financial transparency, this report comes as a welcome contribution. I hope that policy makers, practitioners, and civil society will make good use of this analysis.

The popular uprisings in North Africa are a powerful reminder that integrity is a condition for legitimacy. The fact that many financial centers immediately began work to return assets allegedly stolen by former leaders is a testimony to how stolen assets have become both a symbol of abuse and a rallying point in the calls for justice that are echoing in the international community and among people in the streets.

Let's work together to respond to their call.

Dr. Ngozi Okonjo-Iweala,
Coordinating Minister of Economy and Minister of Finance, Nigeria
former Managing Director, World Bank

Acknowledgments

This study would not have been possible without the participation, guidance, and insights of many individuals, agencies, and organizations around the world who gave generously of their expertise and time.

This publication was written by Emile van der Does de Willebois (team leader, Financial Market Integrity/Transparency and Accountability, World Bank), Professor J. C. Sharman (Griffiths University, Australia), Emily M. Halter (project consultant), Robert A. Harrison (project consultant), and Ji Won Park (project consultant).

The team is especially grateful to Jean Pesme (Coordinator, Stolen Asset Recovery [StAR] Initiative, and Manager, Financial Market Integrity/Transparency and Accountability, World Bank) and Adrian Fozzard (former Coordinator, StAR Initiative) for their ongoing support and guidance of this project. We also greatly appreciated the tireless efforts by Larissa A. Gray (Senior Financial Sector Specialist, Financial Market Integrity/Transparency and Accountability) in providing us with her counsel and incisive editing and tackling of other tasks, to help us reach the finish line.

The team benefited immensely from the peer review process, which was cochaired by Jean Pesme and Adrian Fozzard. The peer reviewers were Elise J. Bean (Staff Director and Chief Counsel, U.S. Senate Permanent Subcommittee on Investigations), Frank Anthony Fariello (Legal Department, World Bank), Agustin Flah (Legal Department, World Bank), Yves Klein (Partner, Monfrini Crettol & Partners), Andrei Mikhnev (*Doing Business*, World Bank), Robert Palmer (Global Witness, United Kingdom), Colin Powell (former Chairman, Jersey Financial Services Commission), Chip Poncy (Director, Office of Strategic Policy for Terrorist Financing and Financial Crimes, U.S. Department of the Treasury), Ric Power (United Nations Office on Drugs and Crime), and Simon Whitfield (Anti-Corruption Team, United Kingdom Department for International Development).

We would also like to gratefully acknowledge the following individuals (as well as those unnamed individuals who preferred to remain anonymous) who shared with us their knowledge, insights, and experiences. These individuals represented a variety of backgrounds and included law enforcement officials, prosecutors, compliance officers from financial institutions, private investigators and attorneys, and academics (please note:

country affiliation does not mean that this person's participation necessarily represented the views of the designated country).

For the Registry Project, Dobromir Christow, Andrei Mikhnev, and Laura Pop; as well as Lanston Connor and the Registrar of Companies of Anguilla; Kim Holmes and the Australian Securities and Investments Commission; Gian C. Gandhi and the Belize Companies and Corporate Affairs Registry; Cindy Jefferson-Bulgin and the General Registry of the Cayman Islands; Christos Nicolaou and the Department of Registrar of Companies and Official Receiver of Cyprus; Rick Geisenberger and the Delaware Department of State Division of Corporations; Natella Safar Ali and the Registrar of Companies of the Dubai International Financial Centre; Karon Beyer and the Florida Department of State Division of Corporations; Jennifer C. Wiley and the Companies House of Gibraltar; Helen Proudlove-Gains and the Guernsey Registry; Ivy Poon and the Companies Registry of Hong Kong SAR, China; Andrew Le Brun, Barry Faudemer, Debbie Sebire, and the Jersey Financial Services Commission; Bernd Hammermann and the Office of Land and Public Registration of Liechtenstein; Yves Gonner, Helene Massard, and the Register of Commerce and Companies of Luxembourg; Zoong Chin Tin Loi and the Companies Division of the Ministry of Finance and Economic Development of Mauritius; Dilkusheen Jayawardene, Amanda Buttigieg, and the Companies and Personal Property Security Branch of the Ministry of Government Services of Ontario; K. Latha and the Accounting and Corporate Regulatory Authority of Singapore; Christa Klokow and the Companies and Intellectual Property Commission (formerly CIPRO) of South Africa; Lester Martyr and the Registry of International Business Companies Pinnacle of St. Lucia; Karen Jackson and the International Financial Services Authority of St. Vincent and the Grenadines; Adrian Tagmann, the Federal Office of Justice, and the commercial registers of Switzerland; John James and the Financial Services Commission of Turks and Caicos Islands; and Gail Richards and the Companies House of the United Kingdom; and Rachelle Boyle (Organisation for Economic Co-operation and Development).

For the Bankers Project, Gemma Aiolfi (Switzerland), Todd Bancroft (Hong Kong SAR, China), Brian Conway (Jersey), Jean-Marc Futterknecht (Switzerland), Shamsuddin Ali Hussin (Malaysia), Oliver Jost (Germany), Keen Yew Kwan (Malaysia), Vincent Li (Hong Kong SAR, China), Frank Meister (United States), Amanda Parmenter (United Kingdom), Paul Shevlin (Jersey), Katy Smith (Australia), Vikas Tandon (India), and Susan Wright (United Kingdom).

For the Investigators Project, Emmanuel Akomaye (Nigeria), Victor Charles Banda (Malawi), Maurice Barrett (Jamaica), Robert Broekhuijsen (The Netherlands), Ruben Carranza (The Philippines), Nikoloz Chinkorashvili (Georgia), Greg Christie (Jamaica), Martin Comley (United Kingdom), Edward H. Davis, Jr. (United States), Yara Esquivel (Integrity Vice Presidency, World Bank), Andre Luis Felicio (Brazil), Financial Intelligence Office of the Macau Special Administrative Region of China, Leonardo Costa Franco (Uruguay), Robin Gazawi (United States), Anibal Gutierrez (International Commission against Impunity in Guatemala), Gene Hann (Canada), Tom Hansen (Canada),

Latoya Harris (Jamaica), Edward Hosea (Tanzania), Guillermo Jorge (Argentina), Adam S. Kaufmann (United States), Martin S. Kenney (British Virgin Islands), Bernd H. Klose (Germany), Arnoldo B. Lacayo (United States), Douglas A. Leff (United States), Robert Lindquist (Canada, United States), Silvio Antonio Marques (Brazil), Peter D. Maynard (Bahamas), Keith McCarthy (United Kingdom), Deborah Morrisey (United States), D. C. Page (United States), Abdul Razak bin Hamzah (Malaysia), Juan G. Ronderos (formerly Integrity Vice Presidency, World Bank; currently, Inter-American Development Bank), Wellington Cabral Saraiva (Brazil), Jean-Bernard Schmid (Switzerland), Maria Schnebli (Switzerland), Galvin Shiu (Hong Kong SAR, China), Craig Sorrie (Canada), Arnold Tenusaar (Estonia), Richard Weber (United States), Joseph J. Wielebinski (United States), and Gary Wilson (British Virgin Islands).

Richard Chalmers (The Financial Services Authority, United Kingdom), Professor Rose-Marie Belle Antoine (Barbados), and Professor Richard K. Gordon (United States) also provided valuable guidance.

The World Bank Law Library and the U.S. Law Library of Congress provided invaluable research assistance and support in the collection of legal documents from around the world.

A special thanks also to Allison Battiste, Jan van Koningsveld, Frederick Lah, Nicolas G. Troncoso, and Matteo Vaccani, who worked on the study in its early stages and to Thelma Ayamel, Michael Geller, Maria Orellano, and Miguel Nicolas de la Riva for their support in the administration of the project.

Abbreviations

AML	Anti–Money Laundering
BO	Beneficial Owner
CAC	Client Acceptance Committee
CDD	Customer Due Diligence
CFATF	Caribbean Financial Action Task Force
CFT	Combating the Financing of Terrorism
CV	corporate vehicle
DNFBP	Designated Non-Financial Businesses and Professions
ECJ	European Court of Justice
EIN	Employer Identification Number
FARA	Foreign Agents Registration Act
FATF	Financial Action Task Force on Money Laundering
FCPA	Foreign Corrupt Practices Act
FIU	Financial Intelligence Unit
IBC	International Business Corporation
IC	Introducer Certificate
IRS	Internal Revenue Service (United States)
ITA	International Trust Act
KYC	Know Your Customer
LLC	Limited Liability Company
LP	Limited Partnership
LLP	Limited Liability Partnership
MLA	mutual legal assistance
OECD	Organisation for Economic Co-operation and Development
OFC	Offshore Financial Center
PEP	Politically Exposed Person
TCSP	Trust and Company Service Providers
TIEA	Tax Information Exchange Act
UNCAC	United Nations Convention against Corruption
UNODC	United Nations Office on Drugs and Crime
VISTA	British Virgin Islands Special Trust Act

Executive Summary

- In 2002, the government of Kenya invited bids to replace its passport printing system. Despite receiving a bid for €6 million from a French firm, the Kenyan government signed a contract for five times that amount (€31.89 million) with Anglo-Leasing and Finance Ltd., an unknown U.K. shell company, whose registered address was a post office box in Liverpool. The Kenyan government's decision was taken despite the fact that Anglo-Leasing proposed to subcontract the actual work to the French company. Material leaked to the press by whistle-blowers suggested that corrupt senior politicians planned to pocket the excess funds from the deal. Attempts to investigate these allegations were frustrated, however, when it proved impossible to find out who really controlled Anglo-Leasing.

- In March 2010, Daimler AG and three of its subsidiaries resolved charges related to a Foreign Corrupt Practices Act (FCPA) investigation in the U.S. In part, Daimler AG's Russian subsidiary, DaimlerChrysler Automotive Russia SAO (DCAR), which is now known as Mercedes-Benz Russia SAO, pleaded guilty to one count of conspiracy to bribe foreign officials and one count of bribery of foreign officials. The Statement of Facts agreed to by Daimler as part of the Deferred Prosecution Agreement in US v. Daimler AG noted that "DCAR and DAIMLER made over €3 million [US$4,057,500] in improper payments to Russian government officials employed at their Russian governmental customers, their designees or third-party shell companies that provided no legitimate services to DAIMLER or DCAR with the understanding that the funds would be passed on, in whole or in part, to Russian government officials." The Statement of Facts details 25 sets of improper payments involving (in addition to cash payments) payments to bank accounts held in Latvia, Switzerland, the United States and unnamed jurisdictions; the accounts were held in the name of some of the 27 involved companies (16 named and 11 unnamed) registered or having addresses in 7 different jurisdictions: the Bahamas; Costa Rica; Cyprus; Ireland; Seychelles; United Kingdom; and in United States in California, Delaware and Florida.

A Significant Challenge

Both the Anglo-Leasing and Daimler AG scandals described above graphically illustrate the central role played by corporate vehicles (companies, trusts, foundations, and others) in concealing the abuse of public trust for private financial gain. In neither case has any individual or company been convicted of a corruption offense, despite the millions—even billions—of dollars of illicit payments allegedly involved.

Research carried out for this report shows that these cases of "grand" (that is, large-scale) corruption are not untypical. Such cases can be found around the world, in both industrial and developing countries, whether as the place that the proceeds originate from or as the place they eventually end up. A review of some 150 cases carried out as part of this study showed that they shared a number of common characteristics. In the vast majority of them,

- a corporate vehicle was misused to hide the money trail;
- the corporate vehicle in question was a company or corporation;
- the proceeds and instruments of corruption consisted of funds in a bank account; and
- in cases where the ownership information was available, the corporate vehicle in question was established or managed by a professional intermediary.

This report casts light on how corporate vehicles are misused to conceal the proceeds of grand corruption. It describes how providers of legal, financial and administrative (management) services—including banks, financial institutions, lawyers, accountants, and other professionals that are known as trust and company service providers (TCSPs)—can be employed to facilitate such schemes. While this report focuses on the use of front companies and the abuse of corporate opacity to conceal corruption, the weaknesses highlighted in this report are not specific to corruption. There is evidence of similar misuse of legal entities, legal arrangements as well as charities[1] in the context of other criminal and illicit behaviors, including escaping international sanctions and the funding of terrorist organizations.

Puppet Masters aims to support countries' efforts to meet international standards that were developed in recent years to help combat financial crime, including grand corruption, money laundering and terrorist financing. The two key standard-setting agreements are the United Nations Convention against Corruption (UNCAC), adopted in 2003 and ratified by 100 countries (as of October 2011), and the 2003 recommendations of the Financial Action Task Force (FATF), endorsed by more than 170 jurisdictions. As highlighted by these two documents, there is international consensus on the need to improve the transparency of legal persons and arrangements, and many jurisdictions have already taken steps in that direction.

As the study shows, however, significant hurdles to implementing these standards remain. To support countries as they work to overcome those challenges, the report offers recommendations on how to ensure adequate transparency of corporate vehicles.

There is no lack of theoretical discussion on transparency in the ownership and control of companies, legal arrangements and foundations. Taking a more practical approach, this report draws on an unprecedented depth and breadth of evidence to show:

- where the challenges of the misuse of corporate vehicles lie;
- which laws and standards are effective in practice and which are not; and

---

1. See also Financial Action Task Force Special Recommendation VIII.

- how the shortcomings that currently allow most corrupt officials to successfully launder illicit funds through corporate vehicles can be addressed.

Three types of evidence were collected for this research:

- a database of more than 150 actual cases of grand corruption from a wide range of jurisdictions;
- extensive interviews with practitioners (both service providers and investigators) on the difficulties they encounter when trying to determine beneficial ownership; and
- evidence from a solicitation exercise, whereby researchers posed as would-be customers soliciting shell companies and trusts to hide their financial affairs.

Through analysis of these varied sources of evidence, the report identifies a number of ways in which the misuse of corporate vehicles can be curbed. Specifically, the report—

- makes recommendations regarding the minimum information that corporate registries should collect and make publicly available about the legal and beneficial owners of legal entities seeking registration;
- explores the role that service providers should be required to play in conducting greater due diligence of the persons who exercise effective control over the corporate vehicles (that is, the beneficial owners); and
- calls for investigative capacities to be strengthened (through better training and greater resources) so that investigators will be better equipped to undertake the increasingly complex cross-border investigations required in the 21st century.

The Elusive Beneficial Owner: A Call for a Substantive Approach

Uncertainty and variation exist among jurisdictions about the meaning of beneficial ownership. This report argues that beneficial ownership should be understood as a material, substantive concept—referring to the de facto control over a corporate vehicle—and not a purely legal definition. To be effective and meaningful, beneficial ownership must not be reduced to a legally defined position, such as a director of a company or foundation or a shareholder who owns more than a certain percentage of shares or legal entitlement/benefit of a trust.

In identifying the beneficial owner, the focus should be on two factors: the control exercised and the benefit derived. Control of a corporate vehicle will always depend on context, as control can be exercised in many different ways, including through ownership, contractually or informally. A formal approach to beneficial ownership, based on percentage thresholds of ownership or designated beneficiary of a corporate vehicle under investigation, may yield useful information providing clues to the corporate vehicle's ultimate ownership or control. More generally, it may lead to the identification of people of interest who possess information regarding the beneficial owners. Service providers, however, should be aware of the limitations of such an approach. In suspicious cases, they need to go beyond their basic obligations and find out whether others are really in control or derive benefit.

Wanted: A Government Strategy

Governments have recognized the importance of curbing the misuse of corporate vehicles to conceal beneficial ownership, and in response, they have adopted certain international standards. We have only to look at the evaluations undertaken by the Financial Action Task Force on Money Laundering (FATF) and similar international organizations, however, to see that compliance with these international standards is poor.

The evidence collected for the present study provides—for the first time—direct insight into the substantial gap between the rules on paper and the rules as applied in practice when it comes to corporate vehicles. On this basis, we argue that a more ambitious approach is needed, one that involves adopting a detailed set of policies specifically aimed at improving transparency in the ownership and control and benefit of corporate vehicles. In our view, an effective policy regime will need to address at least five key issues.

> *Issue 1. The information available at company registries should be improved and made more easily accessible.*

The first source of information mentioned by both investigators and service providers when seeking information about an incorporated entity (that is, any corporate vehicle, excluding trusts or similar arrangements) is the company registry.

The vast majority of registries contain information about legal entities that is of some use to investigators, such as the name of the entity, its address, its articles of incorporation (or charter), and details of its directors. This information should be *publicly available* in all company registries. In cases in which a director is acting as a nominee for another person, that fact should be noted in the registry, along with the name of that "shadow director."

Many registries also hold information on the owners, shareholders, and members of a legal entity. All registries should collect and maintain this information, which should cover anyone whose ownership stake is sufficiently large to be deemed a controlling interest. This information should be updated and made accessible in a timely manner to (at least) law enforcement members in the course of their investigations.

Finally, company registries in some jurisdictions—typically held by a securities supervisor, regulatory commission, or some other agency with a comparably proactive approach—are more inclined toward enforcing and supervising legal or regulatory obligations and have sufficient expertise and resources to do so. In such cases, countries could consider requiring their corporate registry to also maintain information on beneficial ownership. Currently, however, few countries have sufficient expertise and resources to be able to do this adequately.

In addition to improving the data content in company registries, countries should strive to make it freely available. Ideally, this would mean providing free online access (without preregistration requirements or subscription fees), complete with search functions that allow for extensive cross-referencing of the data. Access to historical records on the legal entities entered in the register also should be included.

The report, however, recognizes that company registries have serious limitations—in both how they are set up and how they work in practice. Registries are almost invariably archival in nature; they rarely conduct independent verification; and in many cases, they are already stretched for resources. They clearly are not a panacea for the misuse of legal entities. For this reason, although the information supplied by a company registry may be a useful starting point, it needs to be complemented by other sources.

Issue 2. Steps should be taken to ensure that service providers collect beneficial ownership information and allow access to it.

The Advantages of Service Providers

The most important among these other sources are TCSPs and banks. These providers have unique insight into the day-to-day operations and the real "financial life" of the corporate vehicle, that is, the financial flows of funds—which are harder to manipulate and disguise. As a result, banks and service providers are an essential source of information on control and beneficial ownership of a corporate vehicle. The international standards already call on these institutions to be under an obligation to conduct customer due diligence (CDD) of the corporate vehicle to which they are providing a service. Implementation is significantly lagging however. This obligation should extend to establishing the identity of the beneficial owners, both when the business relationship is initially established and during its subsequent life cycle. Ongoing monitoring is important because the true economic reality behind a corporate vehicle becomes more difficult to hide during the course of a longer-term business relationship. In the case of corporate vehicles that are trusts or similar legal arrangements, service providers play an even more important role as source of beneficial ownership information, as few countries have the functional equivalent of a corporate register for trusts.

Why Service Providers Should Be Obligated to Conduct Due Diligence

The international standard on anti-money laundering, laid down in the FATF 40 Recommendations against Money Laundering, requires the collection of information about beneficial ownership. The review, however, carried out as part of this study on what information TCSPs collect in practice, coupled with country evaluations carried out in more than 159 countries, shows that banks (to some extent) and TCSPs (more generally) still do not adequately identify the beneficial owner when establishing a business relationship. For example, U.S. banks are not generally obligated to collect beneficial ownership information when establishing a business relationship. At the very least, an official declaration by the customer as to beneficial ownership could be useful in improving the situation.

More generally, the imposition of due diligence obligations on service providers is important for two reasons. First, it obliges service providers to collect information and conduct due diligence on matters about which they might prefer to remain ignorant. This obligation is important because in the majority of cases in which a corporate vehicle is misused, the intermediary is negligent, willfully blind, or actively complicit. If a service provider is obligated to gather full due diligence information, it becomes impossible for the intermediary to legitimately plead ignorance regarding the background of a client or the source of his or her funds. Second, having all such information duly gathered by the service provider means that investigators have an adequate source of information at their disposal.

Enforcing Compliance

Experience over the past 10 years has shown that imposing due diligence requirements on paper is not enough. Countries need to devote adequate resources to effectively policing compliance, including supervising service providers and imposing civil or criminal penalties for noncompliance. The evidence analyzed in this study shows that TCSPs in certain financial centers more typically considered "onshore" actually exercise less strict due diligence than jurisdictions identified as offshore financial centers (OFCs).

Attorneys and Claims of Attorney-Client Privilege

Policy makers also need to address the problem of gaining access to the information held by service providers and, in particular, the issue of legal privilege. When investigators seek to access information held by attorneys regarding the establishment and operation of a corporate vehicle by one or more of their clients, the attorneys frequently seek to justify their refusal to divulge such information by invoking attorney-client privilege (or "legal professional privilege"). Investigators should guard against the unjustified use of this privilege. Although the claim of legal privilege is valid under certain circumstances, a number of jurisdictions around the world have carved out statutory exceptions to legal privilege in cases in which the attorney is acting as a financial intermediary or in some other strictly fiduciary or transactional capacity, rather than as a legal advocate.

A Two-Track Approach

Substantial debate is ongoing about which entity, person, or institution would be best suited to maintain beneficial ownership information. We believe that service providers and registries both have a vital role to play in enabling law enforcement to access beneficial ownership information, and we acknowledge that this role might differ from jurisdiction to jurisdiction. Having said that, however, we believe that the service provider generally will be the more useful source of beneficial ownership information. As noted by one investigator in a country where both the registry and the service providers maintain beneficial ownership information,

> When we receive an international request for beneficial ownership information, we always refer them to the service provider. The registry would only be able to give you a name, often (though not always) correct; but the service provider will be able to provide so much more—telephone numbers, family, real estate, and all the other bits of information one gathers over the course of a business relationship.

We realize that some countries, unfortunately, may not (yet) be able to impose such CDD regulations on the relevant service providers. The political reality is that pressure groups or other lobbies (for example, a bar association) prevent the passage of such legislation.

In countries where intermediaries are not subject to CDD requirements, other ways to ensure beneficial ownership identification, although second best, nonetheless may prove useful and effective. Under such circumstances, the obvious institution to maintain beneficial ownership information is the company registry (under the conditions described above). How policy makers choose to define beneficial ownership for the purposes of company registration will depend on the level of expertise of company registry staff. Disentangling who, in a particularly complicated structure, qualifies as the beneficial owner may require significant corporate legal expertise, which may not always be available. In such cases, a formal definition (for example, a natural person holding more than 25 percent of the shares, or a natural person holding the most shares) may be more practicable.

> *Issue 3. All beneficial ownership information should be available within the same jurisdiction.*

Another obstacle to obtaining information about a particular corporate vehicle is that the relevant documentation may be deliberately dispersed across different jurisdictions. Collecting information on a particular legal entity that is incorporated or formed under the laws of Country A but administered from Country B often entails first submitting a request in Country A and then submitting a request in Country B. To avoid having to obtain information from different countries—with all the loss of time and resources that entails—countries should ensure that a *resident* person maintains beneficial ownership information on any entity incorporated under its laws. That requirement could be achieved in various ways—for example, by imposing the obligation on a resident director or other corporate officer, or on a resident registered agent or a service provider. That person should receive all financial documentation relating to the legal entity. This obligation would not affect the obligation requiring the service provider (who may well be located in another jurisdiction) to also maintain this information. Certainly, if this service provider is undertaking the daily administration or management of the corporate vehicle, he or she is likely to have more current information.

Issue 4. Bearer shares should be abolished.

Companies that have issued bearer shares and bearer-share warrants continue to be problematic in terms of transparency of ownership and control of corporate vehicles. The person in legal possession of the physical shares is deemed to be their owner and thus the owner of the company. The problem is knowing who owns the shares at any given point in time. Many countries have immobilized these shares—effectively rendering them registered shares—without disrupting legitimate business. No legitimate rationale exists for perpetuating bearer shares and similar bearer instruments. We recommend that all countries immobilize or abolish them.

Issue 5. Investigative capacity should be strengthened.

Why Due Diligence Is Not Enough

The challenge thrown down by those who wish to deceive ultimately calls for a response by those seeking to unmask that deceit. Efforts to counter the misuse of corporate vehicles have, in recent years, focused on introducing new laws and regulations. Although this certainly forms an important part of an effective response to grand corruption, it is by no means enough. Similarly, prevention and information gathering by service providers or company registries, although vital, on their own are insufficient. A company registry, after all, often will not contain the most current information, and a service provider can undertake only so much due diligence. As one compliance officer noted, "Any due diligence system can be beaten."

Enhancing the Skills and Capacity of Investigators

In any complex corruption investigation involving the use of corporate vehicles, an imaginative, tenacious, and expert investigator is indispensable. In our research, we have discerned a wide disparity among investigators in different jurisdictions around the world in terms of their knowledge and expertise, as well as the technological and budgetary resources made available to them to conduct investigations into corporate vehicle misuse schemes. Given the transnational nature of such schemes, however, it is imperative that this gap in knowledge and resources be narrowed. Accordingly, we strongly recommend greater education, development, and training of investigators regarding (a) the nature of corporate vehicles around the world and their potential for misuse, and (b) the most effective investigative skills and techniques for "piercing the corporate veil." Moreover, as transnational schemes generally involve more than one jurisdiction, authorities need to make sufficient resources available so that investigators can respond to requests for assistance from other jurisdictions in an adequate and timely manner.

Transnational Investigations

A concerted effort is required to improve law enforcement's understanding of corporate vehicles, their function, and their rationale to enable proper investigation. Although investigators generally are familiar with some of the basic legal entities and arrangements available under their domestic laws, they are largely unfamiliar with foreign corporate bodies and the rationale for including them in any corporate structure. It is important that these investigators have some basic understanding of common corporate structures under foreign laws and the (often fiscal) rationale for their existence. In this way, they will be better able to distinguish legitimate from illegitimate uses.

Building a Transnational Case

Being able to identify a corporate vehicle misuse scheme is only the first step, however. Investigators also need sufficient resources to be able to travel to the jurisdictions involved and coordinate with local investigators in gathering all the documentary, testimonial, and other forensic evidence that is needed to be able to successfully present cases in court. Because many corporate vehicle misuse cases are transnational in nature, investigators need to work together. To facilitate this international cooperation at both formal and informal levels, legal mechanisms and more informal channels are needed. As one investigator put it, solving a transnational corporate vehicle misuse scheme is like putting together a jigsaw puzzle, with investigators in different jurisdictions each holding separate pieces of the puzzle. To complete the puzzle, an investigator needs to have access to all the pieces.

Conducting Risk Analysis and Typologies

Countries should undertake a risk analysis and conduct typology studies of the misuse of corporate vehicles in their own jurisdictions to identify what entities (of whatever extraction) and arrangements typically are abused. This analysis would give law enforcement (and service providers) useful information on the types of abuse specific to the country. This information should include a succinct overview of legal requirements of the corporate vehicles that can be established or that operate within the jurisdiction, the rationale for these requirements, and where information may be obtained. The risk analysis should inform the efforts made by service providers when identifying beneficial ownership. Publishing the typologies information and the risk analysis and ensuring accessibility to foreign law enforcement and service providers will be important.

Part 1. The Misuse of Corporate Vehicles

"Even so, I am quite clear that [these distinct legal entities] were just the puppets of Dr. Waller-steiner. He controlled their every movement. Each danced to his bidding. He pulled the strings . . . they were his agents to do as he commanded. He was the principal behind them. I am of the opinion that the court should pull aside the corporate veil and treat these concerns as being his creatures."

—Lord Denning[1]

1.1 Introduction

Suppose you want to give someone some money, and because it is for an illegal purpose, you do not want anyone else to know about it. What would you do? You could hand it over in cash—but that might be difficult if it were a large sum of money or if the recipient lived a long way away. Alternatively, you could transfer funds from your bank account to the recipient's—but then your respective banks would know about it. And they might tell the police, or at least they might offer information if the police came knocking. So your ideal solution would involve a bank account that you control, but that no one can link to you—or at least only with the greatest difficulty.

That, in a nutshell, is the starting point for this study: people who are trying to find ways of sending or receiving funds or assets while concealing their involvement. The funds in question derive from bribery, embezzlement of public funds, or other forms of corruption. In the past, people hid their involvement with funds through anonymous bank accounts or accounts in fictitious names. This option, however, is becoming increasingly less available. So now the preferred method is to use a legal entity or arrangement, known (in the terminology of the Organisation for Economic Co-operation and Development [OECD]) as a "corporate vehicle." This term is mainly used to refer to companies (or corporations), foundations and trusts, and national variations of these. As emerged from our research, corrupt officials do not normally establish a corporate vehicle on their own, but rather have others do it for them. Moreover, in many cases, not just one corporate vehicle is involved but a whole web of vehicles that are linked together across several different jurisdictions.

Attempts by individuals to conceal their involvement in corruption and create a "disconnect" between themselves and their illegal assets are triggered by the efforts of law enforcement agencies to detect them. As law enforcement becomes more skillful and better

---

1. Lord Denning in *Wallersteiner v. Moir* [1974] 1 WLR 99, 1013.

trained in the detection of corruption, so too will corrupt parties find more refined and ingenious ways of concealing their ill-gotten gains. Action, in other words, begets a never-ending chain of reactions. It is important to bear this point in mind, for any proposed "solution" to uncovering the concealment, whether through government regulation or otherwise, inevitably will address only the problem as it exists *at that point in time*. New forms of deception will be developed in response. The quest for a silver bullet is illusory.

In addition to examining the ways in which corrupt officials misuse corporate vehicles to conceal their interests, this report takes a closer look at the chain reaction that spurs both the corrupt officials and those seeking to track them down to continuous improvement of their methods. What is law enforcement doing to detect this type of behavior? How can it discover what natural person or persons are hiding behind a network of entities or arrangements? Or, if it already has its eye on an individual, how can it link that person to a company holding the suspicious assets? And how can it provide convincing evidence of that link? What sources of information could be useful to it in its investigations? What are banks doing to help law enforcement? And what about those who assist in setting up the corporate vehicles in question—that is, the specialized professional service providers? And what about the corporate registries that hold potentially relevant information on legal entities? What help could they offer? This report addresses these and similar questions, with the aim of improving our understanding of (a) what information is currently available to investigators and (b) how that information could be improved and made more accessible.

This report is not the first to be written on this topic and undoubtedly will not be the last. In fact, the concern over the misuse of corporate vehicles dates from long before much of the recent discussion on international corruption, tax havens, and offshore centers. In a 1937 letter to then U.S. President Franklin Delano Roosevelt, his secretary of the treasury, Henry Morgenthau Jr., wrote the following about a tax haven jurisdiction like Newfoundland:

> [T]heir corporation laws make it more difficult to ascertain who the actual stockholders are. Moreover, the stockholders have resorted to all manner of devices to prevent the acquisition of information regarding their companies. The companies are frequently organized through foreign lawyers, with dummy incorporators and dummy directors, so that the names of the real parties in interest do not appear.

As a matter of international policy concern, the misuse of corporate vehicles has been on the agenda for well over a decade. Since the United Nations Office on Drugs and Crime (UNODC; at that time the UNODCCP) issued its 1998 report titled *Financial Havens, Banking Secrecy and Money Laundering*, a steady stream of reports on the issue has been forthcoming, notably *Protecting the EU Financial System from the Exploitation of Financial Centres and Offshore Facilities by Organised Crime* (the Euroshore report, 2000), a report commissioned by the European Commission; *Behind the Corporate Veil: Using Corporate Entities for Illicit Purposes* (2001), commissioned by the OECD; *Towards a Level Playing Field: Regulating Corporate Vehicles in Cross-Border Transactions* (2002), commissioned by the International Trade and Investment Organization and the Society of Trust and Estate Practitioners; *The Misuse of Corporate Vehicles* (2006), by the Financial Action Task Force (FATF); and *Money Laundering Using Trust and Company Service Providers on Money Laundering* (2010), a report by the Caribbean Financial Action Task Force.

These reports, and the policy recommendations based on them, have placed the issue firmly on the international agenda and have contributed to the formulation of international standards on transparency of legal entities and arrangements. The FATF 40 Recommendations on Money Laundering (2003), which represent the international standard on this issue, note the importance of ensuring transparency of legal entities and arrangements and of identifying the beneficial owner in various places. According to Recommendations 5 and 12 on customer due diligence (CDD), financial institutions and other economic service providers[2] should be required to establish the identity of the beneficial owner of a legal person or arrangement. Recommendations 33 and 34 oblige countries to ensure that there is adequate, accurate, and timely information on the beneficial ownership and control of legal persons (33) and legal arrangements (34) and to ensure that this information can be obtained or accessed in a timely fashion by competent authorities. Assessments undertaken by FATF and other bodies of 159 countries show that the levels of compliance are very low, particularly with Recommendations 33 and 34 (see appendix A).[3]

This matter has continued to generate considerable debate. At their summit in Pittsburgh, United Sates, in September 2009, the G-20 leaders issued a statement calling on the FATF to "help detect and deter the proceeds of corruption by prioritizing work to strengthen standards on customer due diligence, beneficial ownership and transparency."[4] More recently, in April 2010, a group of leading prosecutors from around the world sent an open letter to the leaders of the G-20 requesting they address this issue as a matter of urgency.[5]

1.2 Objective of This Report

The objective of this report is to contribute to the international policy debate by providing evidence on (a) how corporate vehicles are misused to conceal the identity of their

---

2. "Economic service providers" or "service providers" is a working term used throughout this report. It encompasses the financial and designated nonfinancial service providers referenced in Recommendation 5 and Recommendation 12 of the FATF 40 Recommendations on money laundering. Absent clarifying or narrowing context, it is used as an umbrella term for the deposit-taking and investment banking institutions, corporate or trust creation and management professionals, and legal and accounting professionals who interact with corporate vehicle clients.
3. In fact, in more than 70 percent of the countries evaluated, the lack of a clear requirement to identify the beneficial owner was mentioned as a key factor justifying a less-than-compliant rating for Recommendation 5.
4. "Leaders' Statement, The Pittsburgh Summit, September 24–25, 2009," accessed at www.g20.org/documents/pittsburgh_summit_leaders_statement_250909.pdf (last accessed August 13, 2011).
5. See a copy of the letter urging the G-20 to call on the Financial Action Task Force to report back on specific actions it has taken to detect and deter the proceeds of corruption by prioritizing work to strengthen standards on customer due diligence, beneficial ownership, and transparency (http://www.globalwitness.org/media_library_detail.php/959/en/open_letter_to_heads_of_state_and_finance_minister).

beneficial owners and (b) the problems that banks, other service providers, and investigators face in attempting to obtain relevant information.

The most significant feature of this report is that its findings and conclusions are based on highly specific data gathered from a wide range of primary sources. These sources include court documents; interviews with investigators, financial institutions, service providers, and corporate registries; and the results of a solicitation exercise. But in providing information on the extent of this type of criminal behavior and the methods most often used by its perpetrators, the report aims to do more than simply raise awareness of the issue. Rather, its ultimate objective is to present policy recommendations for the consideration of authorities as they seek ways to deal with misuse of corporate vehicles within their jurisdictions. A comprehensive strategy at both national and international levels to address the weaknesses in legal and regulatory frameworks—with the aim of decreasing the vulnerability of corporate vehicles to misuse—could contribute toward improving the current situation. Our recommendations are summarized in the Executive Summary and are presented in greater detail in the report.

We choose our words carefully: we do not suggest that policy on its own can provide a solution to this problem. To do so would be to set oneself up for failure. Grand corruption is a criminal problem, and it always will require a response from law enforcement, and certainly, through sheer determination, creativity, and expertise, law enforcement has successfully investigated and prosecuted many cases involving the misuse of corporate vehicles. But even so, law enforcement cannot address this problem alone: a coordinated approach, from both policy and law enforcement perspectives, is required.

Addressing the challenge of identifying the beneficial ownership of corporate vehicles is a multifaceted endeavor. To take this into account, we have gathered data from a variety of sources, including court cases, interviews, and reviews of the activities of relevant institutions:

- *Court Cases*
  Compilation and subsequent analysis of a database of 150 grand corruption investigations involving the misuse of corporate vehicles. The database identifies the types of illicit assets involved (roughly US$50 billion in total), the professional intermediaries and the jurisdictions involved, and the location of the bank accounts (where available). Analysis of actual cases helps to establish the facts and identifies areas where the genuine problems lie.

- *Banks*
  An analysis examining how, in practice, 25 banks establish the identity of a beneficial owner, including the information and documents they obtain from their customers and the challenges they face in conducting their due diligence.

- *Trust and Company Service Providers*
  A study of the extent to which, in practice, TCSPs conduct due diligence when establishing corporate vehicles.

- *Registries*
  A review of the information collected and maintained by company registries in 40 jurisdictions.

- *Investigators*
  An examination of the obstacles and challenges faced by investigators[6] in investigating the misuse of corporate vehicles and identifying their beneficial owner(s).

The methods used in the various research activities underlying this study are described in more detail in appendix B. This study makes no claim to assess the full extent of the problem—that would go far beyond its scope and would require different research methods. Instead, the study builds on expert observations and uses these observations to identify and analyze problems that merit the attention of policy makers.

1.3 How to Use This Report

In part 1 of this report, we have sketched the background of the misuse of corporate vehicles and outlined the objectives and scope of this study. The subsequent parts of this report deal with different aspects of the problem. Part 2 examines specific concerns about how we should understand the person hiding behind the corporate vehicle. Then, in part 3, we look at the types of corporate vehicles chosen to hide behind, as well as other strategies used to generate further opacity. Finally, part 4 considers the sources of information available to investigators tasked with uncovering the person hiding behind the corporate vehicle.

The diversity of topics addressed in this report means that at least some readers may encounter unfamiliar content. In that case, they may consult the information provided in the appendixes, which are useful to fill in any gaps in their knowledge needed for appropriate understanding of the report.

---

6. The term "investigators" used throughout the report encompasses a broad and diverse group of experts we consulted in the course of this study. They include investigators in the traditional sense, those who currently work or formerly worked in law enforcement agencies or other government investigative bodies, such as national anticorruption commissions and financial intelligence units. It also includes prosecutors, in recognition of the fact that, in some jurisdictions, it is prosecutors who lead investigations (or share responsibility for doing so with investigators). Forensic accountants and certified fraud examiners were consulted, as they play critical roles in financial crime investigations. Finally, civil practitioners in the field of international fraud and financial crimes also were consulted, including those with experience in successfully recovering stolen assets on behalf of their client governments or other victims.

Appendix A reviews compliance with FATF Recommendations 5, 12, 33, and 34 and provides an outline of the main issues. Appendix B describes the five component projects that helped to inform this report, including the Grand Corruption Database, Bank Beneficial Ownership, Trust and Company Service Provider, Registry, and Investigator Projects. Appendix C describes the corporate vehicles referred to in this study and Appendix D details ten grand corruption cases. Appendix E provides a detailed comparison of corporate vehicles in selected jurisdictions.

Part 2. The Beneficial Owner

"The secret to success is to own nothing, but control everything."

—Nelson Rockefeller

2.1 Introduction

In Part 2, we focus on the beneficial owner(s)—the person (or group of people) who have an interest in or control over ill-gotten gains (property or financial assets) and who are trying to conceal the fact through the misuse of corporate vehicles.

For our purposes, this concealment can be viewed from two angles:

- The narrow perspective of the service provider
- The broad perspective of the investigator.

Service Providers

Service providers normally face the question of who is the beneficial owner of certain assets when first entering into a relationship with a customer. They normally approach the matter by looking first at the legal structure of the customer's entity or arrangement. They have certain facts and documents at their disposal, at least some of which have been provided by the customer, but this is only part of the information they need. Exactly how accurately the information available to them reflects the economic reality of control will become apparent (to a degree) during the course of their business relationship with the customer. In other words, the information available to service providers is highly partial and incomplete.

Investigators

By contrast, when investigators become involved in a case, they already are looking at a wider constellation of facts. They know (or at least strongly suspect) that they are looking at a scheme that has been designed to create an appearance of legitimacy, when in fact, it is a facade. They no longer are deceived by that appearance.

It is important to remember these two different viewpoints as we examine how the various parties approach the problem of identifying the beneficial owners of corporate vehicles.

2.2 Origin of the Term "Beneficial Owner"

The concept of "beneficial ownership" originated in the United Kingdom (see box 2.1). During the development of trust law, the following distinction between two types of ownership—"legal ownership" and "beneficial ownership"—was introduced:

> The legal ownership of the trust-property is in the trustee, but he holds it not for his own benefit but for that of the *cestui que trustent* or the beneficiaries. On the creation of a trust in the strict sense as it was developed by equity, the full ownership in the trust property was split into two constituent elements, which became vested in different persons: the "legal ownership" in the trustee, and what became to be called the "beneficial ownership" in the *cestui que trust* [that is, the beneficiary].[7]

Although the term "beneficial owner" currently is applied in a wide variety of situations that do not involve trusts, the essence of the concept—as referring to the person who ultimately controls an asset and can benefit from it—remains the same. Indeed, in discussions with investigators, the typical response to the question of how to find the beneficial owner is the simple answer so often heard in criminal investigations: "Find out who benefits." The image of someone absent, temporarily abroad but able to retake his lands at any time, provides a helpful illustration of the idea of beneficial ownership, because it reveals not only that he is the one who benefits but also that he is the one who exercises control in the end—not directly and overtly, but indirectly and covertly, invisible to the outside world. This characteristic is essential to the concept of beneficial ownership, certainly as it applies to criminal situations. The beneficial owner may not be on the scene, and it may *appear* that the lands belong to someone else. However, in the final analysis, they are his.

BOX 2.1   The Origin of the Trust

Although the precise historic origins of the trust are uncertain, they were in use in the 12th century during the time of the Crusades:

> Typically the warrior would be away from England for some years and therefore needed his land tended in his absence. It was essential that the person who was left in charge could exercise all of the powers of the legal owner of that land, such as deciding who would farm which part of the land and collecting taxes. However, the crusader wanted to ensure that he would be able to recover all of his rights of ownership when he returned from the war. Consequently, the idea of split ownership of the property emerged, whereby the crusader was treated as the owner of the land by the courts of equity and the person left in charge was treated by the common-law courts as being owner of the land.[a]

Note: a. See Alastair Hudson, *Equity and Trusts*, 4th ed. (London: Cavendish Publishing, 2005), p. 35.

---

7. Lord Diplock in *Ayerst (Inspector of Taxes) v C&K (Construction) Ltd*, H.L. (1975) S.T.C. 345.

2.3 Defining Beneficial Ownership: The Theory

The internationally accepted definition of beneficial ownership, which may usefully serve as the starting point of this discussion, is the one given by the FATF. It reads as follows: "Beneficial owner refers to the natural person(s) who ultimately owns or controls a customer and/or the person on whose behalf a transaction is being conducted. It also incorporates those persons who exercise ultimate effective control over a legal person or arrangement."[8]

Before discussing the details and implications of this definition, it is useful to clarify a terminological point, specifically the use of the terms "customer" and "transaction" in the first sentence of the definition. The FATF definition was developed in the context of a bank or other service provider dealing with a prospective customer and having an obligation to establish the identity of that potential customer's beneficial owner before carrying out any transactions on its behalf. The definition does not intend to suggest that the "customer" is a natural person (see section 2.3.1).

2.3.1 Natural Person versus Legal Person

The first noteworthy (and only unequivocal) element in the definition is that a beneficial owner is always a natural person—a legal person cannot, by definition, be a beneficial owner. The definition therefore also speaks of "ultimate" control: A legal person never can be the ultimate controller—ownership by a legal person is itself always controlled by a natural person.[9]

2.3.2 Beneficial versus Legal Ownership

The defining characteristic of the beneficial owner of an asset is that he holds a degree of control over the asset that allows him to benefit from it. Whether he is the *legal* owner (that is, holds legal title to it) is irrelevant. The essence of beneficial ownership is precisely *not* ownership in the ordinary sense of the word—but rather control. Control and legal title often will lie in the same hands, but in the sorts of situations addressed in this report, that often is not the case. It is important, therefore, not to confuse beneficial ownership with legal ownership. Section 2.3.3 concentrates on the control and ownership of a *corporate vehicle*.

2.3.3 Control—What Is It and Who Has It?

The definition speaks of "the natural person(s) who ultimately . . . controls a customer." The concept of control is a difficult one, given the manifold ways in which it can be

---

8. See Financial Action Task Force on Money Laundering, "FATF 40 Recommendations," p. 15, available online at http://www.fatf-gafi.org/dataoecd/7/40/34849567.pdf.
9. One cannot quite say the same for ownership, because a foundation, for instance, is not "owned" by anyone.

exercised. What does exercising control of a corporate vehicle mean, exactly? Who ultimately controls a corporate vehicle? The answers to these questions depend on the situation. The legal form and actual structure of the corporate vehicle provide a useful starting point, but they do not give us the whole answer. Let us consider who may be said to exercise ultimate control in a number of different corporate vehicles.

Control in Companies

Our analysis of 150 grand corruption cases shows that the main type of corporate vehicle used to conceal beneficial ownership is the company, so let us consider this vehicle first. In a company limited by shares, three groups of people might arguably qualify as having ultimate control:

- The shareholders, who can exercise the voting rights attached to their shares to make changes in how the company operates
- The board of directors, who generally exercise a more immediate level of control over the company, according to terms setting forth their powers of control
- The executive officers (possibly), who exercise day-to-day control and de facto engage in the transactions and activities of the company.

All three parties hold some level of control. In most cases, the shareholders may be said to have the most control over the corporate vehicle. They represent the ultimate level of power, in that they are not controlled by others (assuming they are natural persons acting on their own behalf) and they typically can remove the directors and ultimately enjoy the financial benefits (that is, dividends and net worth) of the company.

Control in Trusts

Companies have a relatively straightforward structure—it is possible to point to the owners (the shareholders). But a significant number of alternative types of corporate vehicles are more problematic in this regard: they cannot be owned, and simply no position is equivalent to the shareholder. In the case of a trust, for instance, several people arguably could qualify as the beneficial owner:

- The *trustee*,[10] because he conducts the day-to-day management of the asset held in trust and could—if he wanted—dispose of it in any way he liked. He is, however, legally bound to act in the interest of the beneficiary as set out in the deed of

---

10. The methodology for assessing the FATF recommendations ("the methodology") stipulates that, when identifying the *customer* who is a legal arrangement (such as a trust), service providers should obtain information concerning the trustees—that is, the trustee qualifies as/is identified with, the customer (see 5.4 (b) of the *Methodology for Assessing Compliance with the FATF 40 Recommendations and the FATF 9 Special Recommendations*, p. 16). When discussing the identification of the *beneficial owner* of a legal arrangement, the methodology stipulates that this includes identifying those who exercise ultimate effective control over a legal arrangement, which for trusts means "identifying the settlor, *the trustee* . . . and the beneficiaries." So the trustee is perceived as being both the customer and the beneficial owner, qualifying both as part of the trust (the customer) and its ultimate controller. (The same point, incidentally, can be made in connection with the director and companies. He similarly qualifies as/is identified with both the customer [company] and—arguably—as part of its "mind and management" and thus as its beneficial owner.)

trust. He is not, therefore, an ultimate controller but rather acts *on behalf of* someone else and is under fiduciary obligations.

- The *settlor*, because he initiated the trust and contributed the asset to the trust in the first place. He, however, is no longer able to exercise control over the trust.
- The *beneficiary*, because he stands to benefit. But he similarly cannot exercise control over the trust.

The concept of beneficial ownership cannot be applied in a straightforward manner in these instances without knowing more about the context.

It is interesting to note that, when discussing the applicability of beneficial ownership obligations to trusts, compliance officers interviewed in connection with this study generally confirmed that all standard parties to the trust (settlor, trustee, and beneficiary) are relevant and should be considered. One can see why: If one person contributes an asset, another manages it, and yet another will benefit from it, who really is in control? In whom should a compliance officer be most interested? When a service provider is dealing with a prospective client, he does not know at that point (at the beginning of a relationship) what the relationship will involve in practice. All he or she has is some information provided by his or her client. In that case, the wisest course is to gather information on all parties who could be relevant.

Control in Foundations

The vehicle of the foundation could be subjected to a similar analysis as a trust: It also cannot be *owned* by someone else. Although control might appear less problematic in this case (the director or board of the foundation is the obvious first point to look at), in the context of a private foundation with a private beneficiary, such a first-round analysis would be too simplistic—the private beneficiary is also of interest.

The Relationship between Ownership and Control

The FATF definition also refers to "the natural person(s) who ultimately owns . . . a customer." Because natural persons cannot be owned, the "customer" mentioned as being "owned" can only refer to a corporate vehicle. But what does ultimate ownership of a corporate vehicle really mean? The definition stipulates that, in such cases, the beneficial owner includes all people who have "ultimate effective control." According to the FATF methodology, for companies, this normally would entail identifying the people who have a controlling interest and those who make up "the mind and management of a company."[11] So the definition moves from someone who *owns* a corporate entity to someone who holds a *controlling interest* in it. In other words, ownership is a proxy for control and, in this context, is only relevant to the extent that control can be inferred from it.

---

11. See 5.5.2 (b) of the *Methodology for Assessing Compliance with the FATF 40 Recommendations and the FATF 9 Special Recommendations*, p. 16, available online at http://www.fatf-gafi.org/dataoecd/16/54/40339628.pdf.

When Ownership Does Not Automatically Imply Control:
The Company Example

The most common type of owner of a corporate vehicle is the shareholder in a company. The assumption that control automatically can be inferred from ownership requires further analysis. In the United States context, Section 405 of the Exchange Act defines control as "the possession, direct or indirect, of the power to direct or cause the direction of the management and policies of a person, whether through the ownership of voting securities, by contract, or otherwise." The clear implication is that it is possible to exercise control in ways other than through owning "voting securities" (that is, shares).

We have mentioned the control that can be exercised by people in certain positions within the company (for example, board members, executives, and financial officers). Outsiders (that is, those without legal title) also can exercise control if they possess certain contractual rights. Creditors, for instance, can exercise control if they have been given the right to block or approve certain significant transactions of the company or to convert their debt into stock at the occurrence of a particular event. In addition, options and other convertible securities may vest a *potential* for control in certain individuals without vesting them with *actual* control.

The converse situation also arises. Just as it is possible to exercise control over a company without having any legal title to it, so too is it possible to have legal title but be unable to exercise ultimate control. For example, suppose only a minority of the directors is up for election in a particular year. A majority shareholder would then not be able to vote out the board of directors at one election. Or suppose the company in question has issued stocks that carry no voting rights but entail certain economic advantages (such as preferred shares).[12]

In other words, although shareholders with a sizable stake in a company normally may expect to have a certain amount of control over it, they may find that many other people, for totally legitimate reasons, have an overriding say in the company's affairs, such as to render those people, and not the shareholder, the true beneficial owner.

The Ultimate Solicitor: A Hidden Controller

In the FATF definition, the wording "person on whose behalf a transaction is conducted" is intended to ensure that a service provider finds out whether the natural person with whom he or she engages is acting of his or her own accord or is representing the interests of a third party, who consequently also needs to be identified. It could be argued that this concept is covered by the earlier wording "person who ultimately controls the customer." A different way of reading it, however, is of particular interest in the context of this study.

---

12. For a comprehensive discussion of the ways in which control of a corporate entity is distinguished from ownership, see Rafael LaPorta, Florencio Lopez de Silanes, Andrei Shleifer, "Corporate Ownership Around the World," Harvard Institute of Economic Research, Paper No. 1840, available at http://papers.ssrn.com/sol3/papers.cfm?abstract_id=103130. See also J. W. Verret, "Terrorism Finance, Business Associations and the Incorporation Transparency Act," George Mason University School of Law, *Louisiana Law Review* 70, no. 3 (Spring 2010), pp. 857–910.

In dealing with a multinational company, for example, a service provider may find it useful to know who ultimately owns or controls the company but is unlikely to pose much money laundering risk. After all, information about major shareholders and the board of management is in the public domain. Much more interesting from an anti-corruption, anti-money laundering point of view is the identity of the company employee who, *within* this big corporate structure, is ultimately controlling this particular business relationship. The transaction in question may be designed to facilitate payment of a bribe, to set up a slush fund, or (outside the realm of anticorruption) to defraud the company.

Who ultimately requested it? The answer to this question is not necessarily the beneficial owner of the company as a whole. It may well be someone of much lower rank within the management structure. We may call this person the "ultimate solicitor." In that sense, then, this part of the definition expands the original circle of persons to be identified.

Effective Control

The final element in the FATF definition refers to "those persons who exercise ultimate effective control over a legal person or arrangement." The focus is not on the obligation of service providers to identify the beneficial owner of a vehicle as such, but rather on those people who exercise ultimate *effective* control over a corporate vehicle—that is, the parties who, regardless of any service provision, control what happens to the assets.

2.4 Applying the Concept of Beneficial Ownership in Practice

Fortunately, in the majority of cases, identifying the beneficial owner is easier than the theoretical discussion would suggest. Normally, anyone incorporating a company to engage in business or forming a legal arrangement for legitimate purposes is going to ensure that how control is to be shared is predetermined and understood, and then that it is further delegated, in relation to specific functions, to employees or agents. Each of the relationships mentioned in the previous section often involve an individual or a small group of people, and a service provider consequently will not have too much difficulty in establishing the identity of the beneficial owner or owners. This report, however, focuses on the area of greatest risks—the small proportion of cases in which corporate vehicles are established for illegal purposes—and explores how, in such cases, outsiders may find information about what really is going on.

2.4.1 Two Approaches to Meet Different Needs

How can a service provider whose only dealings with a corporate vehicle are to open a bank account, or to provide some other financial service, obtain sufficient information to be able to say with any degree of certainty who the beneficial owner is? The provider may be able to obtain documents showing the corporate structure (such as the register of shareholders and constitutional documents), and he or she may be able to see management board decisions and inspect identification and trust-related documents. Such a service provider, however, generally will have access to less information than an investigator. Of necessity, the service provider will have to rely on representations by the client and cannot be expected to verify all the information presented. The provider can verify whether the information corresponds with the account activity of a corporate vehicle, but that is about the limit of what the provider can be expected to do.[13] A well-resourced and expert criminal can circumvent any due diligence program, no matter how sophisticated.[14]

To help service providers implement due diligence obligations and to ensure that institutions undertake due diligence of similar scope, many countries have adopted a "formal" approach to beneficial ownership, allowing for the inference of beneficial ownership in cases in which a person fulfills a predefined criterion. In contrast, the approach taken by investigators can be termed a "substantive" approach.

A Formal Approach to Beneficial Ownership
A formal definition of beneficial ownership is one that strictly delineates a set of sufficient conditions that qualify certain owners, controllers, and beneficiaries unequivocally as the beneficial owners of a corporate vehicle. This definition is formed on the basis of the assumption that, in the vast majority of situations, to be able to exercise ultimate effective control over a corporate vehicle, an individual will require a measure of legally acknowledgeable authority. Under this approach, the express focus is not the person who actually is exercising ultimate effective control of the corporate vehicle, but rather the person who normally would have legal authority to do so. The "sufficient condition" most frequently used to qualify someone as a beneficial owner is quantitative—for example, with companies, possession of a certain percentage of ownership or voting rights to a corporate vehicle.

Of the 40 countries surveyed for the purposes of this study, a significant number (14) were found to apply just such a quantitative understanding of beneficial ownership. This understanding took different forms. In some cases, it involved owning a standard minimum percentage of shares (varying from 10 to 25 percent), whereas in one country, an adaptive concept was applied, namely, "ownership amounting to voting rights significant enough to elect a majority of the directors," which (absent any peculiar bylaws indicating to the contrary) one typically would assume to be a much higher threshold (51 percent). In part because of its place in the European Union Third Anti-Money Laundering Directive, a quantitative threshold of 25 percent appears to be rapidly becoming the standard for many nations, both within and outside of Europe, that employ this formal approach.[15]

---

13. Many financial institutions use databases supplied by companies such as World-Check and Factiva to check the background of the people they are dealing with, and in this way gain leads to a potential criminal. The point, however, is to show that *for service providers* the scope for far-reaching verification measures is limited.
14. As was also recognized by some of the compliance officers interviewed for this study.
15. Directive 2005/60/EC of the European Parliament and of the Council of 26 October 2005, article 3 (6). "Beneficial owner means the natural person(s) who ultimately owns or controls the customer and/or the

A Substantive Approach to Beneficial Ownership

With its focus on ultimate control, the FATF definition is a good example of a substantive approach. "Beneficial ownership" pierces through the parties, who (like the corporate vehicles) merely represent the mode by which the will of the final actor is being effected.[16]

This focus is echoed by the Wolfsberg Group of banks:

> The term "beneficial ownership" is conventionally used in anti-money laundering contexts to refer to that level of ownership in funds that, as a practical matter, equates with control over such funds or entitlement to such funds. "Control" or "entitlement" in this practical sense is to be distinguished from mere signature authority or mere legal title. The term reflects a recognition that a person in whose name an account is opened with a bank is not necessarily the person who ultimately controls such funds or who is ultimately entitled to such funds. This distinction is important because the focus of anti-money laundering guidelines—and this is fundamental to the guidelines—needs to be on the person who has this ultimate level of control or entitlement.[17]

Although oriented toward the beneficial ownership of bank accounts, which may be easier to deal with conceptually than that of corporate vehicles, this approach places the emphasis on determining who *actually* is guiding the relevant activity, rather than who theoretically possesses enough of a legal claim to be able to do so. The Wolfsberg Group of banks has aligned itself with the substantive approach to beneficial ownership on the grounds that this approach is more in line with the intention of disrupting money laundering, because it includes those persons who might effect their ultimate control of a corporate vehicle outside of the legal strictures of a more formal definition.

---

natural person on whose behalf a transaction or activity is being conducted. The beneficial owner shall at least include:
(a) in the case of corporate entities:
   (i) the natural person(s) who ultimately owns or controls a legal entity through direct or indirect ownership or control over a sufficient percentage of the shares or voting rights in that legal entity, including through bearer share holdings, other than a company listed on a regulated market that is subject to disclosure requirements consistent with Community legislation or subject to equivalent international standards; a percentage of 25% plus one share shall be deemed sufficient to meet this criterion;
   (ii) the natural person(s) who otherwise exercises control over the management of a legal entity;
(b) in the case of legal entities, such as foundations, and legal arrangements, such as trusts, which administer and distribute funds:
   (i) where the future beneficiaries have already been determined, the natural person(s) who is the beneficiary of 25% or more of the property of a legal arrangement or entity;
   (ii) where the individuals that benefit from the legal arrangement or entity have yet to be determined, the class of persons in whose main interest the legal arrangement or entity is set up or operates;
   (iii) the natural person(s) who exercises control over 25% or more of the property of a legal arrangement or entity."
16. Such natural persons that this description alludes to include the class of nominees, trustees, agents, or any other "front men" who wield legal authority, which may extend to full legal control, authority, or ownership of a corporate vehicle (for example, a TCSP-provided nominee shareholder who legally owns 100 percent of the shares in a company, but only on behalf of the beneficial owner, as his trustee).
17. See http://www.wolfsberg-principles.com/faq-ownership.html.

2.5 The Service Provider's Perspective

Consultations with service providers during this study confirm that they typically use the "shareholders owning the company" understanding of beneficial ownership, because it is the one that applies in most of the situations they are confronted with. This perspective is not surprising, given that the majority of any jurisdiction's corporate vehicles will be companies. Furthermore, such a focus on companies is justifiable when one looks at patterns of misuse. From the review of the 150 grand corruption cases undertaken for this study, three-quarters of all the corporate vehicles that were misused were private companies or corporations. This suggests that ownership is at least a useful criterion, even if it does not always lead to the identification of the person who is (or should be) the object of further investigation.

Banks

When conducting business with another financial institution (for example, transferring money or receiving introduced business), a bank may feel uncomfortable about relying on the other institution's customer due diligence. Although the institution in question may be in good standing and be considered by its jurisdictional authorities to have robust client identification and verification procedures, the institution and the bank may differ in the depth to which they believe they should drill down to establish the beneficial owner. In these circumstances, the bank is faced with three less-than-ideal options: (a) turning down the business, (b) compromising its own internal standards by accepting the other's due diligence at face value, or (c) undertaking its own customer due diligence at its own expense. The costs in terms of potential lost profit, increased exposure to risk, or additional expense are potentially high. These costs can be reduced, however, if the use of quantitative standards becomes widespread and financial institutions use comparable methods and criteria for determining customer due diligence (CDD), creating a level playing field.

This approach has two further benefits. First, it instills confidence in the institutions when asserting to clients that they need to comply with the disclosure demands made on them. And second, the more jurisdictions adhere to the same threshold standard, the less effective institution-shopping and jurisdiction-shopping strategies become—strategies that often are employed by corrupt clients seeking to circumvent beneficial ownership disclosure.

Not all banks are created equal, however. Certain banks engage predominantly in business that generally is considered to present minimal anti-money laundering and combating the financing of terrorism (AML/CFT) risk. Quantitative standards allow such institutions to show that their CDD efforts have been made to the requisite degree and in good faith, even if some residual risk may persist. The converse holds as well. When a bank believes it is at risk of becoming a party to money laundering, then it has to adopt a more substantive approach. The bank needs to go well beyond simply scrutinizing the formal positions in a corporate vehicle and must undertake a more thorough investigation of all of the particulars of a corporate vehicle before agreeing to undertake business on behalf of that vehicle.

For that reason, certain banks interviewed for this study questioned the value of using the percentage-threshold method. Although it may be a perfectly adequate way to identify the beneficial owner in the overwhelming majority of situations, in cases of abuse (they argued) it is unlikely to be helpful in identifying the real beneficial owner. Banks refer to a typology sometimes called the "foot in the door" approach: A corporate account is classified as low risk at the beginning of the relationship. Three months after the account is opened, a previously unknown party appears on the scene, as a beneficiary of certain transactions or as vested with signatory powers to the account. This person has no ostensible connection to the corporate vehicle: he occupies no formal position of control and does not possess any relevant shareholding. A focus on percentage shareholdings or formal control thus would fail to identify this person as being of interest. It is therefore imperative that financial institutions be aware of the shortcomings of such an approach and "dig deeper" when circumstances so dictate—as well as maintain effective ongoing monitoring of business relationships.

The Problem of "Close Associates"

Anxious to secure their ill-gotten wealth, many corrupt parties seek to maintain a measure of control over the corporate vehicles involved in their scheme. To do this, they often use means that, although they would not be revealed under the strictly formal approach, nonetheless are legally enforceable. Fortunately, this legal enforceability enables an investigator to construct a "path" of control, however circuitous and oblique, from the asset to the corrupt official. In other instances, however, that path of legally enforceable control may stop short of reaching the official. Instead, it may stop at one or more "close associates"—that is, individuals in the circle of relatives, friends, and trusted associates and professionals around the corrupt official who can, in some way, exert legal control on his or her behalf. The more powerful the official, the wider the circle may be.[18] And although identifying the primary corrupt official as beneficial owner may be a difficult enough task, determining whether a person belongs to this circle of close associates is even more problematic.[19]

This involvement of other parties in the chain of control is confirmed by our review of three decades of corruption cases (1980–2010). This review demonstrated that the structure of control has trended toward the removal of the primary actor from the legal framework of misused corporate vehicles and the more frequent use of close associates.

---

18. Such a "path of legally enforceable control" cannot always be established. See, for example, the discussion on the use of shell companies, which notes that, in some cases, a criminal is able to use a certain corporate vehicle while having no legal ownership or control of it.

19. For a wider discussion of this topic, see Theodore S. Greenberg, Larissa Gray, Delphine Schantz, Carolin Gardner, and Michael Latham, *Politically Exposed Persons: Preventive Measures for the Banking Sector* (Washington, DC: World Bank, 2010).

One investigator commented on his firsthand experiences with this phenomenon: "The Abacha case, in which the connection between the asset and the principal (that is, the beneficial owner) was relatively easily established, was a crime of the 1990s; corruption cases we see now tend to be significantly more complicated."

One way in which a corrupt official can exert control without revealing himself is by having signatory authority over the corporate vehicle's financial accounts. This authority can be justified to the bank by deceptively listing the corrupt party as a low-level financial employee (see box 2.2). Financial institutions have identified this typology and it features in the case studies (see appendix D). Another strategy is to vest the ownership and control of the corporate vehicle in the hands of a front man who (out of loyalty or fear or on account of a financial incentive) is prepared to do the corrupt party's bidding. As such cases show, under the formal approach, it is perfectly possible for a corrupt party to achieve control of a corporate vehicle, both from within and outside the vehicle's structure, without running the risk of being identified as the beneficial owner.

BOX 2.2   Basic Attempt at a Concealment

The Case of Sweet Pink Inc. and Unlimited Horizon Inc.[a]

From 2004 to 2008, Teodoro Nguema Obiang Mangue, the son of Teodoro Nguema Obiang Mbasogo, the president of Equatorial Guinea, used U.S. lawyers, bankers, real estate agents, and escrow agents to move over US$110 million in suspect funds into the United States. George Nagler was one of the lawyers who, from 2005 to 2007 helped him purchase and manage property in Malibu, California, and incorporated shell companies for him.

According to a U.S. Senate investigation report, Nagler began working for Obiang in September 2005, after being contacted through the Internet by Obiang's executive assistant, Rosalina Romo. Nagler told the Subcommittee that he was asked at that time to form a corporation to "employ individuals at the home the Client maintained before he purchased the Malibu property and to handle payroll and other matters related to the employment of those individuals." In an e-mail dated September 15, 2005, Nagler asked Romo to provide him with two or three names for the corporation. Later that same day, the requested articles of incorporation were filed with the California Secretary of State for "Sweet Pink Inc." The Statement of Information for Sweet Pink Inc. listed Romo as the company's chief executive officer, secretary, and chief financial officer. Obiang is listed as "assistant treasurer," but in a letter by his legal counsel to the Senate subcommittee, Nagler conveyed that it was his understanding that Obiang "was the sole owner" of the corporation and was the "sole source of funding for the corporation." A few days later, Nagler was told that Eve Jeffers, a hip-hop musician and Obiang's then-girlfriend, would become the president of the corporation.

(continued next page)

On September 29, 2005, a checking account in the name of Sweet Pink Inc. was opened at Union Bank of California. Jeffers was a signatory, along with four other persons. Obiang was not on the signature card. During October 2005, two wire transfers, each for nearly US$30,000, were deposited into the account from one of Obiang's Equatorial Guinea companies. Union Bank told the Senate subcommittee that it first became aware of Obiang-related account activity in 2004, after the bank deemed Equatorial Guinea to be a high-risk country and conducted a search for Equatorial Guinea wire transfers. The search identified one large wire transfer in 2001 of US$6.2 million and seven smaller wire transfers from 2003 to 2004. On October 27, 2005, less than one month after the Sweet Pink account had been opened, the bank closed it.

The Senate report also noted that over a 10-month period from 2006 to 2007, Equatorial Guinea wire transfers totaling more than US$1.7 million were deposited into the law office account of another attorney, Michael Berger, who was "instrumental in opening the shell company [Unlimited Horizon Inc.] and law office accounts, moving Obiang funds through them, and masking Obiang's financial activities from the bank."[b] The US$1.7 million in Equatorial Guinea wire transfers sent to the Berger law office account triggered internal bank AML (anti-money laundering) alerts, but the bank was in the midst of negotiating a deferred prosecution agreement with the U.S. Justice Department for order deficiencies in its AML program. In June 2007, the bank finally reviewed the transactions and concluded that the Equatorial Bank wire transfers were suspicious, raising both fraud and AML concerns and subsequently closed all three accounts.

Note: a. U.S. Senate Permanent Subcommittee on Investigations, Majority and Minority Staff Report, "Keeping Foreign Corruption Out of the United States: Four Case Histories," Released in Conjunction with the Permanent Subcommittee on Investigations February 4, 2010, Hearing, pp. 49–50, citing as the source an August 1, 2008, letter from Nagler's legal counsel to the subcommittee, PSI-Nagler-02-0002. Id. at fn. 215. According to the Senate report, Nagler provided documents in response to a subcommittee subpoena and answered written questions from the subcommittee. Id., p. 48. Union Bank of California information from same report at pp. 31–32.
b. Id., p. 31.

2.6 Conclusion and Recommendations

Beneficial ownership is a concept that is relatively straightforward in theory but difficult to apply in practice. The essence is to identify the person who ultimately controls a corporate vehicle. This identification always will be a highly context-dependent, de facto judgment; beneficial ownership cannot be reduced to a legal definition. Even when a service provider takes a substantive approach (that is, goes further than a purely formal approach would require), the provider can do only so much to determine control. With few exceptions, service providers do not have the resources or the access to information they need to really *investigate* a corporate vehicle. Certainly, they can ask questions, search databases for information, and compare whether a vehicle's financial conduct matches its profile. But they cannot do much more than that. In the end, any due diligence system can be beaten.

The difference between the substantive and formal approach is that the substantive approach remains open-minded about who the beneficial owner may be, and it takes the outcome of the formal approach as a working hypothesis rather than as a final, definitive conclusion. In addition, the substantive approach goes beyond making inquiries about office holders and shareholdings, important as these are. The approach requires all economic realities to be considered when determining beneficial ownership—when taking on a new customer and thereafter—constantly reviewing whether this information is coherent with everything else known (or thought to be known) about the customer.

That said, having information on the 25 percent shareholder still has merit. Even if the shareholder is not the beneficial owner, the shareholder certainly is going to be a person of interest in any due diligence and normally would constitute a further source of information.

The above conclusions lead us to make the following four recommendations:

Recommendation 1. Countries should ensure that, whatever definition of beneficial ownership they employ, the beneficial owner is *always* a natural person.

Without adherence to this basic principle, the concept of beneficial ownership is virtually useless. Every legal entity and arrangement is ultimately controlled by a natural person. A policy that does not require a service provider to penetrate to this level is deficient in terms of efficacy, deterrence and justice.

Recommendation 2. Countries should consider introducing an alternative term for those persons currently described under formal approaches as beneficial owners.

Formal approaches, such as those based on percentage thresholds of ownership of legal entities, are certainly able to provide actionable information on persons of interest to law enforcement in a corruption or money laundering investigation. A term that clarifies this distinction will facilitate communication on the topic.[a]

Recommendation 3. Countries should develop a clear formal standard for identifying standard parties likely to be the beneficial owner but should require deeper inquiry in high-risk scenarios.

To maintain the focus on the substantive, economic meaning of beneficial ownership, countries that have adopted a formal approach should make it clear in legislation and guidance that the pertinent threshold is a *minimum* standard. They should also make it clear that reporting institutions (financial institutions, trust and company service providers, and others) have a legal obligation when confronted with suspicious circumstances to undertake further inquiry to identify and record information on other parties who appear relevant.

Recommendation 4. Ongoing due diligence should be used to bridge the gap between the formal and substantive approaches toward collecting beneficial ownership information.

Service providers should be aware of the dangers of relying on evadable standards, confirmed only by client-provided information and public records. They should employ ongoing verification practices to determine whether the information clients provide is consistent with the services requested and the transactions taking place. In suspicious cases, they should dig deeper to find out whether other natural persons (beyond the formal, legally declared power holders) really are in control.

Note: a. The participants in this study used various terminology schemes to describe the distinction between the "formal" and "substantive" beneficial owners referred to here. These included "Nominal/Legal/Registered Owner v. Beneficial Owner," "Beneficial Owner v. Ultimate Beneficial Owner," "Persons of Interest v. Beneficial Owner," and "Beneficial Owner v. Ultimate Controller." None of these proposed dichotomies is without its problems, however: "nominal," "registered," and "legal" are not synonymous, and each has shades of meaning that invite criticism if chosen; the idea of a beneficial owner not being an ultimate beneficial owner seems to be splitting hairs; "persons of interest" is vague and possibly accusatory.

Part 3. Where Does the Beneficial Owner Hide?

"Vice knows she's ugly, so puts on her mask."

— Benjamin Franklin

3.1 Introduction

This study revealed that, in the vast majority of grand corruption cases we analyzed, corporate vehicles—including companies, trusts, foundations, and fictitious entities—are misused to conceal the identities of the people involved in the corruption. Of these corporate vehicles, the company was the most frequently used. Investigators confirmed this misuse, noting that locating information about the person who is in control of a corporate vehicle was essential to any large-scale corruption investigation, and indeed, to almost any large-scale organized-crime investigation. Despite the widespread misuse of corporate vehicles for criminal purposes (including corruption, financing terrorism, money laundering, and fraud), most countries have no coherent strategy to tackle this problem. This chapter identifies the types of corporate vehicles used to conceal the identity of the person involved in the corruption and other obstacles that investigators may face. An overview of each of these corporate vehicles is given in appendix C.

3.2 Corporate Vehicles: Types and Features

This section describes the various types of corporate vehicles that have been used in grand corruption schemes. We distinguish four distinct categories:

- Companies
- Trusts
- Foundations
- Fictitious entities and unincorporated economic organizations.

(Fictitious entities is an outlier category, encompassing sole proprietorships, the various forms of partnerships, and other functionally effective equivalents.) We provide an overview of the main characteristics of these corporate vehicles. Their precise nature, the ways in which they are misused for criminal ends, and the extent to which they are misused vary from jurisdiction to jurisdiction; nonetheless, our study revealed a number of global similarities.

3.2.1 Companies

Companies were used to hide the proceeds of corruption in 128 of the 150 cases of grand corruption reviewed. The legal characteristics distinguishing public from private companies, as well as limited liability companies and more recent offshoots, are given in appendix C. The more relevant distinction made to tackle corruption relates to each company's purpose rather than to their legal definition. In this part of the report, we consider both companies that are intended primarily to hold assets or liabilities and companies that are intended primarily for the purpose of engaging in business activity in some industry.[20]

Shell Companies

In more than half of the cases analyzed that involved any sort of company,[21] that company was a "shell company." For our purposes, a shell company can be defined as a non-operational company—that is, a legal entity that has no independent operations, significant assets, ongoing business activities, or employees.[22] In a case study on money laundering involving Riggs Bank, a U.S. Senate report declared that, "In many instances, a private banker will set up [a] shell corporation for a client and open accounts in the name of that shell corporation, in order to disguise the client's ownership of the account or certain assets."[23] Box 3.1 describes how a shell company is set up.

Nonetheless, as long as compliance officers have access to trustworthy information for due diligence, they are generally comfortable providing financial services for nonoperational

---

20. The terminology used in this section includes some working definitions that at times may be ambiguous. The demarcation between types of companies often is not clear-cut. One type of entity may simultaneously fall into several of the categories distinguished in this part of the report. We have offered industry usage terminology when possible and to clearly contrast our usage with other common usages.

21. For roughly a quarter of the investigated cases involving companies, we were unable to determine with certainty whether the involved corporate vehicles were shell companies; it is at least possible that a number of the unknowns were in fact shell companies.

22. The Financial Action Task Force on Money Laundering (FATF) Recommendations make no use of the term "shell company" per se, but do mention "shell banks" in Recommendation 18, and the glossary definition, "[. . .] a bank incorporated in a jurisdiction in which it has no physical presence and which is unaffiliated with a regulated financial group," comes closer to our intended usage by focusing on tangibility rather than illicit intent. In "Behind the Corporate Veil" (Paris: OECD 2001), p. 17, shell companies are defined as follows: "Companies, which are entities established not to pursue any legitimate business activity but solely to obscure the identity of their beneficial owners and controllers, constitute a substantial proportion of the corporate vehicles established in some OFCs [offshore financial centers]." This definition was unsuitable for our needs because it implies an illicit purpose. Ambiguities remain, as certain businesses necessitate the existence of a holding company that holds the shares in one or more operational companies. Given historical usage, referring to such a company as a "shell" may have a pejorative connotation. As a final point of clarification, "significant assets" refers to operationally necessary assets meant primarily to benefit the company rather than its owners (for example, office space, furniture, computer or industry-specific equipment). The major concern raised by shell companies is that they often possess financial assets—cash, stock, titles to property, and so on.

23. U.S. Senate Permanent Subcommittee on Investigations, Committee on Governmental Affairs, *Money Laundering and Foreign Corruption Enforcement and Effectiveness of the Patriot Act, Case Study Involving Riggs Bank*, July 15, 2004, p. 13.

company clients; as such, "hollow" companies are commonly formed to serve a variety of legitimate economic functions. One such function is to facilitate a merger: two companies will structure this transaction so that they merge under a third, neutral shell company. Companies entering into a joint venture also use shell companies. In a multinational transaction, many companies prefer to seat their international joint-venture company in a neutral jurisdiction to ensure that no one company receives preferential legal treatment. In addition, shell companies are also used to sequester liabilities, to create distinctive equity or debt tranches in a single asset, to serve as a personal holding company, or to serve as a company holding personal or family assets for ease of inheritance or as protection against attachment by creditors.

One specific type of shell company structure is the international business corporation (IBC) (see appendix C). IBCs are typically used for shell companies set up by nonresidents in offshore financial centers (OFCs). By definition, IBCs make ideal shell companies, because they are not permitted to conduct business within the incorporating jurisdiction and generally are exempt from local income taxes.

Unlike normal companies, shell companies have no economic activity, which makes it difficult to find out much information about them. A normal company that is engaged in business will typically market itself, join a chamber of commerce, build a website, buy space in the phonebook, sponsor youth sporting events, and purchase supplies and equipment. It will have employees who can be interrogated, keep meeting minutes that may be consulted, and produce financial data that can be compared with normative industry benchmarks. A non-operational company like a shell company may do some of these things (companies are often obligated to hold a meeting of shareholders once a year), but it probably does not have to.

This study's review of grand corruption cases reveals that shell companies, when used illicitly, are generally used in combination with additional mechanisms to obscure beneficial ownership. The mechanisms include exercising control surreptitiously through contracts (rather than "standard" ownership and control positions), adding layers of corporate vehicles, hiding behind bearer shares, and ensuring that the beneficial owners are located (or the identifying information is stored) in another jurisdiction. See box 3.2 for an example of how a shell company was misused.

BOX 3.2 **Misusing a Shell Company**

The Case of Anthony Seminerio (United States)
   On February 4, 2010, the U.S. Attorney for the Southern District of New York announced that Anthony Seminerio was sentenced to six years in prison for defrauding the people of New York of his honest services as an assemblyman in the New York State legislature. Seminerio was also ordered to pay US$1 million in forfeiture.[a] As described in the Government's Sentencing Submission of November 6, 2009, from about 1998 through about September 2008, Anthony Seminerio engaged in a scheme to defraud the public of his honest services through the use of a purported consulting firm, named "Marc Consultants." Seminerio used Marc Consultants to solicit and receive payments of hundreds of thousands of dollars from persons and entities, in exchange for which Seminerio took official action for the benefit of those entities, resulting in favorable treatment for those entities in the Assembly and by New York state officials.
   Moreover, because New York's Public Officers Law permits a member of the Assembly to report income in the name of a business, rather than in the names of the individual clients of that business, Seminerio used Marc Consultants to conceal these corrupt payments from public scrutiny. In fact, Seminerio did little or no consulting work.[b] The government stated that "bank records demonstrate that Marc Consultants was a shell company." The records for an account held in the name of Marc Consultants demonstrate that Seminerio used the Marc Consultants bank account not to handle payments and receipts relating to a genuine consulting business, but rather as an account through which to receive corrupt payments in connection with official acts and to fund his personal expenses.
   According to bank records,
- the address listed on the Marc Consultants bank account is the home address of Seminerio,
- the sole individuals with signature authority for the Marc Consultants bank account are Seminerio and his wife, and
- no disbursements from the Marc Consultants bank account were made to any employees or to any payroll companies.[c]

Note: a. Federal Bureau of Investigation, New York Field Office Press Release, "Former New York State Assemblyman Sentenced to Six Years in Prison for Public Corruption Crimes," released February 4, 2010; available at http://newyork.fbi.gov/dojpressrel/pressrel10/nyfo020410.htm.
b. US v. Anthony Seminerio, Case No. 1:08-cr-01238-NRB (S.D.N.Y.), Sentencing Submission of the USA, filed on November 6, 2009, at 1.
c. US v. Anthony Seminerio, Case No. 1:08-cr-01238-NRB (S.D.N.Y.), Sentencing Submission of the USA, filed on November 6, 2009, at 5.

Shelf Companies[24]

The term "shelf company" is typically (although not uniformly) applied to a company that (a) is incorporated with a standard memorandum or articles of association; (b) has inactive shareholders, directors, and secretary; and (c) is left dormant—that is, sitting "on a shelf"—for the purpose of later being sold (see box 3.3). When the shelf company is sold, the inactive shareholders transfer their shares to the purchaser, and the directors and secretary submit their resignations. Upon transfer, the purchaser may receive the company's credit and tax history. It is possible that the company director(s) will continue in function as nominees, in which case, the outside world only sees a change of ownership—assuming, that is, that the change in ownership is actually registered somewhere, which is not necessarily the case. Until such time as the purchaser may choose to start up operational activity using the shelf company, it also may be considered a shell company.

BOX 3.3	Using Shelf Companies to Conceal Ownership of Bank Accounts

The Scheme of Raul Salinas (Mexico)[a]

Raul Salinas, brother of former Mexican President Carlos Salinas, transferred to the United States US$100 million in questionable assets using a private banking relationship formed with Citibank. Between 1992 and 1994, Citibank assisted Salinas's transfers and effectively disguised the source and destination of the funds by employing shelf companies. Upon setting up the offshore private investment company, Trocca Ltd., to hold Salinas's assets, Citibank appointed three Panamanian shelf companies—Madeline Investments S.A., Donat Investments S.A., and Hitchcock Investments S.A.—to serve as Trocca's board of directors. All three of these companies had been incorporated in 1979, nearly 15 years before Trocca's incorporation. In addition, another shelf company from the Cayman Islands, Tyler Ltd., incorporated in 1984, was named as a principal shareholder. With the help of Citibank, Salinas avoided his name being connected to the scheme by circumventing the incorporation process, and thus no documentation identified Salinas as beneficial owner of the accounts.

Note: a. U.S. General Accounting Office (now known as Government Accountability Office), Report to the Ranking Minority Member, Permanent Subcommittee on Investigations, Committee on Governmental Affairs, U.S. Senate, "Private Banking: Raul Salinas, Citibank and Alleged Money Laundering," GAO/OSI-99-1 (October 1998); United States Senate Permanent Subcommittee on Investigations, S. Hrg. 106–428, "Private Banking and Money Laundering: A Case Study of Opportunities and Vulnerabilities," November 9 and 10, 1999, Government Printing Office, available at http://www.gpo.gov/congress/senate/senate12sh106.html.

---

24. It was not possible to determine the exact number of shelf companies involved in the cases in our grand corruption database. We were able to establish that a shelf company was involved in a small number of cases (six) in which a considerable amount of time lapsed between the company being established and it being used in a scheme (see, for example, the Salinas case in box 3.3). Because a lot of shelf companies are bought just after having been incorporated, however, the time lapse may be only a few months. It is consequently difficult to know whether one is dealing with a shelf company or a company incorporated by a service provider and sold on, especially when it proves impossible to trace the company's establishment history.

The typical advertisement in box 3.4 mentions the benefits for shelf corporations and aged corporations. The price of an "aged" shelf company available for immediate purchase tends to vary depending on how long it has existed. For example, for a company less than five years old, one might expect to pay US$1,000 per year that the company has existed. In the case of a company more than 10 years old, this sum might increase to US$35,000. Costs increase in cases in which the shelf company offers additional benefits, such as pre-existing lines of credit, maintained records, and bank accounts.

Service providers may hold a stock of shelf companies, purchased in bulk from a company wholesaler. Shelf companies have the advantage that one does not need the time to set up a new corporation. In some jurisdictions, incorporation procedures can be time-consuming, so it is often easier, quicker, and less expensive to transfer ownership of a shelf company than it is to incorporate a new one. In some countries, however, the formalities of setting up a company have been so reduced—in some cases to just completing a simple form online—that the difference in terms of timing between buying a shelf company and setting up a new one are minimal. Consequently, the typical justification for buying a shelf company—"I need a company now, not in six weeks"—is losing validity.

Law enforcement authorities are concerned about shelf companies, because

> criminals can easily throw investigators off the trail by purchasing shelf companies and then never officially transferring the ownership [*i.e.*, registering with the authorities] . . . [I]n such

---

BOX 3.4   A Typical Advertisement for "Shelf Corporations and Aged Corporations"

Establish Immediate Corporate History
    Companies Incorporated holds a list of "pre-filed," **off-the-shelf companies** *that you can acquire. By owning a pre-established corporate identity, you are able to* **take advantage of the following benefits:**

1. *Instant availability and fast delivery*
2. *Immediately own a company with a corporate history*
3. *Show longevity and enhance your image with customers and lenders*
4. *Easier to obtain business credit cards and business credit lines*
5. *Often, lenders require a business to have been in existence from six months to two years or more before lending it money*
6. *Ability to borrow money from banks*
7. *Ability to secure bids on contracts. Many agencies will only sign contracts with a business that has been in business for at least two years.*

All entities are in good standing through maintenance, reinstatement, revival, or the equivalent. Your company name can be changed for a small fee.

Source: CompaniesIncorporated®, "Shelf Corporation & Aged Corporations," http://www.companiesinc.com/corporation/aged (accessed July 20, 2011).

cases the investigation often leads to a [dead-end] formation agent who has long ago sold the company with no records of the purchaser and no obligation to note the ownership change.[25]

Operational Entities

The misuse of legal entities is often regarded almost exclusively as being a problem of non-operational companies. This study's analysis of the grand corruption cases, however, reveals that a significant proportion of the schemes (approximately one in seven) misuse operational companies (that is, "front companies"). Operational entities have inflows and outflows of assets, which enables streams of illicit assets to be mingled with legitimate funds and thereby laundered. Thus, substantial amounts of money can be transferred without raising suspicion. One supervisory authority interviewed for this project indicated that the misuse of operational entities for money laundering purposes is a significant and growing problem. The case described in box 3.5 demonstrates the lengths to which criminals will go to gain control of operational entities (in this case, a bank) that will allow them to pass off their illicit assets as something less malignant.

Front companies may be involved in the giving and receiving of bribes. Although unaffiliated individuals may offer bribes to public officials to court favor, the most financially significant instances of bribery, kickbacks, and self-dealing[26] are undertaken by persons working for big corporations.

The case studies of grand corruption investigations identify two schemes that are typically used in cases in which the bribes or kickbacks take monetary form. In one case, the giver of the bribe either creates or contracts with a consulting company to receive and pass on funds to the bribe receiver, thereby obscuring the chain of payment and creating a plausible explanation for the payments. In the second case, the recipient of the bribe creates a corporate vehicle to hide the assets and any connection that he may have to them. In cases in which the official is given a concealed stake in the venture or the company offering the bribe, these corporate vehicles become the opaque link between the corrupted party and the wealth acquired.

Those responsible for active bribery (that is, giving the bribe) sometimes hide behind the fact that although they are in a position to authorize transactions, they are not the beneficial owner of the company. In at least one-third of the cases in our database, bribery or kickback investigations led to operational companies entering into

---

25. Statement of Jennifer Shasky, then Senior Counsel to the Deputy Attorney before the Committee on Homeland Security and Governmental Affairs, U.S. Senate, "Business Formation and Financial Crime: Finding a Legislative Solution," presented November 5, 2009; available at http://www.google.com/url?sa=t&source=web&cd=1&ved=0CBIQFjAA&url=http%3A%2F%2Fhsgac.senate.gov%2Fpublic%2Findex.cfm%3FFuseAction%3DFiles.View%26FileStore_id%3D1c13f428-29f0-47fa-b5d3-6334f51aac0a&ei=86lyTKbmG8WBlAf3ls2cDw&usg=AFQjCNEx1wZRRI_e49v-45Nk6QOWWgmNoQ&sig2=lbwTpXbVzgfN8oyynXTrzg.
26. The hiding of beneficial interests given to or belonging to those public officials tasked with the award of contracts.

The Case of Pavel Lazarenko, Former Prime Minister (Ukraine)

The European Federal Credit Bank (EuroFed) featured prominently in the U.S. prosecution and conviction of former Ukrainian Prime Minister Pavel Lazarenko on charges of money laundering and conspiracy to commit money laundering.[a] In early 1997, when Lazarenko faced corruption allegations in Ukraine and believed that he soon would lose his post, he and his coconspirator Peter Kiritchenko[b] learned that EuroFed, an offshore bank domiciled in Antigua, was for sale and agreed to buy it.[c] According to an opinion issued by the U.S. District Court for the Northern District of California, "Lazarenko opened his own personal account at EuroFed, and in August 1997, Lazarenko and Kiritchenko purchased a 67 percent interest in the bank." The indictment against Lazarenko had alleged that "It was further part of the conspiracy that in May of 1997, Kiritchenko and Lazarenko began negotiations to purchase, and by August 7, 1997, purchased, a [67 percent][d] share of European Federal Credit Bank in St. John's, Antigua, in order to facilitate the transfer of money and to further conceal and disguise the nature, origin, location, source, ownership and control of the money that was paid for the benefit of Lazarenko."[e] The indictment added that "[B]etween May and September 1997, Lazarenko transferred approximately US$70 million into accounts he and Kiritchenko controlled" at EuroFed.[f] In 2005, the U.S. Department of Justice filed a civil asset forfeiture case to seize Lazarenko's assets, including approximately US$85.5 million alleged to have been formerly on deposit in accounts held for his benefit at EuroFed.[g]

Note: a. US v. Lazarenko, No. 06-10592, 564 F. 3d 1026 (9th Cir. 2009). Lazarenko was prime minister from May 1996 to July 1997.
b. Lazarenko was convicted in the United States of having extorted US$30 million from Peter Kiritchenko, a Ukrainian businessman, who first approached Lazarenko in 1992. However, Kiritchenko soon turned from victim of extortion to co-conspirator, playing a key role in the former prime minister's money laundering scheme, a role that continued after his move to San Francisco in 1994. US v. Lazarenko, 564 F. 3d 1026 (9th Cir. 2009).
c. US v. Lazarenko. Case No. 00-cr-00284-CRB, 575 F. Supp. 2d 1139, 2008 U.S. Dist. LEXIS 71387 (N.D. Cal), Opinion issued on August 22, 2008, at 1141.
d. US v. Lazarenko. Case No. 00-cr-00284-CRB, 575 F. Supp. 2d 1139, 2008 U.S. Dist. LEXIS 71387 (N.D. Cal.), Opinion issued on August 22, 2008, at 1141.
e. US v. Lazarenko, Case No. 00-cr-0284-CRB (N.D. Cal.), Indictment filed May 18, 2000, Count 1 Conspiracy to Commit Money Laundering, at para. 21.
f. Ibid at para. 22. The purchase took place a month after Lazarenko was pressured to step down as prime minister in July 1997. US v. Lazarenko, 564 F, 3d 1026 (N.D. Cal.), Opinion issued on August 22, 2008. In the fall of 1999, acting on a request by the Ukrainian authorities, the Antiguan government began an investigation of EuroFed for alleged money laundering activities and froze its assets.
g. US v. All Assets Held at Bank Julius Baer & Company, Ltd., et al., Case No. 1:04-cv-00798-PLF (D.D.C.), First Amended Verified Complaint for Forfeiture In Rem, filed June 30, 2005.

settlements with or without being convicted by the authorities. In one typical case, IBM accepted a settlement with the U.S. Securities and Exchange Commission when people at IBM's Argentina subsidiary—without the knowledge or approval of U.S. employees or IBM shareholders—engaged in a relationship with a subcontractor to pass along millions of dollars for distribution to directors of Banco de la Nacion.[27]

---

27. In the Matter of International Business Machines Corp., Administrative Proceeding File No. 3-13097, Rel. No. 34-43761, Dec. 21, 2000 (settlement), pp. 2–3. In instances such as this, the corporations

In these instances, the company provides an essential veil, but the overarching legitimate activities of the company are what truly provide the cover for transactions used to bribe officials. These transactions are usually small enough not to attract the attention of internal control, management, or shareholders. Therefore, it is not the beneficial ownership of the legal entity as a whole that is important, but rather the control over specific transactions.

Companies with Bearer Shares or Share Warrants

Bearer shares often come up for discussion in the context of anti-money laundering (AML) measures because they allow for anonymous transfers of control. Bearer shares are company shares that exist in certificate form, and whoever is in physical possession of the bearer shares is deemed to be their owner. Transfer requires only the delivery of the instrument from person to person (in some cases, combined with endorsement on the back of the instrument). Box 3.6 shows just how easy it is to set up a company with this type of instrument. Unlike "registered" shares (for which ownership is determined by entry in a register[28]), bearer shares typically give the person in possession of the certificate (the bearer) voting rights or rights to dividend. Almost identical in terms of function are unregistered "share warrants."[29] A share warrant may be thought of as a voucher entitling the holder to the right to acquire shares. Concerns have been raised in AML forums that companies that issue bearer shares are used extensively for illegal activities, such as tax evasion and money laundering (see box 3.7).[30]

In most jurisdictions, bearer-share statutes have generally been undergoing a process of reform and elimination, typically being phased out through "dematerialization" or "immobilization." Dematerialization requires bearer shares to be computerized and registered in company ledgers, thereby negating their status as an "unregistered" instrument.[31] Immobilization requires the bearer share to be placed with a custodial agent,

---

themselves (for example, IBM and others) are not included in our database because, unlike the intermediate companies, they were not themselves used to conceal payments.

28. Although the register may have a certificate of the security evidencing title, possession of this certificate is not relevant to legal ownership. Transfer of a registered security is effected by an amendment of the register.

29. "There is a slight distinction between 'share warrants to bearer' and 'bearer shares'. The former give the bearer an entitlement to the share therein specified, whereas the latter refer to negotiable instruments that accord ownership in a corporation to the person who possesses the bearer share certificate." *Tax Cooperation 2009: Towards a Level Playing Field* (Paris: OECD, 2009), p. 213.

30. Without doubt, such a reputation arises in part from the terms by which some businesses market these entities, for example: "The trick behind Bearer Shares, however, is that they must be issued properly by a qualified and knowledgeable corporate director. *As long as you do not have them in your possession at the time you are questioned, you can legally and truthfully say under oath, 'I am not the owner of that corporation.'* [. . .] If your nominee officer is ever questioned about your corporation, *he can say the same thing: 'Bearer shares were issued, I don't know who owns the company, and I can prove it.'* [. . .] *it is impossible to know for certain who the shareholders of the company are.* Because a transfer of the shares can be made by simply handing them to another person, bearer shares can be transferred more easily than non-bearer shares" (italics added). Coddan Companies Formation Worldwide, http://www.coddan.co.uk/s-9-uk-bearer-shares-company-formation.html (accessed July 22, 2011).

31. For example, a Belgian law of December 14, 2005, provides for the phasing out of bearer shares in all domestic companies.

André Pascal Enterprises (England and Wales)

André Pascal Enterprises[a] was an England and Wales Private Company Limited by Shares (with bearer-share warrants) set up by a U.K. corporate service provider. Upon payment and submission of the order to set up the company, the provider electronically lodged the application with U.K. Companies House. The provider became the initial shareholder of the company and subscriber to the Memorandum and Articles of Association for the purposes of government records. Upon receipt of signed documents from the client—but without requiring or requesting the client to provide any supporting identification—the provider issued bearer-share warrants, erasing the provider's name from the share registry without substituting any other. André Pascal Enterprises had a nominee director and nominee secretary (courtesy of the provider), again providing separation from the beneficial owner. The incorporation process took less than a day, filling out the online forms took 45 minutes, and the total cost was £515.95.

Note: a. This company was set up as part of the TCSP project.

The Case of Former President Frederick Chiluba (Zambia)[a]

Iqbal Meer, a London-based solicitor, was among the defendants in a private civil asset recovery action brought by the Zambian attorney general in the U.K. High Court against his law firm and others for their role in assisting President Frederick Chiluba and his director general of the Zambian Security and Intelligence Services (ZSIS), X. F. Chungu, to funnel funds stolen from the Zambian government. In his judgment delivered on May 4, 2007, Mr. Justice Peter Smith held that Meer had incorporated a British Virgin Islands International Business Company, Harptree Holdings Ltd., with the company's bearer shares held in trust by a nominee at Bachmann Trust Company Ltd. Harptree Holdings had been formed to purchase real estate in Belgium—a block of flats and an apartment hotel—to pay off one of the co-conspirators in the case, Faustin Kabwe, who was identified in the court's judgment as a close friend and financial adviser to Chiluba and Chungu. This involved the transfer of funds from Zambia's ministry of finance to an account in London (referred to as the Zamtrop account) and from that account to a Zambian financial services company, in which Kabwe was one of the main controlling officers. Suspicions of Meer's involvement in this Zamtrop conspiracy (as it later became known) resulted in the U.K. Office for the Supervision of Solicitors paying Meer a visit in April 2003. They asked him specifically about the ownership of Harptree. He responded, "I have no idea whether Kabwe is holding the bearer shares in his hands or whether somebody else is holding

(continued next page)

BOX 3.7   *(continued)*

[the] bearer shares"—demonstrating clearly how a bearer-share construction can allow someone to easily and accurately deny knowledge of ownership of a legal entity.

Mr. Justice Smith concluded:

In my view it is obvious. The (. . .) purchase was FK's [Faustin Kabwe's] pay-off for his role in the conspiracy. IM [Iqbal Meer], whilst he did not know the overarching conspiracy details, took instructions from FK on behalf of Harptree, because he believed it belonged to him beneficially. Yet he knew that the purchase was funded by government monies via the Zamtrop account but did not question FK's entitlement to them. That failure (even if his case that it was a ZSIS purchase is to be believed) and the failure to record that matter in any document are actions again which an honest solicitor would not do. Such a large purchase of a block of flats and an apartment hotel cannot conceivably have been regarded as a purchase for ZSIS operations. Equally, the labyrinthine routing of the ownership of the properties—via a BVI holding company with nominee directors and bearer shares and a Luxembourg company interposed—shows that the whole operation was to hide things.

Source: Supplemented by additional details from the Approved Judgment of Justice Peter Smith in the matter of *AG of Zambia v Meer Care & Desai and Others*, [2007] EWHC 952 (Ch). Case No: HC04C03129. Dramatis Personae, ¶¶593–601.
Note: a. While Iqbal Meer was originally found liable for dishonest assistance, this portion of the ruling was overturned on appeal on the grounds that only negligence had been demonstrated (Zambia v Meer Care & Desai [2008] EWCA Civ 1007).

who holds the share for the beneficial owner, thereby preventing the holder from making unrecorded transfers.[32]

Financial compliance officers and company service providers report that bearer shares have generally been frozen out of the financial sector even if they are still permitted by the laws of a particular jurisdiction. No bank with any sort of due diligence standards is willing to conduct business with a company that has free-floating bearer shares. Companies that are not required under their own laws to have bearer shares immobilized will typically have to place the share in the trust of an agent of the bank, as a condition of being accepted as a customer.

Some jurisdictions require the involvement of intermediaries in the transfer of bearer shares for the transfer to be lawful and thus ensure that each change in ownership is

---

32. In the British Virgin Islands, companies incorporated since January 1, 2005, had been required to lodge bearer-share certificates with custodians. Companies incorporated before that date had not been subject to such immobilization procedures, but as of 2010, they became subject to more stringent regulations: they generally would be deemed to no longer have any ability to issue bearer shares, and any existing bearer shares had to be deposited with a recognized or authorized custodian. Furthermore, the deposit with the custodian would not be deemed valid until a registered agent had received notification or proof of the deposit from an authorized custodian. See BVI Business Companies (Amendment) Act 2005, Sections 67–77.

registered. Panama remains a noteworthy exception to this trend, because thus far, it has not implemented any policy to immobilize or dematerialize bearer shares.[33] Investigators noted, however, that Panamanian banks generally refuse to conduct business with companies with bearer securities, and the director of such a company must sign a notarized declaration of knowledge of the beneficially interested shareholder to be able to conduct business with a bank.

Given the legislative reforms of the past decade and the fact that bearer shares or share warrants featured in roughly 1 percent of the grand corruption cases we reviewed, one might be inclined to consider bearer securities to be a problem of the past. Investigators interviewed for this study from Latin America and the Caribbean disagree, however. They maintain that bearer-share companies are still a problem for money laundering investigations, that their anonymity prevents detection and impedes prosecution, and that corrupt individuals still can gain access to financial systems and undertake anonymous transactions involving considerable sums.

In practice, there is scant business rationale for the continued use of bearer securities. The claims that bearer securities are necessary to facilitate transfer of ownership and enhance liquidity no longer hold for the vast majority of countries. An electronic system of registered shares is clearly a more efficient platform for transferring equity interests. In this case, the risks outweigh the benefits.

3.2.2 Trusts

Our review of grand corruption investigations suggests that trusts are used infrequently. In fact, only 5 percent of the corporate vehicles identified were trusts, appearing in only about 15 percent of the investigations. The misuse of trusts was found in schemes originating with corrupt government officials in all parts of the world. It appeared most in Latin America, the Caribbean, and high-income nations. Unfortunately, in most cases, the legal documentation available failed to identify the jurisdiction of origin (that is, the country under whose laws the trusts were organized). In cases in which the jurisdiction could be identified, however, these schemes were found predominantly in the U.S. states, the Bahamas, the Cayman Islands, and Jersey.

---

33. "Decree 524 of 2005 establishes the registration requirement for associations and non-profit foundations. Except for this development, none of the actions recommended in the evaluation report have been taken: (a) corporate services providers (mostly lawyers) are not subject to an adequate AML/CFT [anti-money laundering/combating the financing of terrorism] regime; (b) no measures have been taken to avoid the possible use of bearer shares for unlawful purposes; (c) no obligation has been imposed to update information on the ownership of legal persons in the public registry of property, or for the strengthening of registration to enable more timely and accurate information to be provided; and (d) corporate law has not been revised to ensure that operators of justice and other authorities can access useful information on the beneficial ownership of legal entities established in Panama." Caribbean Financial Action Task Force, "Panama: Follow-up Report to Mutual Evaluation Approved September 2006," February 2009, p. 4, available at http://www.cfatf-gafic.org/.../Panama_1st_Follow-Up_Report_(Final)_English.pdf (accessed July 21, 2011).

In principle, a trust service provider will serve as trustee and thereby have effective control over the trust. In practice, the originator of the trust ("the settlor") may share in these responsibilities or exert influence through other mechanisms. Although it was once considered to be a guiding principle of trust law that a settlor must give up effective control of any assets placed into a trust, many jurisdictions have fundamentally modified this requirement.[34] These modifications make it possible for a settlor not only to be listed as a beneficiary, but also to maintain control over the trust by serving as a co-trustee or protector, with the power to veto trustee decisions or even to replace them.[35] The modifications also make it possible for a trust to be created by a settlor but funded by some other party (the "economic settlor"), whose name need not appear on any documents pertaining to the trust.

The relatively small numbers of grand corruption investigations in this study involving the abuse of trusts seemingly contradicts a popular perception that those perpetrating illicit activities find trusts and similar legal arrangements particularly useful and frequently misuse them for that purpose.[36] Indeed, service providers approached for the audit studies often recommended the use of stand-alone trusts or a combination of a company and a trust for holding assets. The design of trust laws in many jurisdictions may make it difficult for creditors to sue, prevail in court, or collect awarded monies. For example, authorities may not recognize the laws of other jurisdictions, may not recognize and enforce foreign judgments,[37] and may fail to apply laws against transferring assets to avoid creditors.

Investigators interviewed as part of this study argued that the grand corruption investigations in our database failed to capture the true extent to which trusts are used. Trusts, they said, prove such a hurdle to investigation, prosecution (or civil judgment), and asset recovery that they are seldom prioritized in corruption investigations.

---

34. "[O]ne ought not control and benefit from property and at the same time shield it from one's creditors." Elena Marty-Nelson, "Offshore Asset Protection Trusts: Having Your Cake and Eating it Too," *Rutgers L. Rev.* 47, no. 11 (1994–95), p.15.

35. See, for instance, the Nevis International Trust Ordinance. Initial legislative assessment efforts found only two nations (out of 40 reviewed) that, by statute, restrict a settlor's powers in trust administration.

36. "[T]rusts which hide the identity of the grantors and the beneficiaries have become a standard part of money laundering arrangements." Jack A. Blum, Esq., Prof. Michael Levi, Prof. R. Thomas Naylor, and Prof. Phil Williams, *Financial Havens, Banking Secrecy and Money Laundering* (United Nations Office for Drug Control and Crime Prevention, Global Programme Against Money Laundering, 1998), p. 95. See also European Commission and Transcrime, University of Trento (Italy), *Euroshore: Protecting the EU Financial System from the Exploitation of Financial Centres and Off-shore Facilities by Organized Crime* (January 2000), p. 46: "Trusts can be easily exploited for money laundering purposes, considering the rules governing them," such as those that do not require the disclosure of the identity of the beneficiary or of the settlor, those which do not require any governmental license to operate. Some jurisdictions allow for a "flee clause," "pursuant to which "the trustee is able to move the trust from one jurisdiction to another in the event of criminal investigation." See also the FATF Typologies Report on the Misuse of Corporate Vehicles (2006), p. 61: "Responses to the questionnaires [sent out for the purposes of this study] support the conclusion that Trusts and Private companies are the vehicles that are most susceptible to abuse."

37. See, for example, Anguilla Trusts Act, Bermuda Trust (Special Provisions) Amendment Act 2004, Trusts (Guernsey) Law 2007, and Nevis International Trust Ordinance.

The Case of Diepreye Alamieyeseigha, Former Governor of Delta State (Nigeria)

In May 2001, on the advice of UBS bank (UBS), Diepreye Alamieyeseigha settled a Bahamian[a] trust—the "Salo Trust"—for the benefit of himself[b] and his family.[c] He contended that, because the UBS account, although legally in his name, was a trustee account for the benefit of his wife and children (he was purportedly unaware of his own status as a trust beneficiary), he did not list the account on his Declaration of Assets form that all Nigerian state governors are constitutionally required to submit.[d] Alamieyeseigha thus admitted to being (a) the settlor; (b) the trustee (insofar as the UBS account, legally opened and controlled in his own name, was held to be a trustee account); and (c) a beneficiary. Clearly, this was a trust in name only, with no effective legal separation between himself and the asset.

In the first claim made against Alamieyeseigha and his companies in early 2007, Mr. Justice Lewison held that it was established by documentation that, in 1999, Alamieyeseigha opened a London account with UBS with an initial deposit of US$35,000 and a balance in 2005 of US$535,812 from various sources (economic settlors), often recorded simply as "Foreign Money Deposit."[e] Alamieyeseigha claimed such funds were "contributions from friends and political associates towards the education of my children," which Mr. Justice Morgan would later find dubious in light of the governor's inconsistent and changing explanations.[f] Notably, this account received suspect funds of at least US$1.5 million in two 2001 deposits by Aliyu Abubakar. Those funds were immediately converted into bonds,[g] which were transferred to the portfolio holdings of the Bahamian[h] company Falcon Flights, Inc. (purchased or incorporated by the trustees of the Salo Trust, pursuant to the trust agreement[i]) in January of 2002, burying Alamieyeseigha's control over the assets within a nested corporate vehicle structure.[j]

Note: a. Judgment, *Nigeria v. Santolina Investment Corporation & Ors* [2007] EWHC 437 (Ch) (07 March 2007), ¶¶13 and 39. See also Judgment, Nigeria v. Santolina Investment Corporation & Ors [2007] EWHC 3053 (QB) (03 Dec 2007), ¶34(3).
b. *Nigeria v. Santolina Investment Corporation & Ors*, Case No. HC 05C 03602, Defence of the Third Defendant [Dieprey (sic) Solomon Peter Alamieyeseigha], served May 3, 2007, ¶¶10.1 and 37.
c. Id, ¶10.1.
d. Judgment, *Nigeria v. Santolina Investment Corporation & Ors* [2007] EWHC 437 (Ch) (07 March 2007), ¶39.
e. Id. , ¶¶26 and 38.
f. Judgment, *Nigeria v. Santolina Investment Corporation & Ors* [2007] EWHC 3053 (QB) (03 Dec 2007), ¶70.
g. Judgment, *Nigeria v. Santolina Investment Corporation & Ors* [2007] EWHC 437 (Ch) (07 March 2007), ¶¶26 and 28.
h. Judgment, in *Nigeria v. Santolina Investment Corporation & Ors* [2007] EWHC 3053 (QB) (03 Dec 2007).
i. *Nigeria v. Santolina Investment Corporation & Ors*, Case No. HC 05C 03602, Defence of the Third Defendant [Dieprey (sic) Solomon Peter Alamieyeseigha], served May 3, 2007, ¶10.2.
j. Judgment, *Nigeria v. Santolina Investment Corporation & Ors* [2007] EWHC 437 (Ch) (07 March 2007), ¶¶26, 28 and 38.

Investigators and prosecutors tend not to bring charges against trusts, because of the difficulty in proving their role in the crime. Instead, they prefer to concentrate on more firmly established aspects of the case. As a result, even if trusts holding illicit assets may well have been used in a given case, they may not actually be mentioned in formal charges and court documents, and consequently their misuse goes underreported. Unless a clear trail exists, with the proceeds of corruption going into a clearly identified trust account (or unless someone involved in the scheme with knowledge of the trust misuse furnishes sufficient evidence), investigators find it difficult to acquire, through normal legal channels, even the most minimal evidence required to pursue an investigation (and gain a judgment). The extent to which the investigation and prosecution of trusts constitutes a real obstacle may depend on the jurisdiction involved. For example, in jurisdictions where trustees are regulated for AML purposes and the provision of information by such individuals to law enforcement is a well-established practice, a trust may not prove unduly problematic. As one investigator in such a jurisdiction put it, "If you've identified a trust in your investigation, you've hit the jackpot." The perception that trusts are impenetrable may not always reflect the reality of the situation.

Conversely, using trusts to conceal assets does have some potential drawbacks, which may contribute to its low incidence. Professional trustees (who are required to follow standard financial compliance practice) tend to be more inquisitive about the source of funds to be vested in a trust than they would be if establishing a company. They are inquisitive because they face the risk of exposure to legal action, either by outside parties arguing claims against the trust or trust assets, or by settlors and beneficiaries for breach of fiduciary duties. Defending the trust from a suit can prove a costly undertaking for a trustee. Consequently, professional trustees may have a stronger incentive than a company service provider[38] to avoid suspicious clients and ensure that the assets to be placed in trust are indeed owned by the settlor and are of legitimate origin. Furthermore, most service providers nowadays request proof of the source of the funds (for example, a copy of a will or a letter from an attorney for an inheritance, a receipt of sale for funds derived from property or shares, or pay slips).

3.2.3 Foundations

Foundations are a form of "unowned" economic entity, in which asset contributors cede rights of ownership, control, and beneficial interest to the foundation.[39] This corporate form is often used for nonprofit and charitable undertakings. Some jurisdictions have specific laws governing foundations, notably the Liechtenstein *Anstalt* and the Panamanian Private Interest Foundation (see appendix 3). In many other jurisdictions, a foundation is merely a naming convention used for any corporate vehicle (usually a company or a trust) that is intended to benefit a cause,[40] rather than to provide a return on investment to contributors.

---

38. A service provider is unlikely to face such liability when establishing a company. Legal action would be taken against the assets and the beneficial owners of the company itself, rather than the provider who established the company. The service provider's liability is likely to be limited to its capacity as a nominee director. Consequently, such service providers have less incentive to determine whether or not the client is legitimate.

39. As in the case of trusts, such a cession of rights proves to be more theoretical than concrete, as in practice it may be circumvented to varying degrees by allowing the foundation's council to be composed of the asset contributors themselves (or corporate persons controlled by them) or by specifying that the object of the foundation is to financially assist the asset contributors (through wealth management or estate distribution and others).

40. This cause need not always be charitable in nature. See the discussion of the Panamanian Private Interest Foundation in appendix C.

The compliance officers interviewed for this study did not point to foundations as an area of concern, although in a small number of jurisdictions, certain banks indicated a reluctance to enter into financial relationships with foundations, largely because of a lack of familiarity with this kind of corporate entity.[41]

Roughly 13 percent of the grand corruption investigations studied involved (in aggregate) the misuse of 41 foundations, *Anstalten*, or other nonprofit corporate vehicle types that were identified as foundations in court documents. Approximately half originated in Liechtenstein, although this number was skewed by the scheme of Ferdinand and Imelda Marcos of the Philippines, which alone accounted for 15 *Anstalten*.

With the exception of the Marcos case, most of the schemes involving the misuse of foundations did not use a foundation as a shell entity to hold illicit assets, but instead purported to be operational charitable or public interest foundations. This false appearance of doing good may have been intended to discourage close scrutiny of the use of funds. In some cases, funds actually may have been used for the stated object of the foundation, but corrupt officials nonetheless were able to collect assets (especially bribe payments) into foundations and then divert funds elsewhere (see box 3.9).

BOX 3.9 **Hiding the Proceeds of Corruption in a Charitable Foundation**

The Case of Former President Joseph Estrada (Philippines)
In 2000, Joseph Estrada, then President of the Philippines, set up the Erap Muslim Youth Foundation Inc. to "foster educational opportunities for the poor and underprivileged but deserving Muslim youth and students of the Philippines and support research and advance studies of youth Muslim educators, teachers and scientists."[a] Indeed, according to its website, the foundation had provided many scholarships for students to attend universities in the Philippines.[b] In its September 2007 decision in Estrada's Plunder case, the Sandiganbayan (the Philippines' antigraft court) held that US$4.3 million of the US$11.6 million in protection money that Estrada had collected from illegal "juteng" gambling operators were secretly deposited into the foundation's bank accounts. According to the Sandiganbayan, the protection money had initially been hidden away in secret bank accounts set up by his auditor, Yolanda Ricaforte. When Estrada came under investigation for corruption by the Philippine Congress, however, he directed that some of the funds be deposited into the account of the Erap Muslim Youth Foundation.[c]

Note: a. See http://muslimyouthfoundation.com/about.htm.
b. See http://muslimyouthfoundation.com/scholars.htm.
c. People of the Philippines v. Joseph Ejercito Estrada, et al., Sandiganbayan Criminal Case No. 26558 [for Plunder], September 12, 2007 Decision.

---

41. Dealing with nonprofit companies, however, is more standard fare for compliance officers, because such companies are considered to be a primary concern in relation to the financing of terrorism (addressed in FATF Special Recommendation 8) and the source of the contributed assets tends to be carefully scrutinized by bankers.

3.2.4 Fictitious Entities and Unincorporated Economic Organizations

Although all legal persons (including incorporated companies) are "fictitious" in the broadest sense, the category of corporate vehicle referred to in this subsection includes only those with the most tenuous separation of personality from their controllers: They exist *entirely* as an alternative name under which persons conduct business. The glossary of the FATF 40 recommendations clarifies that guidance given in Recommendation 33 on the need for transparency of legal persons is meant to extend beyond entities that have undergone a formal incorporation process to include "partnerships, or associations, or any similar bodies that can establish a permanent customer relationship with a financial institution or otherwise own property."

These types of fictitious entities provided opacity in a small number of the grand corruption investigations studied. The typical purposes of misuse included serving as the name of a business-class bank account (used to launder or store illicit proceeds) or as a name on a contract (for example, listed as a vendor on a government project), spiriting away funds into foreign bank accounts or putting through cash withdrawals before the fraud was discovered. The benefit of misusing these economic forms is clear: authorities are less aware of the existence of the entity,[42] while the criminals face no more liability[43] than they already were exposed to because of the illicit nature of their activities.

Some of these misused entities were originally legitimate, operational businesses that the owners then misused (see Berry Exports in Case Study 2, Charles Warwick Reid, in appendix D). Others, although devised with criminal intent, were intended to stand up to some level of scrutiny (as in the Hollis Griffin case, see box 3.10, in which the misused general partnership that was created was registered[44] with local authorities). Still others proved to be blatant falsehoods even at the most cursory of checks (for example, several cases involved nonexistent companies that were purportedly incorporated in some jurisdiction but that did not appear—even as shell companies—in any company registry[45]).

---

42. The legitimate benefit of conducting business through an unincorporated entity is that less bureaucratic red tape is involved—such an entity need not be "created" through official government processes.
43. The economic argument against conducting business in such a manner is that these economic forms offer no protection in law against unlimited liability. Although this is a concern that needs to be taken into account by legitimate business owners, it is less so for those whose entire purpose is criminal in nature, because criminal liability is never "limited," regardless of business form.
44. "Registration" consists of providing the business names and parties to the local authority, and it is not to be confused with "incorporation."
45. Although they did not really exist, such "companies" often received government contracts for projects that were (a) vehicles for fraud (the project authorizers never intended the project to be completed, merely using it as a cover-story for paying out funds to the corrupt contractor or recipient); (b) legitimate but never performed (funds were received but performance of the contract was either faked or never attempted); or (c) legitimate but subcontracted out to others (the recipient of the contract hired others to complete it, with the contract recipient's only involvement being to profit from a percentage of the contract value).

The Case of Hollis Griffin, Environmental Protection Director (U.S. Virgin Islands)

One of the only clear instances in which a general partnership was found to have been created for anonymity purposes to launder the proceeds of corruption occurred when Hollis L. Griffin, along with three other unidentified officials of the government of the U.S. Virgin Islands, authorized and awarded more than US$1.4 million in contracts, in exchange for bribes and kickbacks.[a] Less than a year after being appointed director of the U.S. Virgin Islands Department of Planning and Natural Resources (DPNR), Division of Environmental Protection,[b] Griffin and others[c] formed a fictitious business partnership and association under the name "Elite Technical Services" (Elite I).[d]

In May 2000, several of Griffin's conspirators registered Elite I with the Office of the Lieutenant Governor of the U.S. Virgin Islands under the trade name "Elite Technical Services." The Certificate for Registration of Trade Name declared the intended nature of the partnership business to be "Computer Consulting and Systems Consulting" and further contained a forged signature of another high-ranking government official, falsely stating that the official was a partner of Elite I.[e] Several months before registration, the partnership was awarded a no-bid contract by DPNR relating to a building-permit request. Without fulfilling its terms, Elite I was paid US$125,755.34, with approximately US$80,000 cash payments being delivered to Hollis and other officials.[f] Payment was received via two checks paid into a First Bank account, following which the funds were removed from the account in structured cash withdrawals.[g] After this first illicit contract was completed, the Elite I partnership was converted into a U.S. Virgin Islands corporation "Elite Technical Services, Inc." in February 2001.[h]

Note: a. *US v. Hollis L. Griffin*, No. 2006 cr-35 (District Court of the Virgin Islands, St Thomas & St John). Complaint. ¶16(C).
b. Id. ¶2 (3).
c. Id. These others included separately charged co-conspirators Esmond J. Modeste (President and CEO of GBS, Ltd., an accounting firm incorporated and principally conducting business in the state of Georgia [¶¶13-14]) and Earl E. Brewley (a local US Virgin Islands Fire Service firefighter and self-employed taxi driver [¶4]). Griffin, Modeste, and Brewely all pled guilty to the charges. See Press Release: US Department of Justice. "Former Government Official Is Third to Plead Guilty in $1.4 Million Virgin Islands Bribery Scandal," September 26, 2006 [Last accessed 08/20/2010: http://www.justice.gov/opa/pr/2006/September/06_crm_649.html] and were sentenced to jail time, and (fitting for a general partnership) found jointly and severally liable for US$1.1m. Press Release: US Department of Justice. "Two Virgin Islands Commissioners Convicted in $1.4 Million Bribery and Kickback Scheme." February 28, 2008.
d. Id. ¶5.
e. Id. ¶¶5-6, 17 A(2).
f. Id. ¶17 B(4),(5),(6).
g. Id. ¶17 J(1),(2). From the first check of US$43,455.34, the sum of US$33,000 was removed within nine days in four transactions of between US$7,500 and US$9,000 each, while from the second check of US$82,300, the sum of US$59,400 was removed over the course of the following two weeks, US$9,900 at a time, twice a day on three separate occasions.
h. Id. ¶7.

In some cases, access to the financial services for these types of entities was the result of dishonest collusion or negligence on the part of bankers. In other instances, the financial institutions were presented with plausible (although false or forged) evidence that justified the creation of the account and gave what was, for their purposes, a satisfactory explanation for the resulting transactions that occurred through the accounts. Most unincorporated businesses were able to open financial accounts under the protocols that banks allow for dealing with sole proprietorships, partnerships, or the "trading as" (or "doing business as") names that are often used by (natural or corporate) persons

BOX 3.11 Laundering Money through a Sole Proprietorship

The Case of Plateau State Governor Joshua Dariye (Nigeria)[a]

The Federal Republic of Nigeria engaged in civil asset recovery attempts in the United Kingdom in the hopes of recouping £762,000 that had found its way into the U.K. financial system from £2.6 million of Plateau State public funds that represented either misappropriated public funds or secret profits obtained by Gov. Joshua Dariye through the abuse of his position as a public officer.[b] As noted by the U.K. High Court,

"On or about 16 December 1999, in Nigeria, Mr. Dariye applied to the Abuja branch of Allstates Bank Plc to open an account in the name of 'Ebenezer Retnan Ventures'. Mr. Dariye signed the application form as 'Ebenezer Retnan', this name being an alias adopted by him. As he admitted to the Metropolitan Police in an interview on 2 September 2004, the Ebenezer Retnan account was his account. Mr. Dariye did not register Ebenezer Retnan Ventures with the Nigerian Corporate Affairs Commission and he requested the management of the Allstates Trust Bank Plc to waive all account-opening requirements beyond completion of the application form. The Ebenezer Retnan account was opened as account no. 2502012136 on 22 December 1999, with the first trans-action taking place on 1 March 2000. Mr. Dariye used the Ebenezer Retnan account to receive large sums from Plateau State, of which he was Gover-nor. . . . Mr. Dariye thereby transferred naira (N) 53.6 million from public funds to [the Ebenezer Retnan account]."[c]

Nigeria's Particulars of Claim stated that Mr. Dariye "wrongfully transferred N438.6 million (about £2.6 million) from public funds to his Ebenezer Retnan account."

Note: a. Particulars of Claim filed by the Government of Nigeria in Federal Republic of Nigeria v Joshua Chibi Dariye and Valentina Dariye, Claim No. 07 C00169 filed on 25 Jan 2007; "Case-study: the Dariye proceedings in the United Kingdom. Written by Case Practitioner." <Accessible at: http://www.assetrecovery.org/kc/node/4710f64d-c5fb-11dd-b3f1-fd61180437d9.html> noting that on June 7, 2007, the High Court ordered judgment in favor of Nigeria and against Dariye and his wife for US$5.7m, plus interest (totaling US$8m), affirmed as fact in Federal Republic of Nigeria v Dariye and Another [2007] EWHC 0169 (CH) 7 June 2007 Approved Judgment.
b. Federal Republic of Nigeria v Dariye and Dariye EWHC 0169 (CH), Particulars of Claim, 25 Jan 2007. ¶47
c. Id., ¶¶26-37.

engaging in trade. Generally speaking, it is not mandatory for basic information on such entities to be maintained at the state level, although there are exceptions.[46]

3.2.5 Other Ways to Use Corporate Vehicles to Obscure Control and Hide Money Laundering Activities

Grand corruption schemes involving corporate vehicles often involve the use of additional strategies to add layers of "legal distance" between the corrupt beneficial owner and his

---

46. Nigeria's strict business naming law (see Laws of the Federal Republic of Nigeria 1990, Chapter 59, Companies and Allied Matters Act [CAMA], Part B, Section 656, Business Names) is one such example in which compelling government interest in preventing corruption has resulted in more strict information-gathering policies being implemented. If a natural or corporate person in Nigeria does business under a name other than their natural, full, legal one, it must be registered with the authorities.

assets. These multiple layers render the beneficial owner's connection to money laundering less apparent to investigation. These layers may also allow the owner to plausibly deny ownership or control of such assets if they are discovered. Investigations are particularly complicated when such layers are placed strategically in multiple jurisdictions, because no investigating authority will have the legal compulsory power to procure evidence from all parties involved. This may be accomplished in many different ways. This section discusses the two most commonly used strategies: legal fiction and the use of surrogates.

Separating the Beneficial Owner from Formal Control via a Legal Fiction

In a tiered corporate vehicle structure, layers or "chains" of legal entities and/or arrangements are inserted between the individual beneficial owner(s) or controller(s) and the assets of the primary corporate vehicle. The use of tiered entities affords a beneficial owner further opportunities to pocket integral pieces of relevant legal ownership, control, and assets across multiple jurisdictional boundaries. All this makes it easier for him or her (a) to access financial institutions in the names of different entities, which serve the same ultimate end, and (b) to maintain control over the primary corporate vehicle (that is, the vehicle holding, receiving, or transferring the asset). Tiered entities enable the beneficial owner to meet these goals while remaining wholly obscured by a convolutedly indirect hierarchy.

This type of tiered approach appeared most commonly in our grand corruption database in situations in which legal entities were listed as (a) the legal shareholders or (b) the directors of companies or (c) both. When discussing such cases, the investigators we talked to said that their efforts to ascertain who truly controlled a suspect entity were frequently frustrated, especially when they were pursuing such information outside their own jurisdictions. Despite having gathered considerable information about an entity, the investigator may still not have been able to reconstruct the control framework; on the contrary, a new layer of opacity may have appeared. For example, if, as part of a money laundering investigation, the authorities in Country A manage to successfully cooperate through the appropriate formal channels with the authorities of Country B to discover the shareholders of a corporation registered in that jurisdiction, they may well find that the listed shareholders of that corporation are in fact corporations registered in Countries C and D.

It is a widely held view that corrupt officials particularly like to hide away their ill-gotten gains using corporate vehicles established in offshore centers. It is true that most of the cases reviewed did involve schemes in which corrupt officials used corporate vehicles established under laws other than their own. Offshore jurisdictions by no means have a monopoly of this type of business, however. Corporate vehicles established under what are normally considered "onshore" jurisdictions (such as the United States and the United Kingdom) also feature prominently in the database. The complex, transnational nature of some of the grand corruption schemes analyzed for this study is clearly illustrated by the case of Pavel Lazarenko of Ukraine (See box 3.5). Twelve jurisdictions were implicated, and criminal charges were filed in Ukraine and criminal convictions were obtained in Switzerland and the United States. Lazarenko and his

"Chaining" Corporate Vehicles to Conceal Beneficial Ownership

The Case of Former New York Senate Majority Leader Joseph L. Bruno (United States)[a]
From 1993 to at least 2006, Joseph L. Bruno defrauded the State of New York by exploiting his position as New York senate majority leader for personal enrichment, using his ability to influence official action in return for personal benefit.[b] He also filed faulty annual financial statements about his consulting work for a company called business consultants. This company was used to disguise Bruno's identity.[c] The whole scheme was effected through several corporate vehicles. One of these was Capital Business Consultants LLC, a company incorporated by Bruno, which never performed any real function other than to serve as an alternate name for the bookkeeping of his outside financial activities.[d] The payments for fictional services actually were made out to Capital Business Consultants LLC and Business Consultants, Inc., a fictional subsidiary that never had been formally incorporated.[e] Bruno further used Capital Business Consultants LLC to "purchase"—and thus conceal—his ownership interests in Microknowledge, Inc. (a company holding contracts with the State of New York), which he and Fassler had acquired in 2000.[f]

Note: a. Details taken from Indictment. US v Joseph L. Bruno. (U.S. Dist. Ct., N.D.N.Y., Jan. 23, 2009) and confirmed in: Federal Bureau of Investigation, New York Field Office Press Release. *"Former New York State Senate Majority Leader Joseph L. Bruno Convicted of Scheming to Defraud the Citizens of New York of His Honest Services,"* December 7, 2009. [Last accessed July 5, 2010: http://albany.fbi.gov/dojpressrel/pressrel09/alfo120709a.htm]
b. Indictment. US v Joseph L. Bruno. (U.S. Dist. Ct., N.D.N.Y., Jan. 23, 2009) ¶¶18-21.
c. Indictment. US v Joseph L. Bruno. (U.S. Dist. Ct., N.D.N.Y., Jan. 23, 2009) ¶57(b)(1)(d).
d. Indictment. US v Joseph L. Bruno. (U.S. Dist. Ct., N.D.N.Y., Jan. 23, 2009) ¶39
e. Indictment. US v Joseph L. Bruno. (U.S. Dist. Ct., N.D.N.Y., Jan. 23, 2009) ¶¶41, 43
f. Indictment. US v Joseph L. Bruno. (U.S. Dist. Ct., N.D.N.Y., Jan. 23, 2009) ¶¶46-48

associates were found or alleged to have formed corporate vehicles, held illicit proceeds, and conducted transactions in Antigua and Barbuda, Bahamas, Cyprus, Guernsey, Liechtenstein, Lithuania, Poland, the Russian Federation, Switzerland, Ukraine, the United Kingdom, and the United States.[47] Not every case, however, involves this degree of complexity. A little more than one-third of the cases we reviewed involved officials using corporate vehicles established under the laws of their primary place of residence.

The ability to chain within and across jurisdictions has few restrictions. In all countries, legal persons are allowed to own shares in companies. Additionally, in a majority of the 40 jurisdictions whose registry systems were reviewed as part of this study, legal persons may be registered as the directors of companies. Twelve jurisdictions were found to prohibit corporate directors of this sort outright, whereas five jurisdictions restrict the use of corporate directors in some way—for example, by requiring that a legal person that is a corporate director not itself have any corporate directors but only natural persons; that the corporate director be licensed; or that the corporate director not

---

47. US v. All Assets Held at Bank Julius Baer, et al., Case No. 1:04-CV-00798-PLF (D.D.C.). First amended verified complaint for forfeiture *in rem* (June 30, 2005).

TABLE 3.1	Two Examples in Which the Registration of Corporate Directors Is Addressed in Law	
Guernsey		**Hong Kong SAR, China**
An application for incorporation of a company shall be made to the Registrar, and shall include with respect to directors,[a] where a director is not an individual, the following particulars that must be entered in the register—(a) its corporate or firm name and any former such name it has had within the preceding five years; (b) its registered office (or, if it has no registered office, its principal office); (c) its legal form and the law by which it is governed; and (d), if applicable, the register in which it is entered and its registration number in that register.[b]		A person who wishes to form an incorporated company shall apply to the Registrar in the specified form, which shall contain the following particulars with respect to each person who is to be a director of the company on its incorporation, in the case of a body corporate, its corporate name and registered or principal office.[c]

Note: a. The Companies (Guernsey) Law, 2008, 17(1)–(3), Application for incorporation.
b. The Companies (Guernsey) Law, 2008, 143(5), Register of directors.
c. Hong Kong Companies Ordinance, Chapter 32, §4A(2)(h) and (i), Incorporation form.

include any foreign company or trust.[48] See table 3.1 for two examples in which the registration of corporate directors is addressed in law. Additionally, in cases in which prohibitions were noted, they did not necessarily hold across all legal entity types: a jurisdiction that requires natural persons to undertake the management of one legal entity type (thus disallowing corporate directors in that role) might not do so in the case of another type.[49]

Of course, the chaining of corporate vehicles (in either ownership or control capacities) does not necessarily imply a risk of money laundering activity. The most elaborate tiered-entity ownership and control structure may still seem simple in comparison to what happens in practice in legitimate undertakings.

---

48. For example, in the United Kingdom, since 2008, at least one director of a legal entity must be a natural person, such that directors of an entity may not all be corporate directors. Companies Act 2006, Part 10, Paragraph 155.

49. For example, in Antigua and Barbuda, the International Business Corporations Act (IBCA), at Section 61, only requires resident natural person directors in a limited context (". . . in the case of banking, trust or insurance corporations, . . . at least one director must be a citizen and resident of Antigua and Barbuda . . . and, in the case of banking, trust or insurance corporations, all directors must be natural persons . . ."). At the same time, a corporate trustee is required for organization of a trust under the International Trust Act (ITA). An international trust is one in respect of which at least one of the trustees is either a corporation incorporated under the IBCA or a licensed trust company doing business in Antigua and Barbuda.

Neither does the chaining of corporate vehicles together necessarily obscure the beneficial ownership of a corporate vehicle. For instance, the use of corporate vehicles as owners and controllers is a common feature of government-owned and -operated corporate vehicle structures set up to engage in either public or commercial business on behalf of the state. Similarly, a family business may be an operational company whose ownership and control is vested in further companies, representing the stake of each individual family member. And a publicly traded company may be listed as the owner or controller of as many subsidiaries as allowable by law and operating agreement. In all these examples, a banker, lawyer, accountant, or other service provider can readily ascertain the true beneficial ownership of the corporate vehicle structure. These kinds of tiered entities have virtually no risk of being misused to conceal the identities of any unknown beneficial owner(s). Instead, identification of money laundering risks will depend on the reputations, intentions, and activities of the known end users and agents of the client—in other words, it will depend on where the corporate vehicle's assets come from and go to, on whose orders, and why.

When confronted with a multilayer corporate vehicle structure, most service providers will need to ensure that they understand why such a complex structure makes sense in the circumstances. This assurance is necessary because the absence of a plausible explanation often implies a money laundering risk for economic service providers conducting business with this type of organization. As a number of compliance officers indicated, a complex corporate vehicle structure "passes the smell test" only when there are (a) legitimate business reasons to justify the form of the structure and (b) significant arguments against using less complex options that might have been available.

Excessive complexity in a corporate vehicle structure can be a good "red flag" indicator of risk—but only if one has a good grasp on what constitutes "excessive." Bankers find it difficult to explain to others exactly what excessive is in such cases: it is grasped only through years of experience. Younger, more junior staff may struggle to understand excessive complexity and miss warning signs. Conversely, investigators with limited background in corporate vehicle structures may tend to overestimate complexity; and a tendency to eye all multilayer structures with suspicion may be just as dangerous, as it can potentially result in the inefficient allocation of law enforcement resources. An example of a complex structure that is nonetheless perfectly legitimate can be seen in figure 3.1.

From our discussions with various service providers, we have distilled four good practices (see box 3.13) that will aid staff in developing a good sense of what level of complexity is appropriate and what may be suspicious.

Such measures are virtually useless, however, unless one drills down to natural persons. Compliance officers in countries where institutions are not required to identify beneficial ownership said they did not feel that they were under any obligation to pierce through layers of corporate vehicle structures when conducting due diligence

FIGURE 3.1   Example of a Complex Legitimate Corporate Vehicle Structure

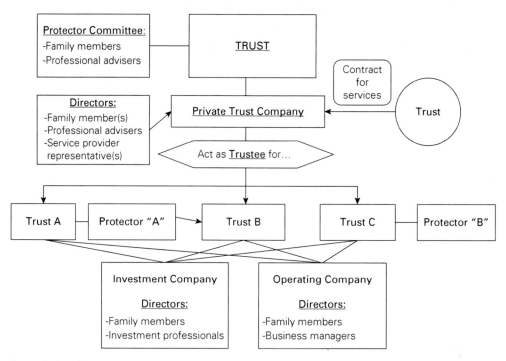

Source: Authors' illustration based on material presented by a member of the Society of Trust and Estate Practitioners (STEP) at the STEP Caribbean Conference CC10 in Bridgetown, Barbados, May 25, 2010.
Note: This example of a complex corporate vehicle structure was devised by a member of the Society of Trust and Estate Practitioners (STEP). It is designed to implement perfectly legitimate goals: to provide segregated asset pools for different investment assets and different family members while ensuring that investment operations be guided by specific instructions (typically of the grantor) with the assistance of outside experts. Clearly, however, unraveling the complexity of this structure would require specific expertise.

BOX 3.13   Developing a "Nose" for Inappropriate Complexity

Following are four good practices to develop the ability to recognize inappropriate complexity:

- **The three-layer test.** One compliance officer suggested an informal "three-layer complexity test" as a quick-and-dirty rule of thumb. Whenever more than three layers of legal entities or arrangements separate the end-user natural persons (substantive beneficial owners) from the immediate ownership or control of a bank account, this test should trigger a particularly steep burden of proof on the part of the potential client to show the legitimacy and necessity of such a complex organization before the bank will consider beginning a relationship.

(continued next page)

BOX 3.13 *(continued)*

- **Expert opinion.** In most legal situations, the rationale for a complex corporate vehicle structure is that it is the most economically advantageous. Often, an expert opinion will certify the legal validity and fiscal appropriateness of the structure. Compliance officers can ask for a copy of that legal opinion (and larger banks can have that opinion validated by their own legal departments).
- **Training.** Many of the bankers who took part in our study asked if the database of grand corruption investigations compiled as part of this study could be made available to them so that they could incorporate sample cases into in-house training sessions with junior staff. The time spent exposing junior staff to novel and atypical instances of corporate vehicle misuse hidden in layered complexity (from formal training sessions to the trading of war stories) is an exceptionally effective way to help investigators develop a keen nose for suspicious indicators.
- **Partnering with professional organizations.** To recognize "excessive" complexity, one needs a good understanding of day-to-day practice and the rationale underlying reasonable (that is, economically sensible and legal) complex corporate vehicle structures. To help to "demystify" the services and products of TCSPs, professional organizations, such as the Society of Trust and Estate Practitioners, are seeking active partnerships with law enforcement and other possible investigators.

in relation to clients.[50] In such cases, they said their financial institution would do no more than simply determine the legitimacy of the corporate vehicles making up the first level of ownership or management, typically by checking the validity of any customer-provided documents by searching in a company registry or using any confirmation materials that could be found online.

Corporate vehicle layering represents a significant problem for investigators. No standard rules of registration make a distinction between (a) a corporate vehicle that owns or controls another (as part of a larger, multi-vehicle structure) and (b) a corporate vehicle that is merely a professional nominee provider. In the absence of clear (or at least suggestive) evidence that a corporate vehicle falls into one or other of these categories, an investigator may find it difficult to know how to proceed. If the jurisdiction of the shareholding entity does not regulate professional nominees, it may not have an immediate way to ascertain the entity's status. If the investigator approaches the entity

---

50. Certain contributors to the project pointed out that the current domestic industry interpretation of beneficial ownership statutes in their jurisdiction allows for the term to be understood as a natural *or* a corporate person, despite having been implemented to address FATF Recommendation 33, which specifically references natural persons.

for information, will the service provider be cooperative—or will it tip off a participant in the scheme?

If an investigator believes that the owners or controllers of the corporate vehicle under investigation are part of some larger, multi-vehicle structure, then he or she will want to analyze the ownership and control of this larger structure, in the expectation that it will bring him or her closer to the beneficial owner(s). To that end, the investigator will seek to obtain evidence that genuinely documents the owners and controllers and the activities of this larger structure. However, if instead the investigator manages to determine that the corporate directors or shareholders are professional nominees, then he or she will give priority to finding out who contracted the nominee services. Relevant evidence will be the trust deeds, indemnification-of-agents contracts, and power-of-attorney declarations whereby the nominee(s) agreed to take legal possession of the shares or to act as the director(s) of the company in question. The investigator can check with the service providers' jurisdiction to see whether it is a regulated business. This will help the investigator decide how best to proceed.[51]

Separating the Beneficial Owner from Formal Control through the Use of Surrogates

In many instances, parties to corruption have found it useful to arrange for other persons (whose names will attract less attention than their own) to be declared the party responsible for a corporate vehicle in some capacity. Out of the 150 grand corruption cases in our database, more than two-thirds involved some form of surrogate—be it in ownership or in management. The use of a surrogate is a particularly effective way of increasing the opacity of a scheme. For example, a legal entity will usually be subject to a registration regime, in which case at least information on management and control is publicly available or accessible to the authorities. The principal actor in a corruption scheme can plant evidence that leads to the surrogate and thereby conceals his or her own connection to the entity.

Most financial institutions consulted for this study said that, in cases in which they suspected that someone else was involved, they did no more than check whether the natural person wishing to enter into a business relationship with them was acting on behalf of some other person. From the names of natural persons or chained corporate vehicles, the number and identification details of directors, or even self-disclosure, it quickly becomes obvious, they say, which accounts are suspect. When pressed on this issue, certain institutions said they adopted a more consistent approach by using a jurisdiction-mandated beneficial ownership disclosure form. In such cases, the

---

51. If the corporate nominee is a regulated TCSP, it probably falls under AML or regulatory regimes that require the company to collect (and make available to the authorities) beneficial ownership information and identification documents, while being legally prohibited from tipping off suspects during an inquiry. If it is a TCSP from an unregulated jurisdiction, however, a more cautious approach would be warranted.

> **BOX 3.14** **Setting up Formal Nominee Arrangements for BCP Consolidated Enterprises (Nevada)[a]**
>
> BCP Consolidated Enterprises was a Nevada corporation set up by a Nevada service provider with a nominee director (officially based in Panama) and nominee shareholders. The name of the beneficial owner appears nowhere on the incorporation documents. With the help of the service provider, BCP Consolidated then opened an online bank account with a major U.S. bank. The cost of establishing the company and the bank account was US$3,695. Neither the original service provider nor the bank required more than an unnotarized scan of the client's driver's license (which happened to show an outdated address).
>
> *Note:* a. This was undertaken in the context of the TCSP project on company service providers.

institutions are always apprised of the beneficial owners of the corporate vehicle's accounts (unless the parties before them are prepared to perjure themselves).

Two different classes of persons actively engage in shielding the beneficial owners or controllers of a corporate vehicle from scrutiny: (a) formal nominees (acting professionally) and (b) front men (acting informally).

Formal Nominees

A nominee is essentially a person who holds a position or assets *in name only* on behalf of someone else. Nominee participation in a corporate vehicle can be devised by trust (typically when holding shares) or by civil contract (typically when registering as a company director) between the nominee and the actual end user.[52] A typical example of how easily formal nominees can be arranged is shown in box 3.14.

Although the reasons for permitting nominee shareholding are apparent in the case of publicly held companies (for example, to facilitate the clearing and settlement of trades by brokers), compelling reasons in a private company context are more debatable. Suppose an individual wants to acquire complete shareholder control of a company that by statute or by law requires two shareholder members. This can, of course, be effected by incorporating a second legal entity to be that second member, or indeed by fundamentally altering the company (in terms of jurisdiction, organization, or bylaw). But it is actually often much cheaper and simpler to hire a company service provider to acquire a negligible "in name only" stake in the company. Service providers most frequently advertise nominee services as a standard component of establishing legal

---

52. Jack A. Blum, Esq., Prof. Michael Levi, Prof. R. Thomas Naylor, and Prof. Phil Williams, *Financial Havens, Banking Secrecy and Money Laundering* (United Nations Office for Drug Control and Crime Prevention, Global Programme Against Money Laundering, 1998), p. 30.

As Described in Typical Advertisements
  Nominee Director Service. Who is a Nominee Director?[a]
  A nominee director is someone who in fact is renting his or her name to you. In other words, the name of this person is used and not yours for the incorporation documents. They are also taking the positions on paper of the company directors. The term of straw man *or* front man *has been used to describe someone who is acting as the nominee. Legally, according to the incorporation documents, the nominee is responsible for the company or entity. In addition, if it is the case of a nominee that is also listed as the nominee shareholder, then they in effect also have the related ownership responsibilities as well.*
  The basic function of the nominee director is to shield working executives of limited and other companies from the public disclosure requirements that exist in the UK and other jurisdictions. It is a perfectly legal device, which preserves the privacy of an individual. It is designed to help a person who would rather not disclose their interest or association with a given corporate body. Anyone performing a company search on a company with a nominee director would be unable to discover in whose name the nominee director was registered.

Note: a. See http://www.ukincorp.co.uk/s-23-uk-nominee-director-advantages.html.

entities, as a way to ensure that the names of the entity's true owners are nowhere to be found on the entity's paper record, thus ensuring privacy. For examples benefits typically cited in advertisements, see box 3.15.

All the national jurisdictions examined for the purposes of this study either explicitly allowed or did not expressly prohibit nominee participation in a legal entity. Guernsey was the only jurisdiction that directly addressed the fact that persons other than those occupying the declared legal management roles of a company may in reality be controlling its activities (although Hong Kong SAR, China, has a provision that perhaps could be interpreted as addressing this matter).[53] See table 3.2 for two examples in which the registration of nominees is addressed in law.

---

53. *The Companies (Guernsey) Law, 2008, § 132:* "(1) In this Law, 'shadow director', in relation to a company, means a person in accordance with whose directions or instructions the directors of the company are accustomed to act. (2) A person is not to be regarded as a shadow director by reason only that the directors act on advice given by him in a professional capacity. (3) For the purposes of sections 160 and 162 to 166, a shadow director is treated as a director." *Hong Kong Companies Ordinance, § 53(B):* "(1) Where the articles of a company authorize a director to appoint an alternate director to act in his place, then, unless the articles contain any provision to the contrary, whether express or implied: (a) an alternate director so appointed shall be deemed to be the agent of the director who appoints him; and (b) a director

TABLE 3.2	Examples in Which Nominees Are Addressed in Law
Turks and Caicos Islands	**Cyprus**
Section 4: Nominee or trust firms, etc: "Where a firm, individual or corporation having a place of business in the Islands carries on the business wholly or mainly as a nominee or trustee of or another person, or other persons, or another corporation, or acts as a general agent for any foreign firm, the first-mentioned firm, individual or corporation shall be registered in manner provided by this Ordinance, and in addition to the other particulars required to be furnished and registered, there shall be furnished and registered in the Schedule to this Ordinance [...] *Schedule (Section 4):* The present Christian or fore name and surname, any former name, nationality, and if that nationality is not the nationality of origin, the nationality of origin, and usual residence or, as the case may be, the corporate name of every person, or corporation on whose behalf the business is carried on: Provided that if the business is carried on under any trust and any of the beneficiaries are a class of children or other persons, a description of the class shall be sufficient."[a]	53(1) Where a firm, individual or corporation is required by paragraph (d) of section 50 to be registered, such registration shall be effected by sending or delivering to the Registrar, within one month of the data the business therein provided has commenced, a statement in writing, in the prescribed form, signed by all the partners of the firm or the individual or corporation, as the case may be, and containing the following particulars, that is to say, the present Christian name or names and surname, any former Christian name or names and surname, nationality and usual residence or, as the case may be, the corporate name, of every person or corporation on whose behalf the business is carried on: Provided that if the business is carried on under any trust and any of the beneficiaries are a class of children or other persons, a description of the class shall be sufficient. 53(2) The particulars required to be furnished and registered under subsection (1) shall be in addition to any other particulars required under this Law to be furnished and registered.[b]

a. Turks and Caicos Islands, Business Names (Registration) Ordinance, §4. Nominees or trust firms, etc and Schedule (§4), available at http://www.tcifsc.tc/Templates/Legislations/Business%20Names%20(Registration)%20Ordinance.pdf (last accessed August 17, 2011).
b. Partnership and Business Names Law, 53(1) and (2), Particulars of registration in case of nominees or trustees.

The grand corruption investigations analyzed for this study show the regular use of professional surrogates in corruption schemes. Often, these were TCSP companies specializing in offering nominees and trustee services; lawyers were also found to fulfill such roles. The consequence of such nominees being registered as a corporate vehicle's owners and controllers is that the identities of the beneficial owners remain concealed.

---

who appoints an alternate director shall be vicariously liable for any tort committed by the alternate director while acting in the capacity of alternate director." The Hong Kong SAR, China, provision may work in reverse of the Guernsey provision on shadow directors. In schemes in which a TCSP director hands over control to a bad actor through a power of attorney or other means, the potential exists that both parties incur liability on the basis of the bad actor's actions.

"Front Men"

Unlike a hired nominee, a front man cannot be said to be just renting his name to an enterprise. Hired nominees acting in a professional capacity may be selected at random, based on cost and the level of secrecy offered. They will seek to insulate themselves by plausible deniability and indemnification agreements. By contrast, a front man is specifically selected, is more likely to be connected to the principal by biographical data than by a contractual paper trail, and usually purports to be the beneficial owner of the corporate vehicle (until legal proceedings are brought against it or the front men). The personal links between the front man and the beneficial owner may be very varied (see box 3.16).

Barring the existence of any exculpatory evidence that proves otherwise, front men face all the risks and liabilities associated with being the true end-user parties in relation to a corporate vehicle, even though they may be doing so for another person. Nearly half of the grand corruption investigations reviewed for this study involved the use of these informal front men. Typically, they appear when the corrupt party holds some public office: he will place the rights to his illicit-asset-holding corporate vehicles in the name of trusted associates or family members (see box 3.17).

One of the ways in which financial institutions are required to identify possible front men is by conducting enhanced due diligence on politically exposed persons (PEPs) *and their family members and close associates* (FATF Recommendation 6). The latter addition was included precisely to identify people in the corrupt person's circle who may be fronting for him or her. Experience shows that, in practice, it is difficult for

---

BOX 3.16	Finding the Front Men: An Insider's View

My experience has taught me that these individuals generally have known someone in the criminal organization for a long period of time, often from school days. There is a strong bond, and the element of trust, between the front man and the criminal, [which are] often reinforced by large and continuing payments and an understanding that the front man will derive financial independence from the arrangement. I have actually looked at high-school yearbooks, and real-estate block records, in order to ascertain who were childhood friends, and/or living in the same neighborhood, as criminal targets. When I was a money launderer, I lived near a major client, which facilitated late-night meetings.[a]

Source: Kenneth Rijock, "From a Different Angle: Money Laundering through Securities and Investments," March 31, 2010, http://www.world-check.com/articles/2010/03/31/money laundering-through-securities-and-investment.
Note: a. This quote, taken from Rijock, a World-Check financial crime consultant, speaks to the people that we include in this section under our working definition of front men.

The Case of Former President Augusto Pinochet (Chile)[a]

Former Chilean president Augusto Pinochet funneled illicit proceeds through foreign corporate vehicles that named his family members and other close associates as the owners and controllers. For instance, Meritor Investments Ltd., Redwing Holdings, and a trust numbered MT-4964 were foreign corporate vehicles beneficially owned by Pinochet's son, Marco Antonio Pinochet Hiriart and his daughter Ines Lucia Pinochet. Bank accounts were also opened under the names of these two persons, as well as another daughter of Pinochet, Maria Veronica Pinochet. Oscar Custodio Aitken Lavancy, an attorney who had ties to Pinochet, controlled six other corporate vehicles involved in the scheme. Pinochet's family members and Aitken effectively served as front men for Pinochet, allowing him to disassociate his name from the scheme while maintaining control over the assets.

Note: a. Facts confirmed in U.S. Senate Committee on Governmental Affairs, Permanent Subcommittee on Investigations, "Money Laundering and Foreign Corruption: Enforcement and Effectiveness of the Patriot Act, Case Study Involving Riggs Bank," Report prepared by the Minority Staff of the Permanent Subcommittee on Investigations (July 15, 2004), available at http://hsgac.senate.gov/public/files/ACF58.pdf (last accessed August 14, 2011).

compliance officers to identify all family members.[54] Commercially available databases may help an institution identify a public official, but it is much harder to find out who belongs to this "circle of trust."

Investigators consulted as part of this study indicated a preference for policies that make corrupt persons more likely to turn to front men for help than professional service providers. A front man cannot hide behind bank secrecy laws or professional privilege because he is ostensibly conducting his own business. As a result, they find that front men usually give up, confess, and cooperate when the police come after them. "It's not like they're under a Mafia code," as one investigator put it. If an investigator wishes to build a case against the ultimate head of a money laundering conspiracy, then catching a front man is an effective move, because it provides the investigator with an informant who can identify the main perpetrator and assist in building the case against him. When family members and close associates own the shares (or perform the management duties) in a network of money laundering companies, it is easier to make a case that the corrupt individual is the "common thread" between all such parties; and when (as is often the case) the beneficiaries are the corrupt individual's spouse and children, it again makes it harder for the corrupt person to argue that he has no connection to the vehicle.

54. For further discussion of the point, see Theodore S. Greenberg, Larissa Gray, Delphine Schantz, Carolin Gardner, and Michael Latham, *Politically Exposed Persons: Preventive Measures for the Banking Sector* (Washington, DC: World Bank, 2010).

BOX 3.18   The Experience of the United States

The United States is one of the world's preeminent providers of corporate vehicles to both domestic and foreign beneficial owners. As such, the strength of its AML regime is of critical importance in the global efforts to counter the misuse of corporate vehicles.

As described in the introduction to this report, concerns in the United States about the misuse of corporate vehicles formed in jurisdictions off its shores can be traced back to a 1937 report by then–Treasury Secretary Henry Morgenthau, Jr. to President Franklin D. Roosevelt. Nearly 70 years later, Secretary Morgenthau's son, then–District Attorney for New York County Robert Morgenthau would endorse U.S. Senate Bill 569, "Incorporation Transparency and Law Enforcement Assistance Act."[a] The key difference, however, was that this proposed legislation (S.569) sought to address the increasing problem of misuse of corporate vehicles formed *within* U.S. borders.

The U.S. Government's National Money Laundering Strategy calls for increased transparency of beneficial owners of legal entities.[b] A 2006 report by the Financial Crimes Enforcement Network of the U.S. Treasury examined the role of domestic shell companies in financial crimes and money laundering.[c] The Government Accountability Office, the auditing arm of the U.S. Congress, also issued reports on the misuse of domestically formed companies for money laundering, and the lack of beneficial ownership information collected by virtually all of the corporate registries operated by the fifty U.S. states.[d]

The Senate Permanent Subcommittee on Investigations, chaired by Sen. Carl Levin, held hearings on the issue in 2006, and the Senate Homeland Security and Governmental Affairs Committee held hearings on S. 569 in 2009. District Attorney Morgenthau and representatives from the U.S. Department of Justice and Department of Homeland Security's Immigration and Customs Enforcement testified that the bill had the support of U.S. law enforcement.[e] A common theme in their testimonies was that the lack of beneficial ownership information collected and held by state corporate registries impeded their investigations as well as their ability to respond to requests for investigative assistance by foreign law enforcement agencies.

Corporate registries in the U.S. typically come under the purview of each state's Secretary of State. At the June 2009 hearings, the National Association of Secretaries of State (NASS), represented by the co-chair of the Company Formation Task Force testified, "NASS and a number of other prominent organizations are currently on record in opposition to this bill, including: the Uniform Law Commissioners, the American Bar Association (ABA), and the National Conference of State Legislatures (NCSL)."[f] The opposition by NASS centered around what it described as the bill's effort to move corporate registries beyond their current ministerial role and the financial costs that states would have to bear to implement the bill's record-collection and record-keeping obligations.

The United States has no legal requirement that companies be formed through a company service provider. Individuals may form and register companies on their own. Moreover, U.S. Trust and Company Service Providers—including attorneys, accountants, and other professionals who perform such services — are not

(continued next page)

BOX 3.18 *(continued)*

considered covered entities under the U.S. AML regime, subject to such requirements as client due diligence and suspicious activity reporting beyond what is already required under criminal law. The ABA, in particular, has been a strong opponent of efforts, including by the Financial Action Task Force's Gatekeeper Initiative, to impose AML regulations on lawyers. Instead, in 2010, the ABA issued a "Voluntary Good Practices Guidance for Lawyers to Detect and Combat Money Laundering and Terrorist Financing."[g]

S. 569, which did not pass in the 111th Congress, was reintroduced in the 112th Congress, in August 2011.[h]

Notes: a. Robert M. Morgenthau, "Tax Evasion Nation," The American Interest Online, September-October 2008, available at http://www.the-american-interest.com/article-bd.cfm?piece=465 (last accessed on July 20, 2011); Written testimony by the Honorable Robert M. Morgenthau, District Attorney for New York County, Delivered by Assistant District Attorney Adam S. Kaufmann, Chief of Investigation Division Central, New York County District Attorney's Office, before the United States Senate Committee on Homeland Security and Governmental Affairs, Permanent Subcommittee on Investigations (Washington, D.C., June 18, 2009), http://www.the-american-interest.com/article-bd.cfm?piece=465. The text of S. 569 can be accessed at the website of the U.S. Library of Congress at http://thomas.loc.gov/cgi-bin/query/z?c111:S.569:, last accessed on July 20, 2011).
b. U.S. 2007 Money Laundering Strategy, available at http://fincen.gov/news_room/rp/files/nmls_2007.pdf, at 8 (last accessed on July 20, 2011).
c. U.S. Department of Treasury, Financial Crimes Enforcement Network, "The Role of Domestic Shell Companies in Financial Crime and Money Laundering: Limited Liability Companies," available at http://www.fincen.gov/news_room/rp/files/LLCAssessment_FINAL.pdf (last accessed on July 20, 2011).
d. Government Accountability Office, "Company Formations: Minimal Ownership Information Is Collected and Available" (GAO-06-376, April 2006), accessed at http://www.gao.gov/new.items/d06376.pdf (last accessed on July 20, 2011); "Suspicious Banking Activities: Possible Money Laundering by U.S. Corporations Formed for Russian Entities" (GAO-01-120, October 2000), accessed at http://www.gao.gov/new.items/d01120.pdf (last accessed on July 20, 2011).
e. Testimonies of Mr. Morgenthau (delivered by Adam Kaufmann), Jennifer Shasky Calvery (Department of Justice), and Janice Ayala (Department of Homeland Security) available at http://hsgac.senate.gov/public/index.cfm?FuseAction=Hearings.Hearing&Hearing_ID=ef10e125-2c1d-4344-baf1-07f6061611c1 (last accessed on July 20, 2011).
f. Testimony of the Honorable Elaine F. Marshall, Secretary of State, State of North Carolina and Co-chair, National Association of Secretaries of State (NASS) Committee Formation Task Force, available at http://hsgac.senate.gov/public/index.cfm?FuseAction=Hearings.Hearing&Hearing_ID=ef10e125-2c1d-4344-baf1-07f6061611c1 (last accessed on July 20, 2011).
g. Various Committees of the American Bar Association, "Voluntary Good Practices Guidance for Lawyers to Detect and Combat Money Laundering and Terrorist Financing," April 23, 2010, available at http://www.acrel.org/Documents/PublicDocuments/voluntary%20good%20practices%20guidance%20final%2009142010.pdf (last accessed on July 20, 2011). See also, Statement of Kevin L. Shepherd, Member, Task Force on Gatekeeper Regulation and the Profession, on behalf of the American Bar Association, before the Senate Committee on Homeland Security, on S. 569, November 5, 2009, available at http://hsgac.senate.gov/public/index.cfm?FuseAction=Search.Home&site=hsgac&num=10&filter=0&q=kevin+shepherd (last accessed on July 20, 2011).
h. Summary and text of the bill, "Incorporation Transparency and Law Enforcement Act," available at http://levin.senate.gov/newsroom/press/release/summary-of-the-incorporation-transparency-and-law-enforcement-assistance-act.

3.3 Conclusion and Recommendations

Corporate vehicles, of whatever form, are an essential part of the economy. They are the instruments through which individuals choose to invest or run an enterprise, manage wealth or pass it on to their children and collect funds for charitable activity. As with any instrument, the use that is made of them depends on the person using them. In the overwhelming majority of cases, this use will be legal, but corporate vehicles can also be used for illegal ends. It is that very small proportion of cases that concerns us here. We draw the following conclusions:

- In cases where the ownership information was available, most cases of large-scale corruption involve the use of one or more corporate vehicles to conceal beneficial ownership.

- The precise patterns of misuse vary from country to country, although the corporate vehicle most commonly used globally is the company.
- Shelf companies pose a particular problem, as they provide criminally inclined individuals with a company history and set of company officials, all entirely unrelated to the corrupt individual.
- Most companies used to conceal beneficial ownership are non-operational, although operational companies are also used, particularly for paying bribes.
- The use of professional nominees and front men increases the lack of transparency of corporate vehicle structures.
- Bearer shares, although still used to conceal beneficial ownership, are being used less frequently than they were in the past.
- A tiered structure of corporate vehicles owning or controlling others can be particularly effective in hiding beneficial ownership. Information about the beneficial owner will be either unavailable or accessible only at a specific location. Bits of information will need to be pieced together from different sources in different jurisdictions. This significantly increases the cost, time, and risk of achieving a successful outcome in a corruption investigation.
- To be able to identify suspicious, economically unsound structures, law enforcement needs to understand the rationale behind legitimate structures. At the moment, law enforcement's understanding of corporate law is limited.

On the basis of our examination of the use of corporate vehicles to conceal beneficial ownership, we make five specific recommendations:

Recommendation 1. Jurisdictions should perform a systematic risk analysis of the cases in which corporate vehicles are being used for criminal purposes within their jurisdiction, to determine typologies that indicate a heightened risk.

This risk analysis—identifying the risk associated with types of entities, specific jurisdictions, specific service providers, and so on—should inform the guidance provided by the authorities to those dealing with corporate vehicles on a daily basis (whether investigating them or providing services) so that they become aware of possible misuse and are better able to assess the risks.[a]

Recommendation 2. Countries should attempt to develop a consensus definition as to what constitutes a shelf company, and should take measures to render this type of company more visible to the authorities and less desirable to illicit actors.

Given that the time and effort required to incorporate a company have been reduced substantially in all relevant jurisdictions, the legitimate advantages of having shelf companies available have all but disappeared. Fraud risks are highest with those shelf companies that are "aged," as they give a false sense of continued existence. Countries should attempt to identify shelf-type companies incorporated under their laws and pinpoint them as higher risk (for example, through irregular business activity, such as unexplained simultaneous changes in key positions or prolonged periods of no account activity). It will probably not be possible to prohibit the trade in shelf companies as such, because it is essentially merely the transfer of shares in a company.

Recommendation 3. Jurisdictions should require that registered members of a legal entity disclose (be it in documents disclosed to the registry or held by the registered agent) whether they are acting on their own behalf or in the interests of another, undisclosed beneficial owner. A "Declaration of Beneficial Ownership," made by the client to a financial institution or service provider, is a useful tool to identify the possible involvement of hidden beneficial owners and should be required universally.

By taking this small step, authorities will be able to determine at a glance whether a listed member of a legal entity is a nominee.

For a more thorough discussion on the benefits of beneficial ownership declaration forms, we refer to the Stolen Asset Recovery (StAR) publication *Politically Exposed Persons: Preventive Measures for the Banking Sector.*[b] Jurisdictions may consider requiring such a form to be kept on file with their registrar, a licensed TCSP, or domestically registered agent of the legal entity. This would mean that the jurisdiction would need to have developed a clear formal definition of beneficial ownership for the vehicle type. Such a declaration could not, of course, be seen as providing conclusive evidence of the identity of the substantive beneficial owner.

Recommendation 4. Countries that have not taken measures to immobilize, dematerialize, or abolish bearer shares (and share warrants) should do so.

For most countries, the initial rationale for the use of bearer shares is no longer valid, and consequently the abolition or dematerialization would not cause any adverse economic consequences.

Recommendation 5. Countries should develop a platform to bring together law enforcement and TCSPs to serve as a framework within which relevant service providers and specialized units in law enforcement can be educated on the types of corporate vehicles and constructions used, and the rationale for them.

This framework would help investigators and service providers to distinguish more easily between what is and what is not suspicious. It also would help to dissipate the deep distrust of the TCSP sector that is common among law enforcement.[c]

Note: a. Although such responsibilities should be extended to all service providers, the financial sector's responsibilities concerning high-value and PEP financial accounts—even specifically addressing corporate vehicles—are already enshrined in the United Nations Convention against Corruption (UNCAC), Article 52 ("Prevention and detection of transfers of proceeds of crime") at 2(a): "[State Parties shall] *Issue advisories regarding the types of natural or legal person to whose accounts financial institutions within its jurisdiction will be expected to apply enhanced scrutiny, the types of accounts and transactions to which to pay particular attention and appropriate account-opening, maintenance and record-keeping measures to take concerning such accounts.*"
b. Theodore S. Greenberg, Larissa Gray, Delphine Schantz, Carolin Gardner, and Michael Latham, *Politically Exposed Persons: Preventive Measures for the Banking Sector* (Washington, DC: World Bank, 2010). pp. 35–39. This report provides particularly instructive advice on the ways in which beneficial ownerships forms give service providers a benchmark against which to test subsequent (financial) conduct of an accepted customer as well as incontrovertible evidence of a customer's statements in criminal and civil proceedings.
c. In many criminal cases, investigators tend to regard TCSPs, as a group, not as neutral service providers but as parties who are at least negligent in the conduct of their due diligence and at worst complicit in criminal behavior.

Part 4. Finding the Beneficial Owner

"You may seek it with thimbles—and seek it with care; You may hunt it with forks and hope; You may threaten its life with a railway-share; You may charm it with smiles and soap—"

—Lewis Carroll ("The Hunting of the Snark")

4.1 Introduction

In this part, we describe the relevant actors and institutions that can (a) help to identify the corrupt persons behind a corruption scheme once it has been discovered or (b) establish a link between a known target and certain assets. We deal in turn with company registries (and other repositories of information), trust and corporate service providers, and financial institutions.

4.2 Company Registries

4.2.1 The Role of Company Registries and the Services They Provide

When corporate vehicles that have a separate legal personality (that is, excluding trusts) are formed and registered, they are granted the legal individuality that allows them to be controlled, owned, financed, and otherwise used for either legal or illegal purposes—in the latter case, often by unacknowledged beneficial owners. It is the task of central company registries to collect and store information on the structural makeup and particulars of such registered entities.

A company registry's main functions are four-fold:

- To record the "birth" of a new legal entity
- To compile the information required by the registry or by law (see section 4.2.2)
- To keep the registry up to date
- To make certain information available to the public.

The information on companies held by the registry serves multiple purposes:

- To identify tax contributors
- To provide statistical information for the government and the public

- To protect consumers and investors against fraudulent entities[55] and
- To allow potential business counterparts to verify the powers and competences of the person they are contracting with.

Several international associations of registries (also called registers) exchange information and ideas concerning the role of corporate registries at both national and global level:

- International Association of Commercial Administrators (IACA) (http://www.iaca.org/)
- Corporate Registers Forum (CRF) (http://www.corporateregistersforum.org/)
- European Business Register (EBR) (http://www.ebr.org/section/4/index.html)
- European Commerce Registers' Forum (http://www.ecrforum.org/)
- Canadian Association of Corporate Law Administrators (CACLA)
- Association of Registrars of Latin America and the Caribbean (ASORLAC) (http://www.asorlac.org/ingles/portal/default.aspx).

Unlike most other potential sources of information on beneficial ownership, corporate registries typically have no specified functions under AML legislation. Their actual function in this regard—as a source for due diligence or investigation—is purely a by-product of their well-established place in the corporate and financial sectors. Nonetheless, both the investigators and the compliance officers interviewed for this study indicated that registries are generally the most valuable and accessible sources of information for investigations, for due diligence, and for identifying trends or recurring patterns (such as cases in which one individual, who is not a service provider, is listed as director for a large number of companies).

The importance of company registries was mentioned frequently during the consultations undertaken for this study. Many financial institutions, for example, reported that they keep track of which registries they trust as a source of certain types of information, and the extent to which they are accurate.

The value of company registries has its limitations. For example, most registries are government depositories and inherently archival in nature. Indeed, all the registry representatives with whom we spoke were involved in almost exclusively receiving and logging information, rather than undertaking any quality controls or verifying the information received from incorporators. Registries have limited scope. With very few exceptions, they do not cover non-incorporated corporate vehicles (that is, legal arrangements such as trusts). Such arrangements are not registered in company registries, and they do not have another equivalent register. Finally, the information available at registries may well be incomplete and out of date.

---

55. Liliana de Sa, *Business Registration Start-Up: A Concept Note* (Washington, DC: International Finance Corporation and World Bank, 2005), p. 3, available at http://rru.worldbank.org/Documents/PapersLinks/BizRegistrationStart-Up_ConceptNote.pdf.

4.2.2 What Information Can Company Registries Usefully Gather to Fulfill Their Duties?

Adequate Information

The type and amount of information on a legal entity captured in a central registry varies from jurisdiction to jurisdiction, but generally it is a combination of the following:

- *Almost always:* The legal status and existence—name, legal entity type (corporation), registration date and (where applicable) date of dissolution or date when the company was struck from the registry, and formation documents, such as the memorandum or articles of incorporation, and related bylaws
- *Almost always:* The addresses of a registered office (which could be a trust or company service provider) or the physical location or principal place of business of the legal entity itself
- *Almost always:* The names and addresses of a registered agent, person authorized to accept service of process, or a resident secretary
- *In the majority of cases:* The names and addresses of persons in positions of legal control within the legal entity (directors and officers);
- *Sometimes:* The names and addresses of persons in positions of legal ownership (shareholders or members);
- *Very Rarely:* The name of the beneficial owner.

As part of this study, legislation establishing company registry requirements was reviewed in 40 jurisdictions. From these 40 jurisdictions, a total of 325 different forms of legal entities (hereinafter "LE types") were aggregated for analysis to determine the information that was required upon registration and that subsequently would be available to banks and authorities (see figure 4.1).

About one-quarter (26 percent) of all LE types file information on the physical location of the place of business, more than half (63 percent) file the address of a registered office, and more than one-third (38 percent) file the address of a registered agent. A little more than half (59 percent) file particulars of a formal position of control (management), and just over one-third (36 percent) file particulars of formal positions of ownership (legal ownership). In cases in which the register of shareholders is not kept at the central registry, it is often found with the legal entity or with the registered office, agent, or representative service provider, whose locations are always required to be recorded in the registry and regularly updated. This can give authorities a quick way to pinpoint who to approach and where to find them.

Of the 40 jurisdictions reviewed, only one—Jersey—requires the beneficial owner to be identified and recorded by a government body, the Companies Registry within the Financial Services Commission, which is responsible for the regulation and

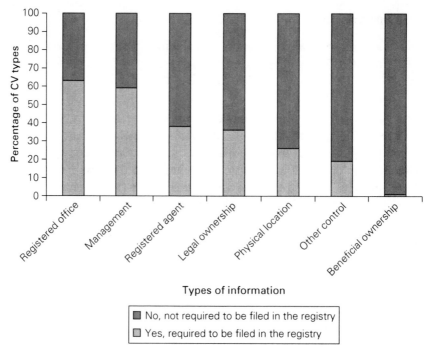

Source: Authors' illustration.

supervision of the financial services industry. Generally registries do not maintain beneficial ownership information, but they do record relevant particulars of legal entities, such as the registered office, the name of the agent, and the management, all of which enhance the potential usefulness of the registry in providing leads to the beneficial owner.

A significant obstacle, however, to the usefulness of the registry is the existence of nominee arrangements, whereby individuals assume a management or ownership position on behalf of an unnamed principal. The majority of registries maintain information about the use or existence of nominee arrangements in the case of but a few LE types: Only a small minority of LE types examined were required to disclose the existence or use of nominee shareholdings, and only a subsection of those were required to disclose the existence of nominee directors.

Accurate and Timely Information

Besides the question of whether information about legal entities is recorded and documented, it is also important to consider the quality and accuracy of that information. Registries rarely verify information or ensure that it is kept up to date. The responsibility for verifying information, notifying changes in particulars, and submitting all the appropriate forms always lies with the legal entity.

Registries generally take information on good faith, with most documents and filings being accepted "as is" unless an omission of information is blatant. On-site visits and data verification fall well outside the typical duties of registries. The information is usually in the form of self-declarations by applicants and subscribers. Quality assurance and updating are the responsibility of the legal entity, and this obligation is reinforced by the threat of sanctions. Providing misleading information is an offense under the relevant regulations in almost all jurisdictions; and in an instance of misuse, this may constitute corroborative evidence in building a criminal case. Nonetheless, registries consulted for this study reported that some companies still fail to comply, simply because they have not understood their requirements and responsibilities. In such cases, they are either asked to amend their information or are referred for enforcement to the respective authorities.

Most registries require changes in information to be updated within 14 days. Requirements vary significantly, however, and the requirements are often formulated vaguely (for example, from "immediately effective upon filing" and "promptly" to "at least every three years" and "from time to time"). Although most registries do take some type of administrative action in the event a company is found to be non-compliant with updating requirements (for example, by revoking registration), they generally cannot actively enforce such compliance.

Because the responsibility to update information lies with the legal entity and compliance tends to be poor, information in the registry may be out of date. Typically, most registered legal entities submit annual returns that allow the registry to note the changes in information or the entity's activities. Almost all registries reported frequent delays in processing and updating information in their databases, however, because of the sheer quantity of companies being registered each year, the high volume of changes filed daily, and the lack of staff to process them.

One of the registries surveyed, for instance, is accountable for a growing register of more than 800,000 existing companies, in addition to 100,000 companies newly registered each year. Although companies remain primarily responsible for complying with their statutory obligations, the registry is continuing its efforts to promote compliance and ensure that up-to-date information is recorded for public search. Similarly, another registry processes and stores such a high volume of paper documents that (as it pointed out) providing access to such information is ineffective and costly for customers and for the registry. Another registry also mentioned that competition with the private sector makes it difficult to recruit and retain qualified, competent, and skilled personnel. For many registries, this combination of large processing quantities and low human resources is preventing them from providing a prompt turnaround of information. Most registries said they have to strike a balance between maintaining the integrity of the register and running a cost-effective operation (see figure 4.2). When seeking information from registries, both financial institutions and investigators should carefully bear these trade-offs in mind. As one investigator put it, "One must take registry information with all its limitations."

FIGURE 4.2   The Balancing Act of the Corporate Registry

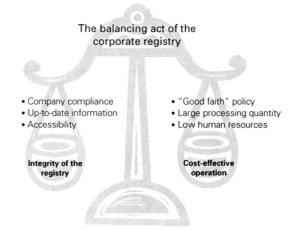

The balancing act of the
corporate registry

- Company compliance
- Up-to-date information
- Accessibility

**Integrity of the
registry**

- "Good faith" policy
- Large processing quantity
- Low human resources

**Cost-effective
operation**

Source: Authors' illustration.

4.2.3 Capacity and Resources—Registering Beneficial Ownership

Several parties[56] have suggested that company registries should expand the information they maintain on corporate vehicles to include beneficial ownership. Clearly, that information would be a potentially useful tool for investigators and service providers alike. To be useful in practice, however, some guarantee is needed that the information is accurate. We therefore believe it will be possible to expand registry information to include information on beneficial ownership only if steps are taken ensure that accuracy.

A Hands-On, Well-Funded Registry

In current practice, registries are archival and passive in nature. Information supplied by applicants is logged, not verified. To ensure that any information on beneficial ownership that it receives is correct, the registry should verify that information (either for every application or on a risk-sensitive basis). For most registries, this would require a significant change in approach and funding. In the course of this study, the 40 registries were asked what effect such an expansion of registered information would have on their operations—assuming equal allocation of resources. Overall, they considered inadequate resources to be a major impediment.

Financial constraints are a pervasive concern, of course, but challenges to resource allocation vary among jurisdictions, depending on the size of the economy, the level of development of the jurisdiction, and the regulatory functions particular to each regis-

---

56. Among many others, the London-based nongovernmental organization Global Witness, the Tax Justice Network, and, in an open letter to the G20, several high-profile public prosecutors. Letter available at http://www.globalwitness.org/library/open-letter-heads-state-and-finance-ministers-g20-renews-call-effective-anti-money (last accessed August 16, 2011).

try. For most registries, verifying registry information would require significant extra human and capital resources. Given resource allocation as it currently stands, we do not believe that most registries are in a position to be able to verify information supplied by a malevolent legal entity or someone acting on its behalf.

In a few exceptions, however, sufficient resources are in principle available for improving operations and meeting additional mandates. This category might include agencies that have a broader range of functions than just business registration (for example, a securities regulator). In addition, some registries generate significant revenues from incorporation fees. A 2007 Delaware report, for instance, indicated that the state's registry had raised US$700.8 million from incorporation activities at an operating expense of US$12 million, providing a significant portion of that state's annual revenue.[57] If the cost of acquiring accurate beneficial ownership information was viewed in the context of helping investigators to better fight financial crime, then high-profit registries might be inclined to devote more resources to enforcement priorities.

Apart from such exceptions, if registries are required to obtain beneficial ownership information, then they will need more government funding to be able to verify the information supplied to them. To effect such an increase in funding, countries could consider adding AML (or more generally crime prevention) to the statutory objectives of a registry.

Credible Enforcement Policy

The ability of a registry to verify the information supplied to it is useful only to the extent that it has the legal power to impose sanctions in cases in which it is provided with inaccurate or incomplete information. And because such a power is credible only to the extent that it is actually used, the imposition of sanctions on those who have supplied inaccurate information needs to be routine. Moreover, the sanctions must be applicable to the person supplying the information, which means that the registry must have jurisdiction over that person.

Sufficient Expertise

Finally, discovering the identity of the beneficial owner in a complicated corporate structure is by no means a routine administrative procedure. It can be demanding, and it requires a good understanding and knowledge of corporate law. Not all registries have this expertise available, and therefore they would not be able to verify beneficial ownership information in every situation. As an alternative, such registries could consider applying a simplified or formalized definition of beneficial ownership.

We believe that it makes sense to have a registry collect beneficial ownership information on incorporated entities only if it is sufficiently expert, well-resourced, and proactive, coupled with a credible enforcement policy (see box 4.1 for an example from Jersey).

---

57. Delaware Department of State Division of Corporations, *2007 Annual Report*, available at http://corp .delaware.gov/2007DivCorpAR.pdf.

Conditions under which the company registry can be considered a viable option for providing beneficial ownership information

Condition 1. The registry is active and alert, that is, it verifies the information supplied to it, or checks it for accuracy (can be based on risk).

- *Beneficial ownership information provided at the time of application is checked against an external database (see World-Check, http://www. world-check.com/) and an internal regulatory database. Applicants often need to be (and in practice frequently are) asked to provide additional information.*
- *Jersey publishes a list of activities that they consider to be "sensitive." They make it clear that, in cases in which a company intends to be conducting any of these activities, more information must be provided at the time of application for incorporation. This policy is currently being reviewed, and its scope is likely to be extended to take account of the countries in which the company will conduct its activities and the parties with whom the company will be engaging in those activities.*

Condition 2. The registry enforces compliance with legal registration requirements and with updating requirements when information changes.

Trust companies that fail to provide adequate information and that otherwise fail to comply with obligations set forth in the Companies Law are brought to light in the extensive dialogue that takes place between the Registry and the Trust Company Business division. Only trust companies regulated by the Jersey Financial Services Commission and Jersey-resident individuals are able to file applications to incorporate a Jersey company.

Condition 3. The registry (particularly the staff responsible for reviewing and approving information for acceptance into the registry) is sufficiently expert and knowledgeable on the concept of beneficial ownership and knows how to identify, in a complex corporate structure, the natural person who is the beneficial owner. If the registry is unable to internalize such specialized experience, a simplified definition of beneficial owner (focusing on percentage shareholding or possibly the natural person with the largest share or controlling stake) might be preferable.

- *Applications for registration can be approved only at the director level, where there is sufficient experience to understand beneficial ownership. Jersey recently created a new deputy director post in the Registry to strengthen experience within the division.*

Sources: Authors' interview with Jersey Financial Services Commission. See also Companies (Jersey) Law 1991, available at http://www.jerseyfsc.org/registry/legislation/index.asp.

4.2.4 Online Accessibility

Various parties consulted for this study expressed a particular preference for online registry databases. The registry databases currently online vary in sophistication and in the amount of information they make available. The simplest allow you to search within a given jurisdiction by entity name, and they show whether the entity is registered in that jurisdiction or not. By contrast, the most developed online databases have extensive search-engine capabilities, with the ability to search by numerous categories. Such advanced registries also store PDFs and document scans relating to the company, which are available for viewing either free of charge or for a fee.

Although many registries can be searched only by a few categories of information (for example, entity name and entity registration number), others make it possible to apply search criteria for all types of information collected by the registry. See, for example, the numerous search facilities made available to the public by the Company Register of Dubai International Financial Centre (DIFC) (figure 4.3) and the ICRIS Cyber Search Centre in Hong Kong SAR, China (figure 4.4).

4.2.5 Information Recorded in Registries

In the registries we studied, the information most commonly recorded per jurisdiction was company name, date of incorporation, entity type (for example, partnership) and status (for example, active) (see figure 4.5). Almost half the registries also made management information publicly accessible, although few made information on legal ownership available. Many registries maintained historical data on inactive, dissolved, or struck-off companies, either in the form of archived documents, name history, or dates of changes in addresses, managers, or officers (see examples in boxes 4.2, 4.3, and 4.4). The amount of information available without requiring a fee or user login also was found to vary.

4.2.6 Access to Information

When capacity and resources allow, access can and is being improved. Many registries, for instance, have begun to upgrade their systems to take advantage of recent developments in digitalization and electronic processing. This is expected to improve efficiency in a number of important respects: accelerating the process of receiving and retrieving information, facilitating timely disclosure, enabling instantaneous incorporation, and generally improving access to corporate registries. These are all important in making the registry an even more useful tool in combating money laundering, as rapid, efficient access to information can save valuable time in a criminal investigation.

4.2.7 Other Repositories of Information

Other repositories of corporate vehicle information that may be useful for investigators and compliance officers include commercial databases, tax databases, and land and property registries.

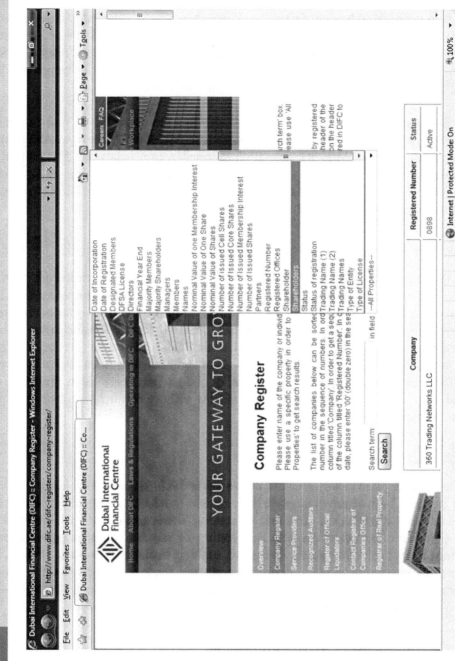

Source: Available at www.difc.ae/difc-registers/company-register/.

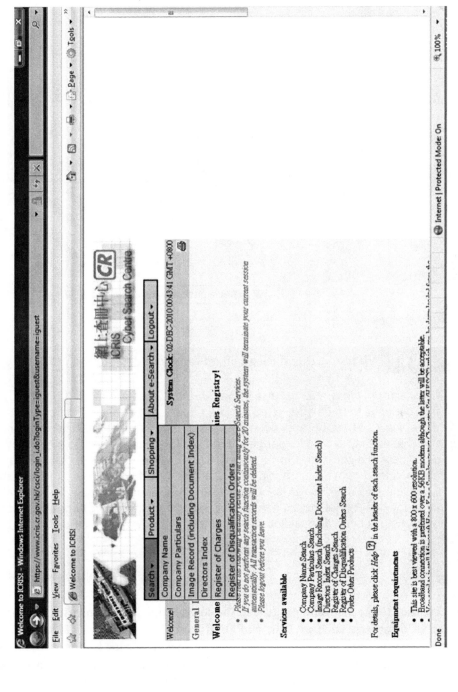

Source: Available at www.icris.cr.gov.hk/csci/.

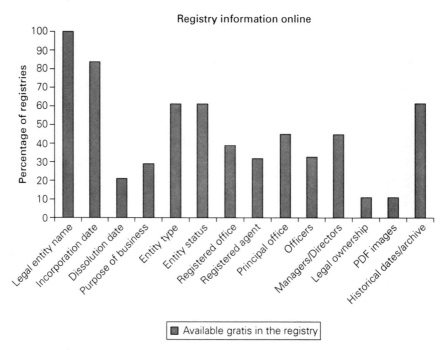

Registry information online

Source: Authors' illustration.

Company directors may be disqualified in the United Kingdom if, for example, they continue to trade after going bankrupt (to the detriment of their creditors), or if they have not kept proper accounts or submitted tax returns. The disqualification means they can no longer be a director of a company, set up a company, or participate in a company. Some disqualified directors ignore the disqualification, however, and continue in business—and therefore form a threat to the public. Companies House, the U.K. company registry, offers a handy search feature whereby one can search by name or by town of residence to track down someone who has been disqualified as a director.

Source: www.companieshouse.gov.uk; "Disqualified Directors Register," available at http://wck2.companieshouse.gov.uk/98864a 48430c353f0286633918c43a0c/dirsec.

In contrast to the depository nature of the central (that is, government) registry, commercial databases, such as Dun and Bradstreet (www.dnb.com), Bureau van Dijk (www.bvdinfo.com), and others, are designed specifically for business solutions, risk management, and client prospecting, and they actively gather their data from a variety of sources. Investigators in several jurisdictions also mentioned the existence of company registries that were wholly maintained by business federations, such as the local chamber of commerce.

The Directors Index: Hong Kong SAR, China

Information about all companies registered in Hong Kong SAR, China, is available online for public search, 24/7. Moreover, information regarding directors of limited companies can be obtained by conducting a search in the Directors Index, through the Registry's Cyber Search Centre (www.icris.cr.gov.hk) or at the Public Search Centre of the Registry (13th floor, Queensway Government Offices, 66 Queensway, Hong Kong SAR, China). Hence, anyone wishing to know which companies a given person currently directs, for instance, can simply conduct a search in the Directors Index.

Source: www.icris.cr.gov.hk/csci/DS_SearchType.jsp

Information Sharing and Financial Reporting Systems: Singapore

Information Sharing—The BizFile Service

Singapore's Accounting and Corporate Regulatory Authority (ACRA) has streamlined and standardized the data file formats it uses to register information about business entities (companies, businesses, limited liability partnerships [LLPs], limited partnerships [LPs], and so on) and developed a highly effective and efficient system to facilitate information sharing with both private and public agencies. Previously, users had to purchase the complete documentation relating to a company to see the item of information they needed. In the new system, individual items of data (such as registered office address, business activities, or directors' particulars) are extracted from the database and are prepackaged into a variety of information products. One-time purchases can be obtained from iShop@ACRA, while government agencies can obtain secure information in bulk through the BizFile subscription system. Interested parties can see what information is available and immediately access only what they need, thus eliminating unnecessary cost. This transformation has made it much easier, both for government agencies and the private sector, to obtain information that meets their business and operational needs.

Financial Information—Using XBRL Data

As of November 2007, companies in Singapore have had to file their annual accounts with ACRA in XBRL (eXtensible Business Reporting Language) format, rather than PDF. XBRL allows data to be read by machines and extracted for analysis. In this way, the business community has an extra source of information at its disposal. These data have a number of important advantages over data in traditional formats. They can be analyzed dynamically to assist in decision making; they are available for analysis as soon as the accounts are filed; and the system conducts validation checks, ensuring the accuracy of the data. Several interactive web-based tools are available for use with ACRA's XBRL data, including Open Analytics and Singapore Financials Direct. In addition to making a useful service available to businesses and banks, the use of XBRL makes it easier for authorities and investigators to scrutinize companies' financial information for regulatory and surveillance purposes.

Sources: Authors' compilation. See also www.acra.gov.sg, BizFile at https://www.psi.gov.sg/NASApp/tmf/TMFServlet?app=RCB-BIZFILE-LOGIN-1B, and XBRL available at https://www.fsm.acra.gov.sg.

Tax databases can prove useful for investigative purposes. The nature of tax information available about a given corporate vehicle will depend on the type of tax regime operating within the jurisdiction. For instance, the tax information available in a tax haven jurisdiction may consist of no more than a certification of continued exemption status. Even in that case, however, a filing will have been made claiming the exemption, and that in itself can provide useful information. The degree to which tax authorities will have developed sophisticated knowledge of and intimate familiarity with corporate vehicles will probably depend on their tax regime. In jurisdictions that offer blanket exemptions from taxation to entice foreign customers to incorporate in their country, the tax authorities may possess little practical knowledge of corporate vehicles. In other jurisdictions, which pursue a more aggressive stance toward enforcement of their taxation laws, much more extensive information may be present.

In addition, if a bilateral tax information exchange agreement is in place, investigators may obtain tax information held by authorities in another jurisdiction.[58] A briefing paper by the Organisation for Economic Co-operation and Development (OECD) of August 2010 describes the significant progress that has been made in this area, noting that some 600 bilateral tax conventions have been entered into by both OECD and non-OECD member countries.[59] The standards for the exchange of information in such conventions include, among other points, "Exchange of information on request, where it is 'foreseeably relevant' to the administration and enforcement of the domestic laws of the treaty partner" and "No restrictions on exchange caused by bank secrecy or domestic tax interest requirements."[60] As the briefing paper explains,

> The scope of the information that may be requested, however, is extremely broad. Where the information requested is 'foreseeably relevant', then this will cover any and all information that relates to the enforcement and administration of the requesting jurisdiction's tax laws, including information relating to interest, dividends or capital gains, bank information, fiduciary information relating to trusts, or ownership information of companies.[61]

---

58. In addition to Tax Information Exchange Agreements, Double Tax Conventions typically achieve the same goal.
59. OECD, " The Global Forum on Transparency and Exchange of Information for Tax Purposes: Information Brief " (OECD, August 10, 2010), at 3, available at http://www.oecd.org/dataoecd/32/45/43757434.pdf.
60. Ibid.
61. Ibid.

Land and real estate registries also may be valuable sources of information. These registries can be perused for records of title transfers when trying to connect assets possibly hidden in property to a certain party of interest.

4.2.8 Asset Disclosures

An additional source of information that can be consulted in the event of an investigation is a jurisdiction's asset disclosures, in which public officials (for example, members of parliament, heads of state, cabinet members, or senior civil servants) declare their financial and business interests.[62] Although asset disclosure systems are not a recent governance development, the adoption of disclosure provisions has gained rapid momentum in the past two decades. These systems have been found to be widespread across countries and regions, and their prevalence is growing as the importance of transparency also increases. Currently, more than 120 countries around the world implement disclosure regulations. Although their content varies, asset disclosure forms often require registration of shares and securities. Frequently, the company name and the value of all types of stocks, whether held domestically or abroad, have to be disclosed. In other cases, only shares in local companies will need to be disclosed. In certain instances, only the value of the stock or only the name of the company will be required.

As with corporate registries, access to asset disclosures may vary. In many cases, asset declarations are published in an official gazette, or in the media. They also may be made available through nongovernmental organizations (NGOs), and in some cases, they may be available online through the official websites of anticorruption agencies, parliaments, or the like. Frequently, the public is permitted only partial access to the contents of the disclosure statement, while investigators and financial institutions may request full access from the agencies responsible for collecting or verifying them. Asset disclosure systems can be an important supplementary tool to help investigators make appropriate links and discern trends or patterns in an investigation: They are available and not all are confidential.[63]

4.2.9 Unique Identifiers

Another useful tool that can facilitate the gathering of information across different government agencies and institutions and help to eliminate false positives generated by corporate vehicles having similar names, is the assignment of unique identifiers. This is particularly useful in the case of entities that are operational, because typically they will interact with a wider range of government agencies than would mere shell entities.

---

62. Asset disclosures may be collected, verified, and held by a variety of agencies (for example, anticorruption commissions, commissions that focus exclusively on asset disclosures, tax authorities, parliamentary commissions, supreme courts, ombudsmen, and so on).

63. See Djankov, Simeon, Rafael La Porta, Florencio Lopez-de-Silanes, and Andrei Shleifer, "Disclosure by Politicians," *American Economic Journal: Applied Economics* 2, no. 2 (2010): 179–209, available at http://www.aeaweb.org/articles.php?doi=10.1257/app.2.2.179.

4.3 Trust and Company Service Providers

TCSPs are businesses that create and provide administrative services for corporate vehicles.[64] In some jurisdictions, TCSPs are the only means for those looking to establish certain kinds of vehicles, such as international business corporations (IBCs), although in certain countries, customers can choose to form a legal entity through a TCSP or directly through the registry (via an application for incorporation). In certain civil law countries, corporate entities (such as companies and foundations) require a notarial deed for their establishment, meaning that the founders need to enlist the services of a notary. In most of the cases examined in this study, an outside service provider was used to establish or manage (administer) the corporate vehicle.

TCSPs are crucial actors in both the legitimate and the illicit use of corporate vehicles, and, as such, it is essential that investigators and regulators know how they work. These service providers perform a variety of administrative procedures necessary for establishing a company or other corporate vehicle. These procedures include checking for the availability of the desired name, lodging the required documents, and paying fees. Assuming the vehicle is to be maintained for more than a year (about a quarter to one-third are not), TCSPs will handle renewal fees accordingly and fulfill any required annual reporting obligations on behalf of the company. They may also provide services such as mail-forwarding or virtual office facilities. As part of their typical package, many TCSPs routinely act as registered agents or resident secretaries for foreign and domestic companies, as well as provide nominee services (such as nominee directors or shareholders, trustees, or foundation council members). In addition, TCSPs will commonly act as the intermediaries or introducers between their clients and the respective financial institution or bank where the customer wishes to establish the corporate account. A simple transaction—setting up a single company—might cost US$1,000–$2,000, depending on the options, of which US$100–$300 would be the government fee for registering the company.

Although some TCSPs may only offer corporate vehicles domiciled in their local jurisdiction, it is not uncommon for TCSPs to be able to furnish customers with vehicles from a wide menu of foreign jurisdictions. At the moment, for instance, large TCSPs can act as registered agents for companies incorporated under the laws of the British Virgin Islands (BVI). This means that they form BVI companies (typically IBCs) for clients, but keep clients' due diligence information on file elsewhere. This makes it more difficult for BVI regulators to access that information. The BVI regulator does conduct random assessments, however, asking TCSPs for beneficial ownership information on

---

64. According to the FATF definition, TCSPs provide any or all of the following services: acting as a formation agent of legal persons; acting as (or arranging for another person to act as) a director or secretary of a company, a partner of a partnership, or a similar position in relation to other legal persons; providing a registered office, business address or accommodation, correspondence, or administrative address for a company, a partnership, or any other legal person or arrangement; acting as (or arranging for another person to act as) a trustee of an express trust; acting as (or arranging for another person to act as) a nominee shareholder for another person.

IBCs, besides making specific requests. If a TCSP were unable to produce this information, the BVI government would revoke its registered agent status.[65]

4.3.1 Diversity in Size and Nature

As institutions, banks are relatively uniform; it is generally clear what a bank is and what it does. The term "TCSPs," however, covers a wide variety of service providers both in size and in nature. For example, they may differ in terms of the profession of the provider, the services they offer, the number and type of clients they engage with, and the relationship they maintain with those clients. Generic references to a "typical" TCSP therefore are highly misleading. At one end of the spectrum, they may be a single individual operating through a website, or a small law or accounting firm for whom forming companies is only a minor sideline, their core business being something else. At the other end of the spectrum, some of the most well-established TCSPs employ hundreds of people, administering tens of thousands of companies at any one time and holding up to 10 percent of the total market in companies formed in offshore jurisdictions. In some cases, these large TCSPs have written the company legislation for the smaller jurisdictions that are more recent entrants to the market for offshore companies.

Moreover, TCSPs may cater to individual customers, institutional customers, or both; and transactions may involve just one TCSP or multiple TCSPs. As in most other sectors of the financial services industry, they also have a substantial degree of specialization. This specialization may create challenges for regulators and investigators. Even in the case of a simple transaction, such as a private client wishing to form a single company, it is common for more than one TCSP to be involved. TCSPs can be roughly divided into "wholesale" TCSPs and "retail" TCSPs. A large TCSP may form and sell thousands of companies to dozens of other, smaller TCSPs, which then sell them to their private clients. For example, one TCSP in our study reported that it deals with several thousand intermediary TCSPs—law firms and accountancy firms—which sell companies to individual clients. The "wholesalers" often supply the "retailers" with companies on a one-by-one basis; and the companies may be either ready-made shelf companies or companies tailor made specifically for the client (see box 4.5).

4.3.2 Regulation

Over the past decade, TCSPs in most offshore jurisdictions have increasingly become subject to formal licensing and regulation. They now often need to meet consumer

---

65. The BVI is an important "supplier of corporate vehicles" for certain jurisdictions. The most popular corporate vehicle in Hong Kong SAR, China, for instance, is a BVI IBC. The success of the BVI is in large part a product of timing. Launched in 1984, the BVI IBCs came on to the market at the time just after the British government had agreed to hand Hong Kong SAR, China, back to mainland China, which created a massive demand for asset protection among people who spoke English and were familiar with the British legal system. The previous leader in the field of shell companies, Panama, was suffering from the mismanagement of the Noriega regime and increasingly strict U.S. sanctions. Simple, flexible, and cheap, BVI IBCs became, from this initial advantage, the default choice in Hong Kong SAR, China, and with increased liberalization, for mainland China as well.

Gruppo 20 Enterprises was established as a Seychelles International Business Company with a nominee director, authorized share capital of US$1 million, and bearer shares. It was supplied by a Singaporean service provider (the retailer), but it had been formed for this Singaporean service provider by another service provider (the wholesaler). Before forming the company, the retailing TCSP required a notarized copy of a passport. The accompanying bank account for Gruppo 20 was in Cyprus, picked on the advice of the first service provider because of this bank's willingness to accept bearer share companies. The bank insisted on taking physical possession of the sole bearer share issued. Establishing the company and opening the account cost €1,754.

Note: a. Undertaken in the context of the TCSP Project.

protection requirements, be audited by the authorities, and meet AML reporting requirements, and their directors need to pass a "fit-and-proper-person" test. By contrast, TCSPs in onshore jurisdictions are frequently not regulated. As a result, the number of TCSPs operating in such jurisdictions is unclear, and there is no clear dividing line between them and other financial services or legal firms.

In cases in which TCSPs *are* regulated, however, they are commonly responsible for obtaining and updating beneficial ownership information of the corporate vehicles they administer. This makes TCSPs important parties when it comes to preventing the misuse of corporate vehicles. In fact, in some cases, they can be more important than either registries or banks. As noted, corporate registries usually contain (at best) only legal ownership and management information; and although banks collect beneficial ownership information on corporate entities holding accounts, not all vehicles have a bank account but rather hold real estate assets instead. Compared with these, then, TCSPs provide a significant point of leverage for increasing the availability of beneficial ownership information.

4.3.3 Due Diligence Information Gathered by TCSPs

TCSPs vary considerably in the types of services they provide and the persons to whom they provide them. If a potential client approaches a TCSP for services with an established corporate vehicle, the TCSP will need to identify the natural person behind the corporate vehicle before delivering any services. (In a few jurisdictions, identification of the beneficial owner may take place later, provided it occurs shortly after the initiation of services.) As described by one of the TCSPs in our study, in the case of a complex structure (such as a BVI company owned by a Jersey trust), the procedure would be to perform personal due diligence on the following:

- The directors and shareholders (including the ultimate controllers, if the directors and shareholders are nominees)

- The trustees and (if they are corporate trustees) the beneficial ownership of the company
- The settlor (unless deceased)
- The beneficiaries (although they may be unborn)
- The protector (if applicable).

The beneficiaries would be, first, the principal beneficiaries and then anyone to whom a distribution is made. The performance of due diligence on the protector would depend on the protector's power. If this power was considerable, including, for instance, the power to move funds, then due diligence certainly would be performed. All this information (on all parties) has to be kept up to date. In unusually complex cases, the fee for conducting due diligence is payable by the client; otherwise it forms part of the service.

Not infrequently, a TCSP may ask another TCSP to conduct the due diligence on its behalf. This might occur, for instance, because the TCSP is not in a position to conduct the due diligence himself because the client is located in a different country. One of the TCSPs in our study considered such delegation of CDD to third-party TCSPs in other jurisdictions quite common. It is effected in the relevant jurisdiction through Introducer Certificates (ICs), usually with trust companies, law firms, and banks. (This arrangement is only available if the introducer is a licensed entity in a well-regulated jurisdiction—that is, "well-regulated" in the sense that the regulator in the original TCSP's jurisdiction has judged it to have proper AML procedures in place.) Ideally, each transaction requires a separate IC; but sometimes a general IC is issued, covering all business done with a particular intermediary. The certificates show the name of the intermediary and details of its license, as well as the same details of the client. They commit the intermediary to hold and update as necessary beneficial ownership information on the underlying client and provide it promptly upon request.

4.3.4 The Information Gathered by TCSPs

To find out to what extent due diligence information is gathered in practice, Case Western Reserve School of Law, as part of background work for this study,[66] contacted TCSPs, requesting advice on possible corporate vehicles for holding funds. The results of the first and second audit studies are presented in the following paragraphs. Although the enquiries with TCSPs were carried out a year apart and used slightly different approach letters, both rely on the same logic and the results are comparable.

The first and second round of inquiries yielded valid responses from a total of 102 TCSPs. Of these, 60 said that, before they could supply corporate services, they needed to see a photo ID, while one required a personal visit by the client. The ID documentation consisted of (at least) a photocopy of the face page of a passport, usually notarized, apostilled, or otherwise certified as a true copy of the original. In addition, proof of

---

66. For the general logic of audit studies in economics, see David Neumark, "Detecting Discrimination in Audit and Correspondence Studies" (National Bureau of Economic Research Working Paper No. 16448, NBER, Cambridge, MA, October 2010). See Appendix B, TCSP Project.

residence (in the form of a recent, original utility statement or a recent bank statement) was often requested. Some TCSPs also required a business plan for the company to be established and a short *curriculum vitae* of the client (who, not acting on anyone else's behalf, is also the beneficial owner). These 61 respondents (60 requiring photo ID and one a personal visit) can be considered to have conducted sufficient due diligence to establish the beneficial owner when establishing a corporate vehicle: They had taken reasonable steps to establish the owner's identity, and these documents were held on file and presumably accessible to investigative authorities.[67]

The remaining 41 TCSPs cannot be considered to have undertaken sufficient due diligence, because they had no ID documentation on the beneficial owner. In most cases, the applicant simply had to complete an online form (no more complex than that used to buy a plane ticket). The TCSPs apparently trusted applicants to enter their true names and addresses. It is difficult to see how TCSPs (or by extension, the authorities) could determine the beneficial ownership of the companies established in this way with any degree of certainty.

The 60 percent of TCSPs in the survey that apparently performed adequate due diligence may suggest an artificially positive picture, given the possibilities of linking together chains of corporate vehicles, the possibilities of a more thorough-going and high-budget search for anonymous vehicles, and the ability to practice regulatory arbitrage to exploit those jurisdictions performing the least due diligence. In most cases in which a trust was to be formed, and almost always when a bank account was to be opened, some evidence as to the source of wealth was requested. This might take the form of a simple declaration that the wealth was not the product of illicit activities. More often, however, providers asked for a letter from a lawyer (for inheritance), proof of sale (if the funds were derived from property or other asset sales), or copies of recent pay slips (if the wealth was from salary).

Only a few of the application forms asked about politically exposed persons (PEP) issues (for example, about whether the customer or any of the customer's relatives held elected office). According to interviews with service providers, most run potential customers' names through software like World-Check or, at least, Google.

This level of due diligence notwithstanding, many of the respondents emphasized in their correspondence and on their websites that one of the main reasons for forming a company or trust was the anonymity and secrecy it offers. Five providers explicitly recommended a structure combining a trust and company to increase both secrecy and asset protection. As one of the TCSPs advocating such a combined trust-company structure notes on its website,

> [The trust can] serve as beneficial owner when opening financial accounts: Today, due to the global scare of terrorism, etc., most offshore tax-haven jurisdictions have implemented laws

---

67. It was beyond the scope of this project to look into the safeguards that may be applied to protect against the use of false documentation (for example, independent checks against government databases to which the service provider may have access, or databases of lost and stolen travel documents).

that require their banks to obtain "declarations of beneficial ownership" when establishing corporate bank accounts . . . [I]f you do not wish to sign the declaration as the beneficial owner when establishing your corporate accounts, the Trust can serve as the beneficial owner for these declaration purposes, and the nominee Trust council can sign the declarations on behalf of the Trust.

Many of the respondents (including the one quoted) explicitly noted their duty to collect, and if necessary hand over, beneficial ownership information in the event of money laundering activity.

Forty-one TCSPs communicated their willingness to create corporate vehicles without the need for any supporting identity documentation from the beneficial owner. The process of forming a company consisted of typing the preferred name and other details of the company (for example, options for nominee shareholders and directors, mail and phone forwarding, corporate stationery, and so on) into a simple online form. For this reason, the authorities would never be able to compel these TCSPs to provide any information on the underlying owners, no matter how strong their investigative powers might be, because the TCSPs never collected such information in the first place. Indeed, a couple of respondents explicitly mentioned this point among the advantages of their service. If the customers had paid the TCSP for its services using a credit card, tracing this might provide some leads, but it would not be difficult for a customer to use an anonymous prepaid debit card—after all, the incorporation fees are quite modest. Alternatively, after forming one anonymous company using a personal credit card, it would be possible to go to a different TCSP and get them to create a second anonymous company, using a corporate credit card issued in the name of the first company.

4.3.5 Examples

This situation reinforces the conclusion that criminals and anyone else intent on lowering the "corporate veil" would only need to carry out a relatively casual search to quickly and easily gain access to anonymous shell companies. Before looking at the overall pattern of results from the first and second sets of inquiries, it may be useful to explore some examples in detail.

First, let us look at a provider in Dominica and another in the United Kingdom. Both the text and design of their websites suggest that it is highly likely that these providers are prepared to incorporate companies without requiring any supporting due diligence material. Both have a purely web-based order form. The customer enters the preferred name of the company, desired optional extras, and credit card details. Although the Dominica provider offers only Dominican companies, the U.K. provider is a much larger operation, offering customer support in eight languages. It sells companies from the Seychelles and British Virgin Islands, as well as from England and Wales. Finally, this provider offers a new, proposed European Private Company, which would be able to be redomiciled to any EU member state. Nowhere, throughout the ordering process on these two providers' websites, is there any mention of the need to supply supporting documentation—and from the whole context of the sites, it is quite clear that indeed none was required. These providers were among the cheapest in the sample, offering anonymous shell companies (that is, no beneficial ownership information held on file, nominee shareholders and directors) for US$1,200–$1,500.

The next example is the most clear-cut in terms of offering anonymous companies (and trusts). This example is unusual in that it is featured in other inquiries, enabling us to place its business model in a wider context. The following e-mail exchange with this provider, which is based in the United States with a secondary office in the Bahamas, is clear enough:

> Customer: *Could you please provide guidance as to what documentation is needed to set up the company or trust and to open the bank account in Nevis or any other appropriate jurisdiction?*
>
> TCSP: *There is no documentation needed to form an offshore company or trust. To open an offshore bank account, you'll need a copy of an ID (like a license or passport) and a copy of a recent bill or statement (like a cable bill, electric bill, bank statement, etc.) that shows your name and address on it.*

The provider's website explicitly confirms that in forming companies (and trusts), no identity documentation is required. It also states, however, that to open a bank account, the standard suite of documentation will be required. In this way, customers can form companies domiciled in Belize ($1,500), the British Virgin Islands ($1,950), Nevis ($1,850), Panama ($1,950), and the Seychelles ($1,650), as well as set up a Bahamian trust ($1,000). The provider cannot know for whom the companies are being established, and no requests from law enforcement would be able to yield information on the underlying beneficial owner, because no such information was collected.

We can place this provider in a broader context. He—it is largely a one-man operation—testified before U.S. Senate Permanent Subcommittee on Investigations, and this testimony was later included in the 2006 report, "Tax Haven Abuses: The Enablers, the Tools and Secrecy." According to that report, over the preceding six-year period, this provider had set up offshore structures for more than 900 individual clients, largely from the United States, all via e-mail and the website. These structures were mainly used for asset protection purposes, although the report gives strong hints that some clients used them to evade tax obligations. According to the report, the business "grossed several hundred thousand dollars in this way in 2003 and 2004." Confirming the evidence that emerged during interviews on the importance of networks to TCSPs, this provider depended on other parties in various offshore jurisdictions to perform the roles of trustee, trust protector, and company director.

Significantly, this provider confirmed in an e-mail exchange in 2010 that its due diligence procedures for company formation (or the lack thereof) had not changed since 2005. Although identity documentation, a bank reference, and proof of address were required for all offshore banks, no documentation was required for companies or trusts. The provider offered his services to anyone—except those who volunteered the information that they were in the pornography business or came from the Islamic Republic of Iran or Cuba.

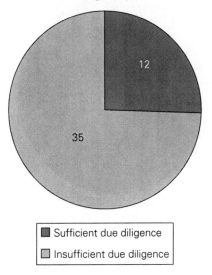

Sampled OECD countries total: Requirement to provide ID in forming companies [47 TCSPs]

■ Sufficient due diligence
☐ Insufficient due diligence

Source: Authors' illustration.

4.3.6 Common Patterns

The pattern that stands out most clearly in our data is that TCSPs from sampled OECD countries (figure 4.6) do not conduct CDD to the same extent as those in other countries (figure 4.7). Whereas 47 out of 53 providers in this latter group conducted proper due diligence, only 12 out of 47 did so in the sampled OECD countries. Some specific examples were discussed above in relation to André Pascal Enterprises (see box 3.6) and BCP Consolidated Enterprises (see box 3.14).

Positive findings on identification were particularly high among those TCSPs from jurisdictions identified as tax havens by the OECD in 2000 as part of its Harmful Tax Competition initiative (see figure 4.7). These jurisdictions have been portrayed as offering corporate secrecy and generally being underregulated. The results of the two studies show exactly the reverse, that is, that TCSPs from those tax havens have higher standards in corporate transparency, at least at the company-formation stage, than those in other countries. Although the sample is too small to allow for any firm conclusions, the findings do not support the (reasonable) assumption there is a relationship between the wealth of a country and the rigour of its KYC practices and that compliance is largely a matter of capacity and resources rather than will.[68]

---

68. It is recognized that the size of the sample—both in terms of numbers of TCSPs and countries sampled—does not allow for any conclusions about compliance within the OECD as a whole. A forthcoming study by academics from Brigham Young University and Griffith University of over 3,500 company

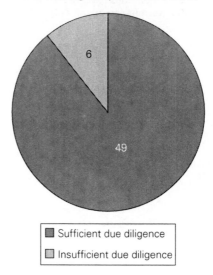

Other countries total: Requirement to provide
ID in forming companies [55 TCSPs]

■ Sufficient due diligence
□ Insufficient due diligence

Source: Authors' illustration.

By far the worst performer of the countries reviewed is the United States. Out of 27 service providers under U.S. jurisdiction returning a valid response, only 3 said they asked for any form of identity documentation, whereas the others (24) were prepared to form companies without conducting any due diligence whatsoever. Although a majority of providers noted that nonresidents would have to obtain an employer identification number (EIN), the associated forms again did not ask for any proof of identification. Furthermore, some providers in Wyoming and Nevada actually offered to use their employees' Social Security numbers to spare clients the need to obtain an EIN. This verdict is strongly confirmed by a number of U.S. government reports,[69] and recent statements from the U.S. Senate Permanent Subcommittee on Investigations. In particular, Subcommittee Chairman Senator Carl Levin noted in November 2009 that "our 50 states are forming nearly 2 million companies each year and, in virtually all cases, doing so without obtaining the names of the people who will control or benefit from those companies."[70]

---

service providers confirms this conclusion. Reference is made to appendix B for further discussion of the method followed.

69. "Company Formations: Minimal Ownership Information is Collected and Available" (Government Accountability Office, Washington, DC, 2006); "The Role of Domestic Shell Companies in Financial Crime and Money Laundering" (Financial Crimes Enforcement Network, Washington, DC, 2006); see also "Money Laundering Threat Assessment" (Money Laundering Threat Assessment Group, Washington, DC, 2005).

70. "Statement of Sen. Carl Levin, D-Mich., on Business Formation and Financial Crime: Finding a Legislative Solution," November 5, 2009, available at http://levin.senate.gov/newsroom/speeches/speech/statement-of-sen-carl-levin-d-mich-on-business-formation-and-financial-crime-finding-a-legislative-solution/?section=alltypes (last access date July 27, 2011).

FIGURE 4.8   Requirement to Provide ID in Forming Companies (Worldwide)

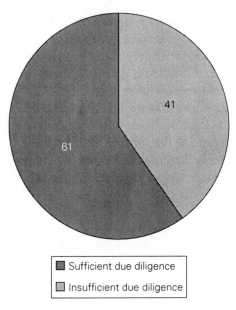

Worldwide total: Requirement to provide ID
in forming companies (102 TCSPs)

41

61

■ Sufficient due diligence
□ Insufficient due diligence

Source: Authors' illustration.

The poor showing is especially troubling given the huge number of legal entities formed in the United States each year—around 10 times more than in all 41 tax haven jurisdictions combined. Because so little information is collected on U.S. companies, it is impossible to tell how many are shell companies and not operational companies, but U.S. law enforcement consistently has indicated that the number is high enough to cause grave concerns.[71] To judge from our interviews with TCSPs and from advertising, U.S. shell companies are a popular choice among non-U.S. residents.

It is possible that the positive picture of countries in which TCSPs did request further information on the client may be skewed because of what some have called "the compliance dance"—a tendency for firms to pay lip-service to every new regulation that comes along, while not really accepting the underlying rationale. If we had engaged those seemingly compliant TCSPs further, perhaps the window dressing would have quickly become apparent as such and we would have discovered, for example, ways to set up a corporate vehicle anonymously. We do not know because such checks were beyond the scope of this project. What we can be certain of, however, is that the converse does not hold. Because TCSPs have no reason to pretend to be noncompliant while being secretly

---

71. See especially "The Role of Domestic Shell Companies in Financial Crime and Money Laundering" (Financial Crimes Enforcement Network, Washington, DC, 2006). See also "Money Laundering Threat Assessment" (Money Laundering Threat Assessment Group, Washington, DC, 2005).

compliant, the low level of compliance we see on the part of TCSPs in some countries surely reflects the situation accurately.

4.3.7 Obstacles to the Provision of Information by TCSPs

All investigators interviewed for this study agreed that a TCSP that establishes a corporate vehicle for a client (or manages or otherwise fulfills a role in it) is in a very good position to obtain the relevant information on the ownership and control structure (at least at the time the vehicle is established). As a result, there can be little excuse for inaccurate information. Law enforcement often views the TCSP sector with a degree of suspicion, however. In many criminal cases, investigators tend to see TCSPs not as neutral service providers, but at least negligent in the conduct of their CDD and at worst complicit in criminal behavior. At the same time, it is clear that investigators do not always have sufficient understanding of the rationale behind many of the constructions involving corporate vehicles in multiple jurisdictions that serve legitimate purposes.

Attorney-Client Privilege

Invariably, almost all of the investigators interviewed for this study mentioned that one of the obstacles to obtaining information from TCSPs was attorney-client privilege (legal professional privilege). The special nature of the relationship between a lawyer (such as a solicitor, an attorney, or an *avocat*) imposes a duty of confidentiality on the part of the lawyer with respect to his client. This is to encourage the complete disclosure of information, without fear of further disclosure to outside parties. The concept of attorney-client privilege is rooted in a fundamental right to counsel and the right to a fair trial, whereby a defendant has the right to legal representation by a lawyer. Although the exact scope of this privilege varies from country to country (in some countries it also applies to the relationship between an *expert comptable* or a notary and his client), there is general agreement among authorities in most countries that the privilege should not apply when the lawyer is performing only purely fiduciary services for the client.

To overcome attorney-client privilege, judicial proceedings often need to be instituted. For instance, in Canada, a privilege hearing is required for the judge to review each piece of paper before it is handed over to the police; in the United States, a *prima facie* case is needed if a lawyer is suspected of misusing the privilege. For that reason, investigators stated, they have to carefully weigh the benefits of information that the lawyer may have against the risk that they would tip off their client.

Other investigators reported that, in cases in which the privilege is invoked to frustrate law enforcement, the investigative trail often stops. In Brazil, even if the investigator manages to find the TCSP that formed the corporate vehicle, that TCSP will often have sold the company to a law firm, which then invokes privilege to avoid disclosing the name of the person who purchased the company. In Germany, in a case in which a lawyer acting for a special purpose vehicle claimed privilege on documents relating to an entity, the investigator instituted insolvency proceedings against the entity and was able to retrieve the released documents from the liquidator. In Hong Kong SAR, China, when suspicion arises that a lawyer formed a trust and may have the trust deed or information in his offices, the investigator needs to obtain a search warrant, but often the solicitor will invoke privilege, compelling law enforcement to go to court. Again, investigators must determine whether it is worth devoting resources to fighting the claim of privilege, especially in cases in which they are not quite sure what they are looking for.

Lawyers working in various capacities and engaged in certain transactional activities on behalf of their clients are in a good position to obtain the relevant information on the ownership and control structure of a corporate vehicle.[72] For that reason, the FATF has subjected lawyers and other legal professionals to due diligence obligations when performing certain services (Recommendation 12) and when they encounter anything suspicious in the course of their service provision (clearly circumscribed) to report any dubious transactions to the Financial Intelligence Unit. Information obtained under circumstances subject to attorney-client privilege, however, is not subject to the same reporting obligations.

Countries have implemented this obligation to various degrees, but on the whole (see appendix A), compliance is low. The most widely discussed reporting obligation is probably the one laid down in the Third EU Money Laundering Directive, which requires independent legal professionals to report suspicious transactions when executing transactions for their client. These transactions include, among others, creating, operating, or managing trusts, companies, or similar structures.

The directive exempts those categories of professions from reporting with regard to information they receive from or obtain on one of their clients, in the course of ascertaining the legal position for their client or performing their task of defending or representing that client in, or concerning, judicial proceedings, including advice on instituting or avoiding proceedings, whether such information is received or obtained before, during or after such proceedings.

Because several bar associations deemed the reporting obligation an infringement of the right to a fair trial and the exemption not sufficiently wide, they initiated legal action against the European Council before the European Court of Justice (ECJ). In an important ruling,[73] the ECJ ruled against them, noting that:

> Given that the requirements implied by the right to a fair trial presuppose, by definition, a link with judicial proceedings, and in view of the fact that the [exemption cited above] exempts lawyers, where their activities are characterised by such a link, from the obligations of information and cooperation [the STR obligation and the obligation to provide information upon request by the authorities], those requirements are respected.

---

72. Notaries and independent legal professionals; see Third EU Directive (Directive 2005/60/EC of the European Parliament and of the Council of October 26, 2005, on the prevention of the use of the financial system for the purpose of money laundering and terrorist financing), and FATF, "RBA Guidance for Legal Professionals" (October 23, 2008), available at: http://www.fatf-gafi.org/dataoecd/5/58/41584211.pdf.
73. See European Court of Justice, Case C-305/05, *Ordre des barreaux francophones et germanophones and Others v Conseil des ministres*, judgment of 26 June 2007, available at: http://eur-lex.europa.eu/LexUriServ/LexUriServ.do?uri=CELEX:62005J0305:EN:HTML.

Inclusion of Lawyers in the AML Framework

One of the arguments against the inclusion of lawyers or other TCSPs in the AML framework is that when lawyers or other TCSPs are facilitating criminal conduct, they rarely do so unwittingly. In those circumstances, what is the point of imposing an obligation to report suspicious transactions? They are unlikely to report anything. From the review of cases in this study, it was difficult to ascertain whether TCSPs were knowingly involved in money laundering activities. In some cases, they were investigated and prosecuted; in many cases, they were not. Investigators considered TCSPs more likely than not to be complicit but indicated that this did not necessarily mean that they would investigate or prosecute them. The burden of proof was often too high, and investigators would rather spend their efforts targeting the principal perpetrators, not the facilitators. In a few cases, the TCSPs involved were considered innocent. Based on investigators' opinions, and having regard to the degree of involvement of TCSPs with their client, it is arguable that a TCSP is often either knowingly involved in or at least willfully blind to the criminal conduct he is facilitating. Unlike a bank, where transactions are automatically processed without human intervention (unless picked up by the bank's system for identifying suspicious transactions), TCSPs provide services that *do* usually require such human intervention, even if remote or minimal.

Being involved (to a greater or lesser degree or merely willfully blind), however, does not mean that inclusion in the AML framework is pointless. First, a minority of the TCSPs will be innocently involved and would file a report if they deemed a transaction to be suspicious. That could be a valuable source of information, and lawyers or other TCSPs who are later found to have been complicit may be penalized for non-reporting. More importantly, however, inclusion in the AML framework implies more than just the reporting obligation. First and foremost, it is about conducting proper due diligence of a client before entering into a business relationship. That means that lawyers or other TCSPs found to have been involved in a money laundering or corruption scheme will no longer be able to claim with impunity that they did not know what was going on. Willful blindness is no longer an option for the lawyer or TCSP willing to look the other way.

Cases in which service providers have been penalized for failing to follow through on their due diligence obligations have certainly been infrequent, but they are effective in encouraging compliance. In one case,[74] a Jersey Court of Appeal ruled in favor of the attorney general that a single provable instance in which a TCSP fails to adhere to due diligence standards[75] meets the criteria for prosecution under the AML laws of the jurisdiction.[76]

---

74. Bell v Att. Gen., 27 Jan 2006, 2006 JLR 61.

75. Failing to comply with Art. 2(1) of the Money Laundering (Jersey) Order 1999, contrary to Art. 37(4) of the Proceeds of Crime (Jersey) Law 1999.

76. "Financial Services—maintenance of anti-money laundering procedures—breach—single breach by financial services provider of requirement in Money Laundering (Jersey) Order 1999, art. 2(1)(a) to maintain procedures may constitute offence under Proceeds of Crime (Jersey) Law 1999—failure need not be systemic—'maintain' requires procedures to be established and also kept in proper working order, to prevent and forestall money laundering whenever business relationship formed or one-off transaction carried out." (http://www.jerseylaw.je/Judgments/JerseyLawReports/Display.aspx?Cases/JLR2006/JLR060061.htm).

On May 8, 2006, a nonpublic judgment (*Tribunal correctionnel de Luxembourg*, no. 1507/2006) was handed down by the *Tribunal d'arrondissement de Luxembourg, 16e Chambre* [District Court of Luxembourg] in which a lawyer received monetary penalties for failing to perform due diligence obligations to identify the beneficial owner of corporate entity clients.[77] The ruling sent a powerful message, because the attorney's clients were not even found to have engaged in money laundering—the breach of CDD obligations on its own was enough to convict.

4.4 Financial Institutions

Many corporate vehicles that are used to launder money are established solely for the purpose of providing anonymous access to financial institutions. The provision by financial institutions of services that may be used for receiving, holding, or conveying the illicit proceeds of corruption is a critical part of the laundering process. Almost all of the cases reviewed involved bank-held assets: The laundering of the proceeds of corruption is virtually impossible without making use of the services provided by banks. Although money launderers can establish legal entities and arrangements to suggest a fake reality, the flows of funds do not lie. In the words of an investigating magistrate, "Transfers of funds through the banking system always leave a footprint that cannot be manipulated. These transfers constitute the backbone of any investigation into economic crime." Financial institutions are in a particularly good position to know what is really going on.

4.4.1 Information Gathered

In many industrial economies, financial institutions have been subject to AML compliance obligations for some time. This includes CDD and suspicious transactions reporting requirements. Investigators interviewed for this study noted that, over the past decade, the quality of information obtainable from banks in the context of a criminal investigation has improved.

The corporate vehicle information recorded by financial institutions usually includes some combination of the following:

- *Almost always:* Visual inspection of true or certified or notarized copies of identity documentation, which may be copied, or checked on a checklist as having been confirmed, and then filed in the customer's file.

---

77. "The District Court of Luxembourg (Tribunal d'arrondissement de Luxembourg, 16e Chambre) has found, in the criminal case against the lawyer, who provided domiciliation services to corporate entities, that the sanction of an infringement of the obligations laid down by the Law of 12 November 2004, does not require the proof that a domiciled corporate entity was actually involved in a money laundering operation": IBA Anti-Money Laundering Forum, Luxembourg, http://www.anti-moneylaundering.org/europe/luxembourg.aspx (last accessed August 16, 2011).

- *Almost always:* A physical address for the customer's account, used for mailing out notices, variably confirmed through, for example, mailings or onsite inspections.
- *Almost always:* Visual inspection of a true or certified or notarized copy documentation that gives the individual before them the capacity to represent the corporate vehicle that is the client (for example, contract, power of attorney, organizational document naming the party as a member, director, or executive agent of a company, trust instrument naming the person as a trustee, and so on).
- *Often:* The natural person holding more than a certain percentage of equitable interest (that is, the formal beneficial owner).
- *Sometimes:* Particulars of the persons making up other various parties with a significant relation to the corporate vehicle in terms of ownership and control (for example, names, IDs, and addresses of shareholders and board members in a company).
- *Sometimes:* Records of a meeting, required in the course of account opening, or normal account business (including attendees).
- *Sometimes:* A highly documented compliance log, evidencing knowledge about the customer, in accordance with a robust and uniformly applied standard, which typically involves name checking, transaction monitoring, and trend analysis.
- *Sometimes:* Information obtained from independent sources to verify customer-provided information. Such sources may include relevant jurisdictional registrar data, organizational websites, credit ratings, web-search collation services (which crawl the Internet looking for the names of the organization and its related persons).
- *Rarely:* The identity of the beneficial owner in substantive terms (although in many legitimate situations, anyone who holds more than a certain percentage of equity will be the beneficial owner in substantive terms).

4.4.2 Strengths and Weaknesses of the Information Gathered

Although the participants in our study were generally in favor of the identification of a formal beneficial owner (that is, based on a percentage shareholding), compliance officers suggested that it would make sense to do this on a risk-sensitive basis. Much of their time and effort performing due diligence is spent on customer accounts that are clearly beyond all possible risk of money laundering yet require due diligence so that "the paperwork is in order." In the converse situation, when there is a clear and significant risk of money laundering activity, stopping at the minimal threshold is not a defensible option. Whenever 25 percent corporate shareholdings trigger beneficial ownership reporting, those who wish to avoid disclosure will list five shareholders, each having 20 percent holdings. And in cases in which the threshold is 20 percent, they will employ six shareholders with 16.7 percent holdings each. Indirect ownership always is going to be employed to ensure that any quantified beneficial ownership system can be beaten by the highest-risk parties of all, that is, those with a mind to hide their ownership and control.

In one jurisdiction where banks are not required by law or guidance to identify the beneficial owner of a customer, they typically do not volunteer to do so, even if their institution does so in other nations where such an obligation is imposed.[78]

In the matter of establishing beneficial ownership, one factor was frequently cited by participants as not receiving enough attention—that is, control of the corporate vehicle. A lack of screening and vetting of directors, officers, and signatories (the day-to-day controllers of a corporate vehicle or its accounts) is likely to create significant blind spots in CDD measures, especially when some of those parties are corporate vehicles rather than natural persons. Learning from experience, banks now require CDD screening of all signatories to the account (or require that the signatory must be part of the disclosed ownership and control structure that the bank has already screened).

Possibly related to the lack of attention to control, the vast majority of participants indicated that the only time they checked whether the natural person seeking to enter into a business relationship with them was acting on behalf of some other person was in those instances in which they had suspicion to believe that such was the case.[79] It was not part and parcel of the initial question posed to a prospective client. Compliance officers indicated that particularly egregious "letter but not the spirit" of the law violations that weaken AML efforts arise when banks are allowed by law to consider an individual to be (for all intents and purposes) the beneficial owner, even when he or she is known to be merely a nominee.

Noticeable deficiencies were identified in identification and verification processes, when an overreliance on data held by the company registry being cross-referenced against self-certified client-provided data. This situation has the unfortunate effect of checking the client's word as provided to the financial institution against the client's word as provided to the company registry. This discrepancy led one compliance officer from an international institution, in discussing the frequent problem of inadequate CDD information, to remark: "It's all built out of a house of cards, ready to tumble over at any minute."

This is not a hypothetical case—the dangers of overreliance on company registry information were illustrated vividly in a case in South Africa. There, several banks relied on compromised CIPRO (the South African company registrar) information, to verify the bona fides of members of an international criminal syndicate. According to the CIPRO, those front men were the authorized representatives of major economic entities and thus able to open bank accounts in the names identical or similar to those companies as

---

78. Because this was only the case in one jurisdiction, it is too small a sample to draw any inferences from this. It may suggest, however, that the impetus for conducting due diligence on the beneficial owner is merely to be compliant, not because of a concern about being involved in possible money laundering.
79. For some, the willingness of nominees to misrepresent themselves as true beneficial owners has led them to conclude that it would be fruitless to implement an across-the-board, yet "toothless," requirement for corporate vehicle customers' representatives to disclose the existence of a nominee relationship.

part of a multimillion-dollar tax refund fraud. The diverted funds were then laundered through pseudo-business activities and consulting contracts into further corporate vehicle accounts.[80]

Some of the best practices described by interviewees to remedy this reliance on self-certification involved gathering information on the client from the widest possible range of resources, for cross-referencing purposes. Financial institutions detailed a variety of checks that they routinely perform in concert. When dealing with an operational entity, for instance, their compliance checks involve looking at credit ratings, public websites, commercial business websites, and online information about the entities' business activities, among other sources.

Requests for certain unusual, country-specific corporate vehicles may lead financial institutions in other countries to decline the business—because of the unfamiliarity of the legal form. If a particular type of vehicle does not exist in their jurisdiction, relationship managers and compliance officers are unlikely to have the experience needed to determine the opacity of such entities.[81] This is particularly a problem for domestic banks with a strong presence in only one country. Many of the larger banks have built up significant know-how on the various corporate vehicles available around the world by leveraging their global reach and ensuring that their well-resourced legal departments develop dossiers on the corporate vehicles with which they commonly deal.

The internal compliance arms of the larger multinational banks (especially when consolidated under a central command) appear quite effective at detecting possible suspicious behavior. These banks have, in effect, developed "in-house financial intelligence units," which process and analyze the significant amount of voluntarily disclosed information from their customer base and allow them to build intelligence hubs. This process allows banks to determine patterns of behavior of certain corporate vehicle customer profiles to enable quick identification of outlier cases that merit compliance investigation.

4.4.3 Building a Compliance Culture

Because relationship managers engage in the first meaningful interaction with a prospective client, it falls to them (if the client is a corporate vehicle) to understand the ownership and control structure of that client. All the financial institutions participating in this study said it was standard practice within their organization to require relationship managers to complete AML compliance training on a regular basis. In particular, those who deal with corporate-vehicle clients undergo specialized training

---

80. See "Hijacking of CIPRO Scares Banks," *Sunday Times*, July 4, 2010, available at http://www.timeslive.co.za/sundaytimes/article532123.ece/.
81. For example, one Indian bank refuses to do business with a Liechtenstein *Anstalt*, regardless of the circumstances, because they do not understand "what it is, why someone would use it, or what business it has in India." For many financial institutions from civil law countries, trust accounts are immediately elevated to high risk, as they are often viewed as inherently alien and thus suspect. Although in such cases the risk of those specific corporate vehicles being misused for money laundering at these particular banks is low, it can hardly be said that this outcome is based on any sort of fact-based risk assessment.

about handling their accounts appropriately, understanding what institutional resources are available to manage their broader CDD requirements, and meeting their responsibilities for completing due diligence. To help foster accountability, institutions create a complete client profile that shows what research efforts have been undertaken and what monitoring has taken place (including compliance incidents). From time to time, relationship managers are confronted with clients who perceive beneficial ownership due diligence as being overly intrusive. This perception is considered an issue of decreasing concern, however, because of the global awareness of money laundering and terrorist financing issues.

Another issue in obtaining client information is that, in some instances, relationship managers undercut their financial institution's compliance efforts, whether because they view compliance as an obstacle to be overcome or, more seriously, because they are actively circumventing their compliance obligations. Financial institutions and compliance departments may deal with this problem by ensuring that employee performance evaluations have a strong compliance-oriented component (and thus affect salary) or by undertaking a review of a relationship manager's entire portfolio upon discovery or suspicion of a lapse. Such measures may be complementary.

The risk always exists that compliance activity devolves into a box-ticking exercise, in which one only verifies the bona fides of (necessarily declared) major shareholders. Compliance departments try to encourage a focus on detecting indicators that seem out of alignment with the typical profile of an account to which the corporate vehicle account most naturally corresponds. (This lack of alignment, when something seems out of place, is often known colloquially as the "smelliness" of an account.) Taken item by item, these characteristics may seem innocuous, but as a whole, they may be suggestive of undisclosed or concealed control or suspect activity.

To enable better detection of "outliers," many banks recruit heavily from seasoned investigators with a practice-honed instinct for those money laundering typologies of concern to the financial institution. Compliance processes should be steered away from the front-end mentality associated with passive corporate registries (in which case assumptions are based on what the client declares to be the case) and toward the back-end mentality that is shared by investigators seeking to understand the general circumstances of the corporate vehicles' usage. Instilling this element of judgment into compliance personnel is critical to assessing the true risk of a corporate vehicle.

Client Acceptance Committee

When a relationship manager and a compliance officer cannot agree on, or are confused about, the true risk level of a client and whether its business is acceptable, most banks pass the decision up to a higher level of responsibility, such as a client acceptance committee (CAC). Thus, banks seek to ensure that compliance is given its appropriate place through a variety of accountability measures. Several participants mentioned the friction between the bank's business and compliance agendas at this level, and one stated that "bad things happen when business holds the final say, and when business strong-arms the compliance department." Most participants had overwhelming confidence that such issues could be overcome with a robust AML policy. Following are some good CAC practices:

- Requiring the unanimous consent of all participating business and compliance CAC members for the client to be accepted;
- Giving the highest-ranking compliance CAC member powers of absolute veto to overrule acceptance of a client;
- Selecting CAC members to represent the business side of the bank who come from other account or product lines, thereby ensuring that they gain no direct benefit from the acceptance and represent a more disinterested, impartial perspective; and
- Fostering accountability by requiring face-to-face committee meetings, instead of allowing back-and-forth e-mail exchanges among CAC members.

4.5 Conclusion and Recommendations

Corporate registries constitute a primary source of information for law enforcement and other authorities in their search for information on the persons connected to a particular legal entity. As repositories of certain basic information, they can directly provide an investigator with useful leads. The value of these registries could be significantly enhanced in at least three ways:

- Online accessibility and online search facilities can save an investigator both time and effort.
- A shift away from the predominantly archival and passive nature of current registries toward a more proactive attitude, one geared toward enforcing registration obligations, would increase the accuracy of registry information (although in most countries this would mean governments would need to make extra resources available to their registry).
- If certain conditions are met, registries could consider including the identity of the beneficial owner.

In addition to corporate registries, other government-held sources of information could provide useful details about corporate vehicles, including, most notably, the tax authorities and asset disclosures.

Evidence from our database of grand corruption cases shows that TCSPs are often involved in establishing and managing the corporate vehicles encountered in grand corruption investigations. The more complex arrangements are rarely established without an international element. For example, the TCSP may be administering a corporate vehicle incorporated or formed under the law of a jurisdiction other than his or her own, or on behalf of a client resident in another jurisdiction. Although their level of engagement during the life span of a corporate vehicle may vary, TCSPs are generally in a position to obtain good information on the natural persons ultimately controlling the corporate vehicle. Currently, level of compliance by TCSPs is low—although this varies among countries.

The services provided by financial institutions are crucial to the money laundering process—without them, it would be impossible to launder funds on a significant scale. An overview of the flow of funds provides a good indication of the person(s) who are really in control of the funds. Thus, financial institutions are important sources of information for investigators seeking to discover evidence of the beneficial owner of certain funds. The policies established to improve the information available at banks have had an effect. It is important to ensure that the fact-gathering process by banks does not degenerate into a box-ticking exercise. In low-risk situations, threshold-based rules on beneficial ownership might ensure a good minimum level of information, but in higher-risk situations, principal actors always can beat those thresholds. Possibly because of the term (beneficial *ownership*), too much attention is paid to ownership and equity, at the expense of concentrating on control.

Recommendation 1. Certain basic information on legal entities should be maintained in corporate registries.

Such basic information must be easily verifiable and unequivocal. At a minimum, the following information should be maintained:

- Entity name (including governmentally unique identifier and alternative names)
- Date of incorporation, formation, or registration
- Entity type (for example, LLC, *sociedad anónima*)
- Entity status (for example, active, inactive, dissolved—if inactive or dissolved, date of dissolution and historical records of the company)
- Address of the principal office or place of business
- Address of the registered office (if different from principal office) or the name and address of the registered agent
- Particulars of formal positions of control, that is, directors or managers and officers (for example, president, secretary)
  — If a natural person—their full name, any former name, residential address, nationality, and birth date
  — If a corporation—the entity name, address of the principal office, address of the registered office, and (if applicable) for foreign corporations, the registered office in its country of origin
- History of filings (for example, formation documents, annual returns, financial filings, change of registered office, change of registered agent, and so on)
- Required annual returns that verify the correctness of each particular required to be filed in the system, even if it has not changed since the last filing date
- To the extent feasible and appropriate, electronic copies of filings and documents associated with the legal entity (for example, formation documents, annual returns, financial filings, change of registered office, change of registered agent, and so on).

Recommendation 2. Where feasible, the transition of company registry systems from passive recipients of data to more active components in jurisdictions' AML regimes is encouraged.

Countries are encouraged to direct more resources to their company registries to ensure that basic information supplied is compliant with the requirements. Registries would benefit from implementing a robust *ongoing* fact-checking component (even if based solely on statistically significant random sampling); those that demonstrate an effective capacity to enforce financial penalties or other punitive measures against noncompliant registered legal entities will contribute to improving the accuracy of data. As a result, investigators would have immediate access to high-quality data rather than the outdated information that they are frequently confronted with. Capacity investment in registries theoretically could transform a registry office (to the extent that the jurisdiction does not already see it as such) into an AML authority in its own right, somewhat akin to how, in some jurisdictions, securities commissions pursue investigations against public companies.

Recommendation 3. Jurisdictions should make technological investments in their corporate registry systems.

If a registry is to become an efficient AML tool, this development, including the upgrading of resources specifically for this purpose, needs to be planned carefully. For the least developed jurisdictions, a computerized registry is preferable to a paper-based one; and an online registry is preferable to a closed-network one. Such investments not only are desirable from an AML perspective, but also make the registry more business friendly.

Recommendation 4. For AML purposes, it is important to be able to conduct Boolean searches in company registries for specific types of information.

Whether a jurisdiction allows its registry to be searchable by supervisory authorities, AML investigators, economic service providers, or the general public, certain search criteria represent the primary starting points by which a lead is pursued. Incorporating a Boolean search feature is a cost-effective measure that allows for the input of multiple pieces of data and can contribute to efficient cross-indexing of known information. Registry systems in general therefore should allow for queries by the following:

- Natural persons, by first name or last name (which will retrieve their related addresses, files, company positions (for example, director), and details of the companies in question)
- Company secretary, registered office, or agent
- Shareholders
- Addresses
- Business activity
- Country of registration
- Date of registration
- Date of incorporation.

Recommendation 5. Countries should assign unique identifiers to legal entities incorporated within their jurisdiction.

This enables investigators to collect evidence from different domestic agencies within the jurisdiction (for example, tax, licensing, or municipal authorities) most efficiently. This is especially pertinent to operational entities, and if the process of receiving a unique identifier is sufficiently streamlined, it may be further applicable to all legal entities in the jurisdiction (including foreign legal entities, which may have only an operational connection or only be administered from that jurisdiction).

Recommendation 6. Trust and company service providers should be held subject to an effectively enforced AML compliance regime.

Regulation, through licensing and a supervisory authority, currently provides the strongest assurance that TCSPs comply with AML standards. TCSPs, at least, should be given clear and explicit AML-oriented obligations, above and beyond generic standards of professional conduct, to both identify *and* store beneficial ownership information of client corporate vehicles. Such an approach will probably require more vigorous and severe enforcement in instances of malfeasance to serve as a real deterrent to noncompliance.

Recommendation 7. Jurisdictions should ensure that all service providers to corporate vehicles—whether in establishing them, administering them, or providing financial services to them—collect beneficial ownership information when establishing business relationships.

Given the difficulty in establishing upfront who the beneficial owner is, service providers should be aware of all persons who appear relevant in relation to a certain corporate vehicle and who may have any bearing on the control or ownership of the corporate vehicle. Obligations should indicate the necessity of continually monitoring relationships and updating information on such "relevant persons."

Recommendation 8. Documented particulars of a legal entity's organization, including those details that indicate beneficial ownership and control,[82] should be held physically or electronically within the jurisdiction under whose laws it has been created.

The root of the problem of the misuse of legal entities is that individuals can form them in foreign jurisdictions. This compels authorities to engage in the complicated and often difficult process of a cross-border (rather than domestic)

---

82. Investigators recommended that, in addition to beneficial ownership information, copies of all banking documents, as well as all powers granted to non-officers, should be kept at the registered domestic address of the legal entities, allowing for law enforcement authorities to find all necessary information in one location.

investigation.[83] Mandating that such information be held within reach of law enforcement's compulsory powers would make it easier for governments to immediately access it for all domestic legal entities. Jurisdictions that require corporate vehicles to be incorporated or administered through TCSPs may impose such identification and record-keeping obligations on their TCSP sector. Alternatively, in jurisdictions in which anyone (or any citizen) may incorporate, the holding of such documents may be mandated for the resident directors or agents (who may be actual members of the corporate vehicle or, if functioning as a nominee, TCSPs).

Recommendation 9. Nonresidents forming or subsequently taking beneficial ownership of a legal entity should be required to go through a service provider operating under the AML compliance regime of the domestic jurisdiction.

That service provider should be required to collect and hold the standard set of documents including a certified copy of an ID and proof of address.

Recommendation 10. Jurisdictions should clarify what is and what is not covered by attorney-client privilege.[84]

Jurisdictions must settle the question of whether attorney-client privilege extends to all services rendered by an attorney (solicitor, advocate), or whether it covers only information obtained in the context of services rendered in relation to any adversarial processes or litigation, and whether it covers all such information including the identity of the client. At the least, privilege should cover no more than the services provided as an advocate and not extend to financial services or fiduciary advice. Clear penalties should be imposed on those service providers that are willfully blind to the purpose of the services requested.

Recommendation 11. Jurisdictions should ensure that financial institutions gather beneficial ownership information and develop and maintain complete beneficial ownership compliance files.

An investigator seeking information from a financial institution (to build a case linking an account, a corporate vehicle, a person of interest, or any combination thereof) will want to know when payments are made, where funds are routed to, who controls the account, and who (if anyone) is controlling that person. Banks can provide answers to all or some of these queries, if they have implemented a robust compliance regime—one capable of ensuring information on

---

83. Even when working through chains of TCSPs in different jurisdictions is an effective option, for each additional link in the chain, costs are inevitable in terms of the time and effort required for authorities to obtain the ownership information. Additionally, there is a danger that TCSPs removed from the originating jurisdiction may renege on earlier commitments to hand over beneficial ownership information.
84. According to investigators, one of the most frequent obstacles to accessing corporate vehicle information (as opposed to its unavailability) is the use of attorney-client privilege to refuse to divulge information relevant to the ownership and control of a certain corporate vehicle. In some cases, the privilege is advertised by TCSPs explicitly to attract clients. Lawyers indicate that the line between what is and what is not privileged is not always clear, and that in cases of doubt, they err on the side of the client.

control is effectively and consistently identified and maintained in records. The record-keeping requirement is central. Data such as e-mail correspondence and minutes of business meetings can help compliance officers and law enforcement determine persons of interest in corporate vehicle activity.

Recommendation 12. Jurisdictions should encourage their banks to develop broad, principle-based compliance policies, as opposed to prescriptive checklist-based policies.

Although bank staff will require a degree of certainty in knowing what rules to follow, compliance departments should continue to emphasize that due diligence rules are guidelines, and they are not a mere question of paperwork to be filed away and forgotten. These rules and guidelines are intended to help staff develop a deeper understanding of the customer.

Recommendation 13. The objective of financial institutions conducting CDD should be to ascertain the natural person who has ultimate control over the corporate vehicle's accounts.

Financial institutions therefore should always check whether customers are acting on their own behalf or on behalf of others and be sure to screen all signatories or others who hold a power of attorney over the account. Unexplained beneficiaries of significant amounts may be indicative of outsider control and cause for further investigation.

Recommendation 14. Jurisdictions should ensure that their domestic financial institutions have sufficiently independent client acceptance practices.

In their organizational structure, banks should ensure that compliance departments can make their voice heard at the highest managerial level. Once compliance has voiced a concern, relationship managers should not have the final say in deciding whether to accept a client.

Appendix A. Compliance with Financial Action Task Force on Money Laundering (FATF) Recommendations 5, 12, 33, and 34

As shown by an evaluation of 159 countries (24 FATF member countries and 135 non-FATF member countries)

Texts of FATF Recommendation 5 and Recommendation 12[85]

B. MEASURES TO BE TAKEN BY FINANCIAL INSTITUTIONS AND NONFINANCIAL BUSINESSES AND PROFESSIONS TO PREVENT MONEY LAUNDERING AND TERRORIST FINANCING

Recommendation 5: Customer Due Diligence and Record-Keeping

Financial institutions should not keep anonymous accounts or accounts in obviously fictitious names.

Financial institutions should undertake customer due diligence measures, including identifying and verifying the identity of their customers when

- establishing business relations;
- carrying out occasional transactions: (i) above the applicable designated threshold; or (ii) that are wire transfers in the circumstances covered by the Interpretative Note to Special Recommendation VII;
- there is a suspicion of money laundering or terrorist financing; or
- the financial institution has doubts about the veracity or adequacy of previously obtained customer identification data.

The customer due diligence (CDD) measures to be taken are as follows:

(a) Identifying the customer and verifying that customer's identity using reliable, independent source documents, data or information.[86]

---

85. Financial Action Task Force, "The 40 Recommendations," Recommendations 5 and 12 available at www.fatf_gafi.org/dataoecd/7/40/34849567.pdf.
86. Reliable, independent source documents, data or information will hereafter be referred to as "identification data."

(b) Identifying the beneficial owner, and taking reasonable measures to verify the identity of the beneficial owner such that the financial institution is satisfied that it knows who the beneficial owner is. For legal persons and arrangements this should include financial institutions taking reasonable measures to understand the ownership and control structure of the customer.

(c) Obtaining information on the purpose and intended nature of the business relationship.

(d) Conducting ongoing due diligence on the business relationship and scrutiny of transactions undertaken throughout the course of that relationship to ensure that the transactions being conducted are consistent with the institution's knowledge of the customer, their business and risk profile, including, where necessary, the source of funds.

Financial institutions should apply each of the CDD measures under (a) to (d) above, but may determine the extent of such measures on a risk sensitive basis depending on the type of customer, business relationship or transaction. The measures that are taken should be consistent with any guidelines issued by competent authorities. For higher-risk categories, financial institutions should perform enhanced due diligence. In certain circumstances, where there are low risks, countries may decide that financial institutions can apply reduced or simplified measures.

Financial institutions should verify the identity of the customer and beneficial owner before or during the course of establishing a business relationship or conducting transactions for occasional customers. Countries may permit financial institutions to complete the verification as soon as reasonably practicable following the establishment of the relationship, where the money laundering risks are effectively managed and where this is essential in order not to interrupt the normal conduct of business.

Where the financial institution is unable to comply with paragraphs (a) to (c) above, it should not open the account, commence business relations or perform the transaction; or should terminate the business relationship; and should consider making a suspicious transactions report in relation to the customer.

These requirements should apply to all new customers, though financial institutions should also apply this Recommendation to existing customers on the basis of materiality and risk, and should conduct due diligence on such existing relationships at appropriate times.

Recommendation 12: Customer Due Diligence and Record-Keeping

The customer due diligence and record-keeping requirements set out in Recommendations 5, 6, and 8 to 11 apply to designated non-financial businesses and professions in the following situations:

(a) Casinos—when customers engage in financial transactions equal to or above the applicable designated threshold.

(b) Real-estate agents—when they are involved in transactions for their client concerning the buying and selling of real estate.

**FATF Recommendation 5
All Evaluated Countries (159)[a]**

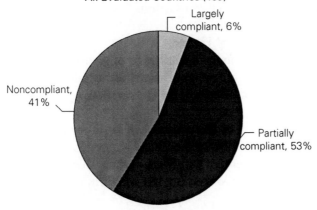

Largely
compliant, 6%

Noncompliant,
41%

Partially
compliant, 53%

**FATF Recommendation 5
FATF Member Countries[b]**

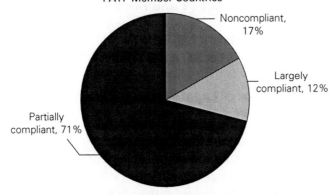

Noncompliant,
17%

Largely
compliant, 12%

Partially
compliant, 71%

**FATF Recommendation 5
Non-FATF Countries (135)[c]**

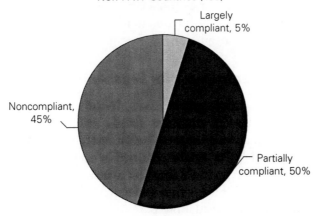

Largely
compliant, 5%

Noncompliant,
45%

Partially
compliant, 50%

Source: Authors' compilation and illustration.
Note: FATF = Financial Action Task Force on Money Laundering.
a. No countries are classified as 'compliant' and this classification does not appear in the figure.
b. No countries are classified as 'compliant' and this classification does not appear in the figure.
c. No countries are classified as 'compliant' and this classification does not appear in the figure.

(c) Dealers in precious metals and dealers in precious stones—when they engage in any cash transaction with a customer equal to or above the applicable designated threshold.

(d) Lawyers, notaries, other independent legal professionals and accountants—when they prepare for or carry out transactions for their client concerning the following activities:
- Buying and selling of real estate;
- Managing of client money, securities or other assets;
- Management of bank, savings or securities accounts;
- Organisation of contributions for the creation, operation or management of companies;
- Creation, operation or management of legal persons or arrangements, and buying and selling of business entities.

(e) Trust and company service providers—when they prepare for or carry out transactions for a client concerning the activities listed in the definition in the Glossary.

Texts of FATF Recommendation 33 and Recommendation 34

C. INSTITUTIONAL AND OTHER MEASURES NECESSARY IN SYSTEMS FOR COMBATING MONEY LAUNDERING AND TERRORIST FINANCING

Recommendation 33: Use of Legal Persons; Beneficial Ownership

Countries should take measures to prevent the unlawful use of legal persons by money launderers. Countries should ensure that there is adequate, accurate and timely information on the beneficial ownership and control of legal persons that can be obtained or accessed in a timely fashion by competent authorities. In particular, countries that have legal persons that are able to issue bearer shares should take appropriate measures to ensure that they are not misused for money laundering and be able to demonstrate the adequacy of those measures. Countries could consider measures to facilitate access to beneficial ownership and control information to financial institutions undertaking the requirements set out in Recommendation 5.

Recommendation 34: Transparency for Legal Arrangements/Trusts

Countries should take measures to prevent the unlawful use of legal arrangements by money launderers. In particular, countries should ensure that there is adequate, accurate and timely information on express trusts, including information on the settlor, trustee and beneficiaries, that can be obtained or accessed in a timely fashion by competent authorities. Countries could consider measures to facilitate access to beneficial ownership and control information to financial institutions undertaking the requirements set out in Recommendation 5.

**FATF Recommendation 12
All Evaluated Countries (159)[a]**

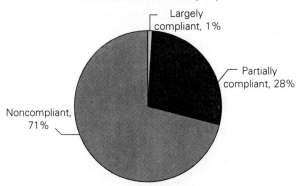

Largely
compliant, 1%

Partially
compliant, 28%

Noncompliant,
71%

**FATF Recommendation 12
FATF member Countries (24)[b]**

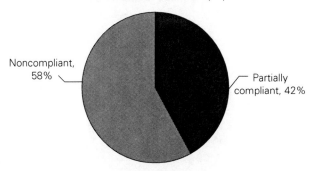

Noncompliant,
58%

Partially
compliant, 42%

**FATF Recommendation 12
Non-FATF Countries (135)[c]**

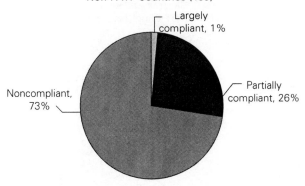

Largely
compliant, 1%

Partially
compliant, 26%

Noncompliant,
73%

Source: Authors' compilation and illustration.
Note: FATF = Financial Action Task Force on Money Laundering.
a. No countries are classified as 'compliant' and this classification does not appear in the figure.
b. No countries are classified as 'compliant' or 'largely compliant' and these classifications do not appear in the figure.
c. No countries are classified as 'compliant' and this classification does not appear in the figure.

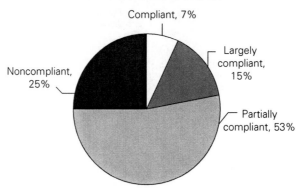

FATF Recommendation 33
All Evaluated Countries (159)

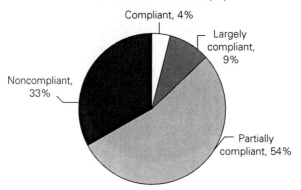

FATF Recommendation 33
FATF member Countries (24)

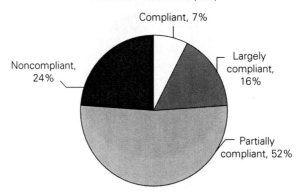

FATF Recommendation 33
Non-FATF Countries (135)

Source: Authors' compilation and illustration.
Note: FATF = Financial Action Task Force on Money Laundering.

FATF Recommendation 34
All Evaluated Countries (159)

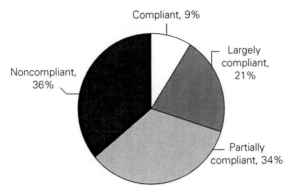

FATF Recommendation 34
FATF member Countries (24)[a]

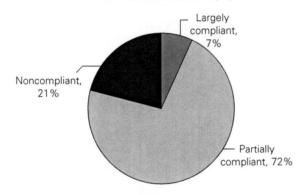

FATF Recommendation 34
Non-FATF Countries (135)

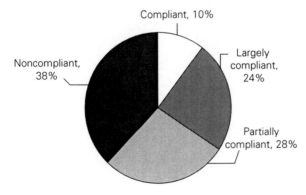

Source: Authors' compilation and illustration.
Note: FATF = Financial Action Task Force on Money Laundering.
a. No countries are classified as 'compliant' and this classification does not appear in the figure.

Appendix B. The Five Component Projects: Methodology and Summary of Findings

Project 1. The Grand Corruption Database Project

1.1 Background

For the Grand Corruption Database Project, 213 grand corruption investigations involving public officials or those with the ability to wield significant power or political influence were examined. These investigations originated from 80 different countries around the world. Initial inquiries revealed 150 instances of the involvement of at least one corporate vehicle that concealed, at least in part, beneficial ownership. In these 150 cases, the approximate total proceeds of corruption amounted to approximately US$56.4 billion, with 15 cases each involving less than US$1 million, 67 cases involving between US$1 million and US$20 million, and 68 cases involving more than US$20 million.[87]

1.2 Methodology

Certain parameters were set to determine which cases would be considered to constitute a "grand corruption case involving the misuse of corporate vehicles." The scheme must have included the misuse of at least one corporate vehicle for which a case could be made that it was used, at least in part, for the anonymity it offered to its beneficial owners. The focus was on those corrupt parties who wanted to obscure their involvement by using a corporate vehicle rather than on those who only sought to use legal features of the corporate vehicle to shield themselves from taxation liabilities or protect their assets. Three additional constraints were placed on the candidate pool. The scheme must have involved a high-level public official or politically exposed person or other party who was able to wield significant influence over a political or bureaucratic process to effect the scheme. Furthermore, the database used a wide time horizon going back 30 years to 1980 to allow for possible analysis of trends over time. Finally, the scheme under consideration must have involved the

---

87. These numbers represent our approximation; where the most precise data available involved a range of suspected corrupt proceeds, we deferred to the lower end of the spectrum. The moneys referenced here represent both misappropriated public assets (by outright theft or the self-dealing of government contracts outside of accepted government norms) and such private funds as were received in breach of public officials' fiduciary duties to their nation (for example, bribes, kickbacks, misuse of position, etc.).

equivalent of more than US$1 million (at the time of the scheme). A few exceptions to this rule were admitted, including instances in which the scheme was particularly expansive or innovative, or when a sum failed to meet the US$1 million threshold but represented a real purchasing power in the particular jurisdiction's economy that was disproportionately greater than what US$1 million would have represented in other parts of the world.

Information on the selected cases was first gathered through publicly available secondary sources, including Internet search engines, academic literature, and reports from national and international bodies pertaining to anticorruption. Subsequently, court documents and other government-sanctioned documents (for example, official government press releases and investigatory hearing reports) were sought to supplement and confirm the information initially gathered. Although many of these documents were obtained through legal research resources,[88] substantial outreach was conducted to secure relevant documentation through contacts, such as prosecutors and attorneys involved in the cases, World Bank country offices, anticorruption agencies, and local courthouses.[89]

In a significant number of instances, the information-gathering process revealed that access to documents (even when purportedly in the public domain) proved for various reasons to be limited and difficult. In a few jurisdictions, the relevant court did not publish the decision sought. For example, upon conducting outreach to various regional experts for a particular lower court decision, the team was informed that lower court decisions were not published in that country. Also, in attempting to access court documents from another case, an attorney informed the team that the courts in that country generally did not publish and distribute public decisions, and that despite the existence of a Freedom of Information Act, accessing the documents from a courthouse could be challenging. In other instances, access to court documents was constrained by surrounding political sensitivities. Finally, court documents for some other cases were simply not available because litigation was ongoing or proceedings were closed to the public. These factors impeded the team's pursuit of court documents in several instances. Because of the lack of access in other venues (or lack of relevant language skills on the team), most of the cases studied have been documented or reported on in English (and Spanish, French, German, and Chinese to a lesser extent) with a substantial proportion being U.S. and U.K. documents. It is arguable that the U.S. and U.K. bias originates in part from the significant number of criminal and civil legal actions against instances of grand corruption have taken place in these jurisdictions. This also goes some way towards explaining the high incidence of those jurisdictions in table B.3. Despite these hurdles, persistent outreach efforts generally proved fruitful. Most prosecutors and other attorneys contacted were willing to assist in the outreach process, whether it was by providing court documents, by leading the team to an alternative contact, or by directly offering valuable insight into their experiences working on grand corruption cases.

---

88. For example, LexisNexis, the World Bank Law Library, and the (U.S.) Law Library of Congress.
89. Each such outreach effort was tracked and recorded for future reference.

Because it often takes a number of years before suspicion of corruption surfaces, and then years more before cases are finally tried, the documentary trail often referred to conduct that predated the documents by several years. In that sense, a database that relies solely on official documentation is bound to be a reflection of a much earlier reality. Cases were included in which a public official may not have been convicted, but in which judicial confirmation of the misuse of a corporate vehicle acknowledged the element or specter of grand corruption. In cases in which final court decisions (not contradicted by legal actions in other jurisdictions) cleared the relevant officials of all wrongdoing, such cases were not deemed to fall within the purview of the study and thus were excluded.

In populating the database, where possible, the exact form (name, entity type, and jurisdiction) of each legal entity or arrangement was recorded and then categorized into streamlined types of entities based on their characteristics. It was not possible to ascertain the jurisdiction of all of corporate vehicles and bank accounts used. This was most often due to a lack of specificity in the relevant source documents. Two of the most common scenarios faced in this matter involve a lack of specificity regarding "companies" and "trusts." Often, court documents implicated a "company" in a jurisdiction that has several variations; without any other independent evidence as to which type of company the courts might have been specifying. In the matter of trusts, these legal arrangements were sometimes specified as being of a certain jurisdiction, but not in many instances. Additionally, many jurisdictions have both common-law and codified variations; again, in the absence of specific evidence, we made no assumptions.

Cases for which evidence of corporate vehicle misuse was not available were excluded from the cases selected; consequently, some of the more sensational and universally known cases of grand corruption were not included in the database, as details of the corporate vehicle misuse were not discovered in the preliminary data-gathering attempts. This does not necessarily mean that corporate vehicles were not used in those cases. A conscious effort to seek cases from all geographic areas (especially in the latter stages of research) means that the 150 cases were not entirely "at random." This was deemed necessary when considering that certain money laundering typologies may be more prevalent (or potentially only occur) in specific regional settings, and such potential omissions outweighed any concern for producing a scientifically rigorous testing method. As with any study based on criminal cases, the data on which the analysis relied may not fully reflect all of the aspects of the relevant criminal behavior and the full extent of the scheme, and we have attempted to give an honest accounting of the extent to which pragmatism and expediency have factored into our findings.

Such caveats notwithstanding, the information was digested and categorized to identify trends among the cases and to test hypotheses regarding correlations between factors. A sizable number of factors were logged, pertaining to, among other things, the jurisdictions of the parties, corporate vehicles, and bank accounts involved, the particular anonymity- and complexity-enhancing methods employed, and the extent to which investigation and prosecution were pursued and effected.

1.3 Summary of Findings

TABLE B.1	Grand Corruption Cases Database: Case Summary
Field Names	
Case Name	
Country of Public Official	
Year scheme began	
Year scheme ended	
Position of Public Official during scheme	
Asset amount in U.S. dollars	
Description	
Type of illicit activity involving Public Official	
Impediments to investigation	
Most recent legal action against Public Official?	
Other legal action / other prosecutions	
Is there a pending case or appeal?	
Jurisdiction(s) of legal action	
Sources	

Source: Authors' compilation.

TABLE B.2	Grand Corruption Cases Database: Corporate Vehicles
Field Names	
Case Name	
Corporate Vehicle (CV) Name	
Jurisdiction of CV Incorporation	
Actual legal form of CV type per jurisdiction (e.g., Sociedad anónima, Anstalt, Stiftung, Aktiengesellschaft, etc.)	
CV type: corporation, trust, foundation, limited liability company, or partnership	
Shell entity?	
Nonprofit?	
Beneficial Owner (BO)	
BO relationship to Public Official: self, nominee, front man, corporate, unknown	
Legal Owner (LO)	
LO relationship to Public Official: self, nominee, front man, corporate, unknown	
Manager of CV	

(continued next page)

TABLE B.2	Grand Corruption Cases Database: Corporate Vehicles *(continued)*			
Manager relationship to Public Official: self, nominee, front man, corporate, unknown				
CV established by public official, professional intermediary, or front man?				
Year of CV incorporation				
CV same jurisdiction as Public Official?				
Jurisdiction of Bank Account (bank name, account name)				
Bank same jurisdiction as Public Official?				
Bank same jurisdiction as CV?				
CV use or role				

Source: Authors' compilation.

Table B.3 shows the key statistics of the database as finally compiled.

TABLE B.3	Grand Corruption Case Database—Key Statistics			
Total No. of Cases	150	**Total No. of Corporate Vehicles (CVs)**		817
Total funds estimated to be involved[a]	US$ 56.4 billion			
Transnational schemes	112[b]	**Total number of persons charged and/or convicted**		118[c]
Jurisdictions of incorporation for the entities involved (Top 20)	**Jurisdiction**	**No. of CVs incorporated**	**Jurisdiction**	**No. of CVs incorporated**
	United States[d]	102	Bermuda	12
	British Virgin Islands	91	Jersey	12
	Panama	50	Cyprus	11
	Liechtenstein	28	Indonesia	8
	Bahamas	27	Tanzania	8
	United Kingdom	24	Trinidad & Tobago	8
	Hong Kong SAR, China	24	United Arab Emirates	8
	Nigeria	20	India	7
	South Africa	16	Isle of Man	7
	Cayman Islands	15	Switzerland	7

(continued next page)

TABLE B.3	Grand Corruption Case Database—Key Statistics *(continued)*		
Types of entities involved	**Type of entity**		**No. of entities in database**
	Company (e.g., corporation, LLC, *sociedad anónima*, etc.)		593
	Trust		43
	Foundation		40
	Partnership		9
	Unidentified/Misc.		132
Bank account jurisdiction (Top 10)	**Jurisdiction**	**No. of CVs with account in this location**	**Jurisdiction**	**No. of CVs with account in this location**
	United States[e]	107	Cyprus	15
	Switzerland	76	Hong Kong SAR, China	14
	United Kingdom	19	Antigua and Barbuda	11
	Nigeria	17	Jersey	11
	Bahamas	18	Liechtenstein	10
Cases with Intermediaries	72[f]	**Cases with Lawyers**	32[g]	**Cases with Bearer Shares**	10

Source: Authors' compilation.
Note: a. Taking the low-end estimate in cases in which an estimated range of amounts was involved.
b. Cases were also considered transnational schemes where it was known that bribe funds originated from a jurisdiction that differed from that of the public official(s).
c. Includes prosecution, civil suit, plea agreement, and indictment.
d. Top five U.S. states for CV incorporation: Florida (20 CVs); California (18 CVs); New York (13 CVs); Delaware (13 CVs); Maryland (6 CVs).
e. Top five U.S. states for CV bank accounts: Florida (31 accounts); New York (16 accounts); California (16 accounts); District of Columbia (3 accounts); Virginia (3 accounts). U.S. Virgin Islands (3 accounts) and Louisiana (3 accounts).
f. Professional service provider that either established a corporate vehicle or held positions of ownership or management through nominee services; of the 150 cases, 59 had insufficient information to definitively determine if an intermediary was involved.
g. Professional legal advisor, solicitor, or attorney who either established a corporate vehicle or held positions of ownership or management.

Project 2. The Bank Beneficial Ownership Project

2.1 Background

The purpose of this study was to gain a clearer insight into the procedures banks use to establish beneficial ownership when providing financial services to corporate clients. The views of banks were solicited on the extent to which they can and do determine beneficial ownership, what methods they employ, and how those methods might be improved upon or what other parties could do to ensure that the information banks obtain is of a higher quality.

The perspective of financial institutions was considered especially valuable in informing this report and in particular, on the contentious matters of the beneficial ownership issue and its place in global standards. Since the adoption of the Financial Action Task Force on Money Laundering (FATF) 40 Recommendations in 2003, regulatory reforms that were designed to bring financial sectors into compliance were among the first changes to be adopted. As a result, implementing beneficial ownership measures for corporate vehicles has improved significantly according to practitioners, although as yet only 3 out of the 31 FATF member countries evaluated obtained a "Largely compliant" rating for Recommendation 5 (which deals with this matter).

2.2 Methodology

To gain practitioners' insight, a multifaceted questionnaire was devised (see figure B.1). It went through several rounds of revision in consultation with anti-money laundering (AML) and regulatory enforcement experts. The questionnaire touches on many aspects of the beneficial ownership issue. In particular, the project team sought to explore what the banks consider to be their beneficial ownership obligations (imposed by their jurisdictions and by the banks themselves) and how these obligations play out in practice, from the initial contact with a client and throughout any subsequent ongoing business relationship. The questionnaire examined the structures of the banks' client evaluation, monitoring, and review processes and sought technical insight into how these processes handle complex corporate vehicle–related scenarios.

Although the questionnaire provided data on how a certain number of global actors dealt with the beneficial ownership issue, it was primarily intended to facilitate a dialogue, to be held at a later time, between the banks' compliance practitioners and the project team. After receiving clearance or acknowledgment from each jurisdiction's financial intelligence unit or central bank, invitations were sent to 11 nations that were either commonly known as major players in the global (or specific regional) financial systems or whose financial systems frequently were mentioned in the Database Project. In each jurisdiction, input was sought from two or three separate financial institutions to (a) take into account the fact that different banks have different market focuses and risk probabilities and (b) identify inconsistent understandings of, or approaches to, shared regulatory obligations. All invited parties accepted the invitation, and 50 compliance personnel from 25 individual banks participated in the exercise.

Upon receipt of the completed questionnaires, interviews were conducted to clarify the answers received and pursue relevant lines of inquiry more thoroughly. To promote frank exchanges, the project team attempted to visit as many of the participating personnel for face-to-face interviews as was feasible. In the end, such meetings occurred with participants from 8 of the 11 jurisdictions. All other interviews were conducted by telephone or videoconference. Given the various sensitivities involved, all participants were guaranteed confidentiality as to the specifics of their contributions to further facilitate a candid exchange.

Organization: _____

Position/Title: _____

Number of years working on anti-money laundering (AML)/combating the financing of terrorism (CFT) issues: _____

City, country: _____

Date: _____

Please note that for the purposes of this questionnaire:

- The term *business relationship* refers to any and all activities or arrangements that your financial institution can engage in, with, or on behalf of a client where Know Your Customer (KYC) and Customer Due Diligence (CDD) protocols apply (including, but not limited to, account opening and service, management activities, one-time transactions, etc.).
- The term *legal entity* refers to any organizations that, for legal purposes are considered capable of engaging in activities and transactions in their own right, separate from any natural person who owns them.
- The term *trust* refers to all arrangements properly so-called and similar arrangements that separate legal and beneficial title to an asset.
- To "identify" a person refers to the process of ascertaining the identity of a person without obtaining further documentation.
- To "verify" the identity of a person refers to the process of using documentation, typically government-issued, to confirm the identity information.
- "Independent verification" refers to the process of conducting verification based on documentation not supplied by clients or their representatives.

For each question, please select all answers that apply, and feel free to alter the length of the response space as required for your answer:

1. Does domestic legislation require, as a part of the customer due diligence process, that financial institutions have procedures for identifying the beneficial owner(s) when establishing a business relationship with a client?

☐ Yes
☐ Laws and regulations do not require it, but our internal policies do
☐ It is not required by laws, regulations, or internal policies

(continued)

2. How does domestic legislation define beneficial owner for the purposes of your institution's customer due diligence process?

- ☐ The physical person(s) who own or control the legal entity
- ☐ The physical person(s) who enjoy the benefits of owning the security or property, regardless of whose name the title is in
- ☐ Any physical person directly or indirectly holding more than ___percent (please provide) of the shares in a company or able to exercise equivalent control
- ☐ Other (please describe if ownership or control is specified differently or beyond the above):

_____

_____

3. Does domestic legislation define beneficial owner in a sufficiently specific manner for you to be able to apply it in practice? Or has your institution (or the group it belongs to) further clarified or expanded upon that definition? If so, how?

- ☐ The definition of beneficial owner in domestic legislation is sufficiently specific to allow direct applicability
- ☐ The definition of beneficial owner in domestic legislation is, on its own, not sufficiently specific to allow direct applicability. However, jurisdictional guidance (please identify the authority providing guidance) has clarified beneficial ownership to mean:

_____

_____

- ☐ Our institution has defined beneficial owner as (please provide institutional definition):

_____

_____

4. What measures (e.g., asking the client, requiring evidentiary documentation and/or client-signed declaration, checking publicly available information, etc.) does your institution use to determine beneficial ownership? If utilized, how helpful do you find publicly available information (such as that found in corporate registries) in identifying beneficial ownership?

_____

_____

(continued)

5. Does your financial institution update beneficial ownership information? If yes, how does it go about doing so?

☐ No

☐ Only in certain circumstances (please specify circumstances and explain how):

_____

_____

☐ Yes (please explain how):

_____

_____

6. Does your institution use a Risk-Based Approach to modify beneficial ownership procedures? If so, please explain: (1) What factors are used to classify those business relationships with legal entities or trusts into different risk levels? (2) Which CDD measures for determining beneficial ownership are affected by this classification? and (3) What percentage of business relationships typically fall into each classification?

☐ No

☐ Yes (please describe):

_____

_____

7. When starting a new business relationship with a client that is a legal entity or repre-senting a trust, are there any situations in which your institution does not identify the beneficial owner(s) (*e.g.*, when an intermediary, such as a lawyer or TCSP, vouches that they have satisfactorily identified the beneficial owner)?

☐ No

☐ Yes (please describe):

_____

_____

8. If domestic legislation or your institution's internal policies require the identification of beneficial owner(s) of clients that are legal entities, does the requirement apply to all such clients or only to some (*e.g.*, high-risk business relationships or other specific categories)?

☐ Not required

☐ All client business relationships in the name of legal entities

☐ Only some business relationships in the name of legal entities (please specify):

_____

_____

(continued)

9. Which parties to trusts (beneficiaries or otherwise, e.g., settlor, trustee or protector) does your domestic legislation or your institution's internal policies require you to identify? Is this requirement applied to all such clients or only some (e.g., required for high-risk business relationships, not required for unit trusts, etc.)?

   ☐ Required to identify all client business relationships in the name of trusts. Please specify which parties to trusts—beneficiary or otherwise: e.g., settlor, trustee or protector—your domestic legislation or your institution's internal policies require you to identify:

   _____

   _____

   ☐ Only required to identify when engaged in business relationships in the name of certain trusts (please specify which). Please specify which parties to trusts (beneficiary or otherwise—e.g., settlor, trustee or protector) your domestic legislation or your institution's internal policies require you to identify:

   _____

10. When establishing a business relationship, does your institution always determine if this relationship is being established on behalf of someone other than the person with whom your institution is dealing? If so, how?

   ☐ No
   ☐ Only if there is reason to believe that outside parties are involved
   ☐ Yes (please explain how):

   _____

   _____

11. When dealing with an intermediary acting on behalf of a principal or corporate legal entity, does your institution verify the existence of the power of attorney?

   ☐ Yes, by requiring the original power of attorney or a certified/notarized copy
   ☐ Yes, by requiring a uncertified/non-notarized copy of the power of attorney
   ☐ Yes, by asking the intermediary if he or she has valid power of attorney to act on behalf of the legal entity (with no further documentation required)
   ☐ Other (please explain):

   _____

   _____

12. In what cases does domestic legislation or your institution's internal policies require your institution to *verify* information on the identity of the beneficial owner(s) provided by clients?

   ☐ All cases
   ☐ None

(continued)

☐ Only some cases (e.g., higher-risk business relationships, foreign business relationships; please specify and describe):

_____

_____

13. What types of information, documents, or requisite courses of actions does your institution typically request in order to verify information on the identity of the beneficial owner(s) provided by clients?

_____

_____

14. In what cases does domestic legislation or your institution's internal policies oblige your institution to conduct *independent* verification of the information on the identity of the beneficial owner(s) provided by clients?

   ☐ All cases
   ☐ None
   ☐ Only some cases (e.g., higher-risk business relationships, foreign business relationships; please specify and describe):

_____

_____

15. What considerations are used to determine whether your institution needs to gather additional information on the identity of the beneficial owner from clients?

   ☐ When we doubt or are dissatisfied with the information provided
   ☐ When the legal entity is considered higher-risk or suspicious (please explain):

_____

_____

   ☐ Other situations (please explain):

_____

_____

16. What sources and types of information does your institution typically use to conduct *independent* verification of the information on beneficial ownership provided by clients?

_____

_____

(continued)

17. Does your institution conduct any extra checks on the authenticity of foreign documentation (e.g., articles of incorporation, registration documents, and powers of attorney)? If so, what types of checks?

    ☐ No, it is impossible for us to do this
    ☐ We try to do so when we know a counterpart in another country who can help us
    ☐ We verify the authenticity of the foreign license and certificate of registration of the legal entity or trust
    ☐ We verify whether the entity is regulated
    ☐ Other (please explain):

    _____

    _____

18. Are there any particular jurisdictions or particular types of legal entities, trusts, or other contractual arrangements that commonly or always pose a challenge in terms of identifying the beneficial owner(s)?

    _____

    _____

19. Approximately how often does your institution decide not to establish a business relationship because you are not satisfied you have identified the beneficial owner?

    ☐ Very rarely (1–2 times a year)
    ☐ Rarely (3–6 times a year)
    ☐ Sometimes (1–2 times a month)
    ☐ Often (several times a month)
    ☐ Very often (daily)

20. If domestic legislation requires you to identify beneficial ownership, does your country's supervisory authority for financial institutions assess compliance with this requirement during onsite inspections?

    ☐ Yes, that is a standard component of onsite inspections
    ☐ Yes, but only rarely
    ☐ No

21. Has your institution ever been subject to supervisory action (in the form of warning letters, fines, etc.) for noncompliance with this requirement? If so, please describe any supervisory or internal remedial actions that have been implemented as a result.

    ☐ No
    ☐ Yes (please describe):

    _____

    _____

(continued)

22. How much time do you estimate is spent by staff at your institution on seeking accurate beneficial ownership information on potential or existing clients (including ongoing CDD in the case of continuing business relationships)?

_____

_____

23. Do you think the time spent on CDD to *verify* identification of beneficial ownership is useful in reducing the risk of AML/CFT-related financial crimes?

_____

_____

24. Broadly speaking, based on your experiences as a compliance officer in dealing with AML/CFT issues, can you think of any modifications to your jurisdiction's legislation or your institution's beneficial ownership procedures that could improve effectiveness?

_____

_____

25. Broadly speaking, based on your experiences as a compliance officer in dealing with AML/CFT issues, can you think of any modifications to the international standards regarding beneficial ownership identification that could improve effectiveness?

_____

_____

26. What are the most vexing and/or recurrent obstacles that your institution experiences when identifying beneficial ownership of legal entities and/or trusts, and what are the most common situations in which these issues arise?

_____

_____

_____

27. Please describe any "good practices" that your financial institution applies when identifying beneficial ownership of legal entities and/or trusts:

_____

_____

_____

Thank you for your participation. Please return the completed questionnaire to Emile van der Does de Willebois, Task Team Leader of the Project.

Once we have compiled the responses from all participants, we will contact you to arrange a face-to-face or videoconference interview in order to discuss our findings and seek your feedback. If permitted at your financial institution, we would appreciate it if you would attach copies of the relevant Customer Due Diligence and Beneficial Ownership Identification guidelines that your institution operates. While not necessary for completion of this survey, such material would be used to help ensure that the matters discussed during our interview are germane.

✶✶✶

2.3 *Summary of Findings*

Questions 1–3: Beneficial Ownership Standards

- The participating compliance personnel stated that the laws of their nation, with the exception of one jurisdiction, require that measures be taken to ascertain the beneficial owner of corporate vehicles in all instances of entering into relationships with corporate vehicle clients. In the exceptional nation, such measures are only deemed necessary in certain circumstances.
- All compliance personnel reported that in their jurisdictions the beneficial owner is considered to refer only to natural persons; however, two participants (from the same jurisdiction) indicated that, contrary to the FATF definition, their national industry standard allows for corporate persons to be considered beneficial owners. Beneficial ownership standards imposed by government, industry, or the institution generally focus on a percentage threshold (most typically in the 20 to 25 percent range) of ownership or control rights (for example, shareholdings or voting rights in a company). All compliance personnel felt that their institutions have sufficient guidance on the topic of beneficial ownership, although quite a few expressed the opinion that, within countries, the standards applied may vary widely among institutions. International banks are the most likely to have broad, self-imposed beneficial ownership definitions, subject to adjustment via a risk-based assessment of the customer.

Questions 4–9, 12–18: Beneficial Ownership Data-Gathering and Verification

- Banks said they rely on client-provided evidence to a significant extent. Most stress, however, that they do not rely on that alone, but rather seek to have collaborative and corroborating evidence available from multiple sources.
- Compliance officers enthusiastically endorsed the idea of Disclosure Forms (whether provided directly to the bank or to a government registry to which the bank has access). Beneficial ownership forms are well thought of, with the caveat that, to avoid accidental misrepresentation, they must be comprehensible to the client and furthermore should be based on the percentage threshold definition of beneficial ownership (usually 25 percent). Consequently, many potential customers that are corporate vehicles do not have beneficial owners in this more technical sense (be that by natural or illicit circumstance), resulting in no such information being gathered. Participants in one nation have full access to shareholders

and directors holdings that domestic companies must file with the government, giving them much more detail than the more standard (although still uncommon among practitioners) beneficial ownership forms.

- Participants reported that company registries are much relied on to cross-check client-provided data. Domestic registries are highly regarded across the board. This is sometimes because of the quantity or quality of information they contain; in other cases, however, it is because they provide easier access to whatever materials they contain, in contrast to foreign registries, which may be difficult to identify or access. Banks with a multinational presence often have less of a problem with foreign corporate vehicles, as (depending on their company's presence in the jurisdiction) they can rely on a sister bank in a foreign nation to forward the relevant information obtained from registry checks. They can sometimes rely on additional "local banker" knowledge about particulars or persons involved. Although other sources (credit checks, company websites, professional references, or hired investigators) are used to varying degrees, company registries are, for all financial institutions, the primary source of non-client-provided ownership and control information.

- Risk-based assessment typically involving politically exposed persons, high net-worth persons, at-risk jurisdictions, and at-risk industries is widely used by financial institutions around the globe. Atypical transactional activity is also used as a risk indicator, with some larger financial institutions monitoring the business volume, account turnover, and other transactional activities of corporate vehicles. These institutions compare the activities of corporate vehicles with industry benchmarks or medians based on other companies of similar size and profile with whom they conduct business. For most banks, risk-based assessment is lauded as the most efficient way to thwart money laundering; it also appears to be the key factor in going above and beyond nationally mandated standards of customer identification in due diligence efforts.

- Trust identification standards are far more rigorous among the majority of banks who are willing to conduct business with international or foreign trusts. Smaller or primarily domestic banks from civil law jurisdictions indicated that accepting such trusts as clients is typically the exception rather than the rule. (A minority expressed the same concerns about foundations, referring to the legally codified variants of such, rather than the generic nonprofits that may also be referenced by the term). Many compliance personnel indicated that the concept of a beneficial owner is a poor choice for a trust client, as beneficially interested parties are (typically) different parties than trust controllers or power-holders (that is, the persons who would seem most likely to misuse the account). All banks indicated a need to identify declared settlors, trustees, beneficiaries, and power-holders as well as a need to ascertain the source of funds or wealth of the declared settlors. None mentioned concerns about "economic settlors" (those persons not legally affiliated with a trust, but who nevertheless contribute assets to the legal arrangement).

- Requirements to verify documents independently generally were found to be underwhelming and to rely primarily on government registries. When these prove unavailable, "sighted" or copied corporate vehicle documentation (of a foreign legal person or arrangement) is usually accepted, on the condition that it is a notarized, certified true copy. Many participants complained about a lack of materials enabling them to confirm client-provided evidence. In fact, those banks that press further indicated that they seldom can be certain that they hold irrefutable, conclusive proof of a (corporate vehicle) customer's beneficial ownership. Instead, they seek comfort by tracing as many unrelated streams of information on the client as can be found, to ensure that the client is presenting a coherent story to all such sources.

Questions 10–11: Verifying the Credentials or Relationship of the Face-to-Face Client Representative

- When faced with a properly credentialed corporate vehicle representative, few banks inquire whether that person ultimately is acting on behalf of (in the beneficial interest of) an undisclosed party. The most common reason given is that, when banks review the credentials presented, such standing usually becomes apparent. A few compliance officers indicate that "straw men" account openers (and the occasional unscrupulous intermediary) are of the mind-set to misrepresent themselves as not acting for an undisclosed party. In other words, they will have come in prepared to lie, no matter what questions they may be asked. In one particular jurisdiction, the financial institutions indicate that national guidance was such that they are allowed to consider the individual before them to be the "beneficial owner" of the account no matter what parties actually own or control the corporate vehicle that he or she is representing—just as long as legal authority is clearly established.
- Generally, any time a party exercises power through a power of attorney over an account, the power of attorney is scrutinized thoroughly, it must be properly notarized, and a copy is kept on file. Recognizing the potential for misuse of powers of attorney to obscure ownership and control to gain access to and control of financial accounts, several compliance personnel state that their institutions do not accept general, all-purpose, or overbroad power-of-attorney holders as signatories on a corporate vehicle account (except those who are regulated trust and company service providers from acceptable jurisdictions).

Questions 19: Refusal to Begin Customer Relationships

- Few institutions keep records of such data, and most contributors supply estimates that are in all cases very low in number. They typically attribute these low estimates to front-end due diligence that might "scare off" bad actors at the inquiry stage or to the inherent low risk of money laundering in their general set of products and services.

Question 20: Supervisory Inspection

- All financial institution personnel indicate that their financial institutions are subject to onsite inspections and assessment by mandated supervisory authorities.

Question 21: Punitive and Cautionary Measures

- Despite the fact that several compliance personnel represent banks that were implicated in major money laundering schemes, only one admits to having received any form of formal reproach. This is potentially attributable to the fact that most respondents' particular branch or territory is distinct from the particular sister company that may have been involved in such cases. The one respondent who admits a case of official sanction indicates that it has acted as an effective call to their organization to strengthen existing beneficial ownership practices. The interviewed financial authority representatives confirm that public censure (causing reputational harm) and punitive fines (causing financial harm), more so than education and training outreach (although also crucial), are the two most effective ways through which to ensure that compliance goals are taken seriously.

Questions 22–24: Efficient Use of Limited Compliance Resources

- Financial institutions generally cannot estimate the average amount of time spent on compliance per account, given the variation that would obtain within any given set of clients and the fact that such efforts are often integrated into (and not particularly assessable separately from) general account opening activities. They generally consider that this time is effectively spent to the betterment of the institution and the local financial system; however, some do complain that when scarce resources must be allocated evenly, without taking into account risk variables, the resulting inefficiency may prevent proper focus on high-risk corporate vehicles.

Questions 25–27: General Guidance

- These questions typically resulted in discussions of lessons learned, corporate commitment to anticorruption goals, effective client acceptance practices, training for front-end staff, the development of in-house information resources, and the effective implementation of risk-based AML strategies; responses were reported in box 3.13 of this report (Developing a "Nose" for Inappropriate Complexity).

Project 3. The Trust and Company Service Providers Project

3.1 Background

This project centered on two audit studies involving the solicitation of offers for shell companies from a range of Trust and Company Service Providers (TCSPs). The data were supplemented with in-depth interviews conducted with TCSPs. The use of a direct approach to testing regulatory compliance in the form of an audit study is unusual. Collecting data by soliciting offers for shell companies is premised on a simple *a fortiori* logic: If it is possible for people who are essentially amateurs to obtain anonymous corporate vehicles for a few thousand dollars via the Internet, then participants in grand corruption schemes, professional money launderers, and others should have no difficulty whatsoever. The project serves two purposes: On the one hand, this effort complements the data of other projects with a "what-happens-in-practice" perspective as to what really occurs when one seeks to obtain corporate vehicles for unseemly purposes. On the other hand, it also addresses the additional issue of the lack of source information on the role of TCSPs in grand corruption cases, occasioned by their (relatively speaking) lower profile when implicated in the aiding of money launderers to obtain corporate vehicles. Thus, the approach adopted in the TCSP Project corresponds to this report's emphasis to go beyond mere examination of such rules-on-the-books as may exist. All fact-gathering for this project was conducted independently of the Stolen Assets and Recovery (StAR) Initiative, from November 2008 to August 2010.

3.2 Methodology

The research for this component developed a substantial evidentiary base amassed through the most direct and powerful technique for judging the availability of companies that leave the identity of the beneficial owner unknown: Seeking offers for such vehicles, and in three cases, purchasing the vehicles in question. Such an approach provides answers to two key questions:

1. How easy or difficult is it for would-be criminals and others to purchase companies while hiding their underlying controlling interest?
2. Does the recommendation that all corporate vehicles should be able to be linked to their beneficial owner really make any difference?

Even if only a few jurisdictions are failing to adhere to the proper standards (compliance with FATF Recommendations 33 and 34) with regard to collecting beneficial ownership, the exceptions may well dominate the rule. In July 2008, the president of the FATF observed the following:

> We live in an increasingly interconnected world and money launderers and terrorist financiers will exploit any gaps between countries. Consistent application of recognised international standards is essential. The weakest link gives the strength of the chain.[90]

Thanks to online incorporation systems, it is likely that criminals, and unscrupulous TCSPs, can effortlessly arbitrage to form companies in the jurisdictions that require the least identification and verification (if any) with regard to the beneficial owners. The rigor of the many may be rendered irrelevant by the laxity of the few.

Early on in the Trust and Company Service Providers Project, a decision was reached that the solicitation of offers by TCSPs would be geared toward obtaining shell entities (that is, corporations, limited liability companies, or jurisdictional variants of the same). Because of pragmatic considerations having to do with ensuring that this subcomponent would be manageable, the omission of other forms of corporate vehicles (trusts, foundations, partnerships, etc.) is nevertheless justifiable for two reasons: (a) the total numbers of such alternate corporate vehicle forms are an order of magnitude smaller compared with total of all types of existing corporate vehicles (at the highest end, there

---

90. FATF e-news, Issue 5, July 2008, available at http:/www.oecd.org/dataoecd/57/19/41094921.pdf.

are only an estimated 40,000 Liechtenstein *Anstalten*[91] and 26,000 Panamanian foundations[92]) and (2) reference to Database Project findings suggests that corporate vehicle misuse in grand corruption cases has most frequently implicated companies.

Decisions as to which TCSPs would be approached were informed to some extent by the distribution of TCSPs and corporate vehicles around the globe. To begin with, a minor note must be made of the conceptual difficulty involved in determining what or who counts as a TCSP. It is typically not possible to strictly delineate between TCSPs and financial institutions and "designated nonfinancial" businesses and professions, because a business may offer one such service as a primary function and the other(s) as an ancillary service, or they may market themselves as a one-stop provider of both (or all three) functions in equal measure. It is easiest to quantify those TCSP providers who fall under the purview of a jurisdiction with a regulated-TCSP regime (most typically found in the "offshore financial centers" [OFCs]—those jurisdictions whose corporate vehicles are primarily used by nonresidents) because, whether as primary or auxiliary function, all those seeking to engage in the provision of such services must be licensed.[93] The larger OFCs usually have 80–120 licensed TCSPs, whereas smaller OFCs may have 6–20. Attempts to count the TCSPs operating in so-called onshore jurisdictions (those jurisdictions whose corporate vehicles primarily are used by domestic individuals) prove more problematic, as most of the onshore jurisdictions do not require TCSPs to obtain licenses within a regulatory framework, and often any range of individuals or companies belonging to the financial, designated non-financial businesses and professions (DNFBPs), or unrelated sectors can engage in the creation and sale of these corporate vehicles as a primary or ancillary service to their clients.

Some of the largest TCSPs are headquartered in the United States, the United Kingdom, Panama, the Isle of Man, and Hong Kong SAR, China.[94] Individually, larger TCSP firms (for example, Offshore Incorporations Limited [OIL], Offshore Company Registration Agents [OCRA], Mossack Fonseca, etc.) may offer company incorporation and management services in up to 30 different jurisdictions and are responsible for incorporating thousands of corporate vehicles each year. Divisions often exist between wholesale and retail TCSPs—the former forming companies in bulk, the latter selling or establishing individual vehicles for particular clients.

The numbers of OFC-based international business companies (IBCs) are relatively well known: the British Virgin Islands has about 40 percent of the market with around 500,000 active companies, and about 70,000 new companies are formed each year.

---

91. Based on a 2007 interview by the Trust and Company Service Provider project leader.
92. According to Offshore Investment Company Formation Survey 2009.
93. Even in these jurisdictions, legal arrangements are seldom regulated to such an extent—perhaps with the exception of certain codified variants. A few countries do register trusts. Liechtenstein, South Africa, and Bahrain are three such exceptions.
94. According to interviews with TCSPs in the United Kingdom; Panama; the Isle of Man; Hong Kong SAR, China; Seychelles; Samoa; and the British Virgin Islands.

Panama is second with perhaps 320,000 total active companies, then Belize, the Seychelles, the Bahamas, and the Caymans with 50,000–75,000 total active companies each.[95] It is relatively safe to assume that most of these are shell companies and that all are owned by nonresidents. The small populations of these jurisdictions and the legal prohibition on IBCs conducting business domestically indicate they are held by nonresidents, as the name international business company suggests. This point is unanimously confirmed in both public documents and interviews with CSPs and regulators in these jurisdictions. Less easy to determine are the data on those shell companies mixed into the sizable numbers of corporate vehicles formed in the onshore jurisdictions. By way of example, the U.S. Senate Permanent Subcommittee on Investigations estimates that 2 million corporations are formed *each year* in the United States,[96] with more than 18 million corporations and limited liability companies currently active.[97] A very large number of U.K. companies are also formed each year, with 362,000 formed in 2009–10.[98] Evidence from interviews with TCSPs and advertising material suggests that a not-insignificant portion of these are formed as shell companies, often by nonresidents and thus are functionally equivalent to the classic OFC-based corporate vehicles. Here, the example of the André Pascal England and Wales company (see box 3.6), set up as part of the first audit study, is illustrative.

Given the uncertainties in the universe of TCSPs and corporate vehicles, the sample of TCSPs that were chosen never could constitute a statistically representative sample. A major focus was on those jurisdictions whose TCSPs are under no specific AML-relevant obligations pertaining to verifiably identifying beneficial ownership. Consideration was given, however, to the possibility that the rules that obtain in theory may often prove ineffectual and irrelevant (for instance, because of failures of implementation or enforcement, driven by a lack of capacity or of political will) in influencing the actual behavior of individuals. So, even in cases in which TCSPs are regulated entities subject to AML requirements, failures of regulation might render them likewise ineffectual. A mix of the two groups was selected from jurisdictions around the globe, with specific providers being identified from advertisements in the specialist investment media, general media outlets, and dedicated online searches.

Once the TCSPs to be included in the study had been identified, the first step of the practical element of this exercise was to compose a short approach e-mail using accounts created for the purpose. This letter was designed to emulate the profile of a representative would-be miscreant, based on recurring elements identified in the various reports. In a manner intended to set off "red flags," this e-mail stressed the need for confidentiality and tax minimization as part of an international consultancy project, as consulting fees often are used as plausible justification for illicit cross-border flows.

---

95. Offshore Investment Company Formation Surveys, 2007, 2008, 2009.
96. The U.S. figure is from Senate Committee on Homeland Security and Governmental Affairs Committee Hearing June 17, 2009, on S.569 Incorporation Transparency and Law Enforcement Assistance Act.
97. J. W. Verret, "Terrorism Finance, Business Associations and the Incorporation Transparency Act," *Louisiana Law Review* 70, no. 3 (Spring 2010): 857–910.
98. *Companies House: Annual Report and Accounts 2009/10*, p. 58.

In two rounds of testing, 217 service providers were contacted, of which 102 returned valid replies.[99] A valid reply consisted of a service provider's recommendation of one or more corporate structures that could achieve the goals set out in the approach letter, together with a pricing schedule. Responses commonly included a brochure specifying further services, and encouraged further contact, which was, wherever possible, carried out via e-mail.

These replies were compiled and coded in terms of the nature and domicile of the corporate vehicle offered, whether the service provider would supply such a corporate vehicle, and what, if any, documentation was required by the TCSP to verify the identity of the beneficial owner for the transaction to move forward. Analysis was then performed to understand what (and in what circumstances) variance of standards may occur: across countries, between different types of countries (for example, OFCs versus onshore jurisdictions) or in line with different regulatory regimes (for example, whether a requirement existed to license TCSPs), thus offering the potential to provide a better diagnosis of where the existing weaknesses lie and to suggest possible solutions.

As a final step, in-depth interviews were conducted with corporate service providers from six major company-formation jurisdictions. These interviews checked and validated the findings of the TCSP component of the study as well as the more general conclusions. A specific focus was given to whether these service providers performed due diligence checks in line with the standards of their home jurisdiction, or according to the standards of the jurisdiction in which companies were being incorporated, or whether they were dictated by separate group standards.

As with the other practitioner consultations, strict confidentiality was assured to ensure forthright participation.

3.3 Summary of Findings

The findings of the TCSP Project (first and second audits, and combined results) are summarized in tables B.4 through B.6.

TABLE B.4	Complete Results of First Audit Study			
Service Provider	Shell Company Jurisdiction	ID Required?	Bank	ID Required?
Bahamas	Anguilla	Yes		
Bahamas	Bahamas	Yes		
Bahamas	Bahamas	Yes		

(continued next page)

99. In the initial round of testing, occurring in 2008–09, 54 service providers were contacted, of whom 45 returned valid responses; in the second round (2010), 163 service providers were contacted, with 57 valid replies. Please note that a forthcoming study by Brigham Young University and Griffith University of over 3,500 company service providers confirm the findings of the present TCSP Project.

Service Provider	Shell Company Jurisdiction	ID Required?	Bank	ID Required?
TABLE B.4	**Complete Results of First Audit Study** *(continued)*			
Belize	Belize	Yes		
Bermuda	Bermuda	Yes		
British Virgin Islands (BVI)	BVI	Yes		
Cayman Islands	Cayman Islands	Yes		
Cayman Islands	Cayman Islands	Yes		
Cyprus	BVI, Panama, St. Vincent and the Grenadines	Yes		
Czech Republic	BVI, Seychelles	Yes		
Dominica	Dominica	Yes		
Gibraltar	Turks and Caicos	Yes		
Gibraltar	BVI, Delaware, Gibraltar, Panama, Wyoming, etc.	Yes		
Hong Kong SAR, China	BVI	Yes		
Hong Kong SAR, China	BVI; Hong Kong SAR, China; Seychelles, etc.	Yes		
Hong Kong SAR, China	BVI	Yes		
Labuan (Malaysia)	Labuan	Yes		
Liechtenstein	Liechtenstein	Yes		
Nauru	Nauru	Yes		
Panama	Panama	Yes		
Panama	Panama	Yes		
Panama	Belize, Nevis, Panama, Seychelles, Vanuatu, etc.	Yes		
São Tomé and Príncipe	São Tomé and Príncipe	Yes		
Seychelles	BVI, Seychelles	Yes		
Singapore	Bahamas, BVI, Delaware	Yes		
Singapore	Singapore	Yes		

(continued next page)

TABLE B.4	Complete Results of First Audit Study *(continued)*			
Service Provider	Shell Company Jurisdiction	ID Required?	Bank	ID Required?
Switzerland	BVI, Delaware, Panama	Yes		
Belize	Belize	No	Belize	Yes
Canada	BVI, Ontario, Panama, Wyoming, etc.	No	Latvia, Panama	Yes
Hong Kong SAR, China	Delaware	No	Hong Kong SAR, China	Yes
Singapore	BVI; Hong Kong SAR, China; Seychelles (Gruppo 20)	No	Cyprus	Yes
Spain	Belize	No	Belize	Yes
United Kingdom	Belize, BVI England, Nevada, Panama, etc.	No	Isle of Man	Yes
United Kingdom	Belize	No	Hong Kong SAR, China	Yes
United Kingdom	Cyprus	No	Cyprus	Yes
United Kingdom	Belize, BVI, Delaware, England, etc.	No	Hong Kong SAR, China	Yes
United Kingdom	England (A. Pascal)	No	Latvia	No (pre-2007), Yes
Uruguay	Seychelles	No	Hong Kong SAR, China; Panama	Yes
United States	Wyoming	No	United States	Yes
United States	Nevis	No	Belize	Yes
Liechtenstein	Somalia	Yes	Somalia	Yes (unnotarized)
United Kingdom	Belize, BVI, Delaware, Nevada, Panama, etc.	No	St. Vincent and the Grenadines	Yes (unnotarized)
United Kingdom	Seychelles	No	Montenegro	Yes (unnotarized)
United States	Nevada (BCP Consolidated)	No	United States	Yes (unnotarized)
United States	Wyoming	No	United States	No (pre-2008), Yes (unnotarized)

Source: Authors' compilation.

TABLE B.5	Complete Results of Second Audit Study (noncompliant responses in italics)	
CSP Jurisdiction	Vehicle Jurisdiction	Photo ID Required?
Malaysia	BVI	Yes
United Kingdom	*Seychelles, BVI, England*	*No*
Jersey	Jersey	Yes
United States	non-U.S. Trust	Yes
United Kingdom	U.K. Trust	Yes
Singapore	Singapore	Yes
Costa Rica	Seychelles, Belize	Yes
United Kingdom	Seychelles, BVI, Belize	Yes
United States	*Nevis, Belize, Bahamas*	*No*
Hong Kong SAR, China	*Nevis*	*No*
Thailand	Thailand	No*
Dominica	Dominica	Yes
Panama	Panama	Yes
Mauritius	Mauritius	Yes
New Zealand	NZ Trust	Yes
Dominica	Dominica	Yes
Cyprus	Seychelles, Cyprus	Yes
United Kingdom	Seychelles	Yes
Barbados	Barbados	Yes
Belize	Belize	Yes
United Kingdom	BVI	Yes
Dominica	*Dominica*	*No*
United States	*Delaware*	*No*
United States	*Delaware*	*No*
United States	*Wyoming*	*No*
United States	Delaware	Yes
United States	*Delaware*	*No*
United States	*Delaware*	*No*
United States	*Delaware*	*No*
Philippines	Philippines	Yes
Seychelles	Seychelles	Yes
New Zealand	Vanuatu	Yes
Panama	Panama	Yes
Neth. Antilles	Neth. Antilles	Yes

(continued next page)

TABLE B.5	Complete Results of Second Audit Study (noncompliant responses in italics) *(continued)*	
CSP Jurisdiction	**Vehicle Jurisdiction**	**Photo ID Required?**
Mauritius	Mauritius	Yes
Mauritius	Mauritius	Yes
New Zealand	New Zealand	Yes
New Zealand	*New Zealand*	*No*
United States	Nevada	Yes
United States	*Nevada*	*No*
United States	*New Mexico*	*No*
United States	*California*	*No*
United States	*Nevada*	*No*
United States	*Nevada*	*No*
United States	*Nevada*	*No*
United States	*Delaware*	*No*
United States	*Nevada*	*No*
United States	*Delaware*	*No*
United States	*Nevada*	*No*
United States	*Nevada*	*No*
United States	*Nevada*	*No*
Singapore	Singapore	Yes
Singapore	Singapore	Yes
Seychelles	Seychelles	Yes
Seychelles	Seychelles	Yes
Hong Kong SAR, China	Hong Kong SAR, China	Yes
United States	*Delaware*	*No*

Source: Authors' compilation.
Note: * The Thai service provider did not require an ID, but did require a personal visit.

TABLE B.6	Combined Results		
	Valid responses	**Compliant**	**Noncompliant**
1. Sampled OECD countries	**47**	**12**	35
(a) United States	*27*	*3*	*24*
(b) Other OECD	**20**	**9**	*11*
2. Other countries	**55**	**49**	6
(a) Tax havens[a]	**36**	**34**	*2*
(b) Non-tax havens	**19**	**15**	*4*
3. Total-Worldwide	102	61	41

Sources: Authors' compilation with some data from J. C. Sharman, "Shopping for Anonymous Shell Companies: An Audit Study of Financial Anonymity and Crime," *Journal of Economic Perspectives* 24 (Fall 2010): 127–140.
Note: OECD = Organisation for Economic Co-operation and Development.
a. Those jurisdictions identified as tax havens by the OECD in 2000.

Project 4. The Registry Project

4.1 Background

The Registry Project aims to provide further clarity regarding the central company registry system and its role in providing information on certain corporate entities. Based on the wording of FATF Recommendations 33 and 34, the following elements served as the existing framework for this project: timely access to adequate, accurate, and beneficial ownership information. These elements should be taken to signify the following:

- The adequacy of information refers to the existence and initial recording of sufficient information to identify the beneficial owner.
- The accuracy of information refers to the appropriate checks conducted to verify the accuracy of the information being recorded.
- The timeliness of information refers to the updating of information when changes in ownership occur, and powers to take action if information is not provided.
- The timely access to information refers to the ability and ease with which competent authorities are able to obtain or access the information in a timely way.

In addition to beneficial ownership information, these elements were extended to include the legislative requirements and availability of supplemental categories of information maintained in a registry that could be useful to an investigation. These categories were as follows: (a) legal status and existence, (b) legal ownership, (c) management, (d) other forms of control, and (e) other characteristics.

4.2 Methodology

To select a set of jurisdictions on which to focus our assessment, the team contacted more than 30 experienced investigators and compliance officers from financial institutions who had proved to be particularly insightful. The team requested from each the names of 5 to 10 jurisdictions for which they would like to have company registry information available, thus ensuring that the project resulted in a tool that was useful to practitioners and that responded to a real need. The top 40 jurisdictions mentioned most frequently by the practitioners constitute the jurisdictions of the sample set. The final list of jurisdictions (unintentionally) encompassed a natural mix of developed and developing, FATF and non-FATF members, and civil and common law countries.[100]

The exact legal forms that were chosen for analysis were jurisdictional variations of the legal persons and arrangements most commonly documented in the Grand Corruption

---

100. The top 40 were Anguilla, Antigua, Australia, Bahamas, Belize, Bermuda, the British Virgin Islands, the Cook Islands, the Cayman Islands, Cyprus, Czech Republic, Delaware (United States), Dubai (United Arab Emirates), Florida (United States), Gibraltar, Guernsey, Hong Kong SAR (China), the Isle of Man, Jersey, Latvia, Liechtenstein, Luxembourg, Mauritius, the Netherlands Antilles, Nevada (United States), Nevis, Ontario (Canada), Panama, the Seychelles, Singapore, South Africa, St. Kitts, St. Lucia, St. Vincent and the Grenadines, Switzerland, the Turks and Caicos Islands, Ukraine, the United Kingdom, Uruguay, and Wyoming (United States).

Database Project to include companies, partnerships, trusts, and nonprofit organizations. On average, nine legal forms were analyzed per jurisdiction.

The legislative assessment was structured as a database, which was composed of four Excel-based documents divided by adequacy, accuracy, timeliness, and timely access. Extensive Internet research was conducted to assemble the current company and trust legislation per jurisdiction, extracting and documenting in the database applicable provisions relevant to each of the four elements. Following the completion of the database, the legislative findings were sent for review by the respective jurisdiction to verify the accuracy of the assessment of their requirements and registration practices. The team then organized the extracted information into individual country reports based on the findings. The textual documents were uniformly drafted and formatted with legal citations.

In addition to preparing the legislative reports, the team drafted a brief questionnaire to capture anecdotal insights into the good practices of registries and any challenges they may face on a day-to-day basis. The questionnaire was formulated around the particular elements guiding the study, namely, timeliness and timely access to information. Meanwhile, during the drafting process, the team had been conducting extensive outreach to each jurisdiction to determine the appropriate person at the registry with whom to work on the study. Once initial contact had been established with the registrar, a packet of documents was sent to each jurisdiction containing an instruction sheet, the individual legislative report for their review and amendment as necessary, and the questionnaire. In most cases, follow-up was needed. In some cases, this was unsuccessful. In total, 22 reports and questionnaires were returned. In some instances, additional follow-up was arranged to clarify their responses.

Once the modified report and completed questionnaires were returned, the team amended its findings in the assessment database in accordance with the jurisdiction's corrections. The information was sorted to derive quantitative findings regarding each element of the study—focusing on figures that may demonstrate the significance of a specific requirement, availability of certain information contained in the registry, or the prevalence of a particular feature. Lastly, the team compiled the tested questionnaires as qualitative findings regarding challenges and good practices for consideration. A combination of numerical and anecdotal findings was used to support the drafting of this report and the subsequent recommendations.

Project 5. The Investigator Project

5.1 Background

The term "investigators" used throughout this report encompasses a broad and diverse group of experts we consulted in the course of our study. It includes investigators in the traditional sense: those currently working or formerly having worked in law enforcement agencies or other government investigative bodies, such as national anti-corruption commissions and financial intelligence units. It also includes prosecutors, in recognition of the fact that in some jurisdictions prosecutors lead investigations or share responsibility for doing so with investigators. Forensic accountants and certified fraud examiners also were consulted, because they play critical roles in financial crimes investigations. Finally, civil practitioners in the field of international fraud and financial crimes were consulted, including those with experience in successfully recovering stolen assets on behalf of their client governments or other victims.

Many of the investigators in our study had experience in investigating grand corruption cases involving the misuse of transnational corporate vehicle structures. Other investigators did not have direct experience in grand corruption cases, but we believed that their experience and expertise in investigating transnational corporate vehicle misuse in the context of other financial crimes, such as narcotics trafficking, tax evasion, and fraud, were highly relevant to our inquiry—which, at its core, is about understanding how to unravel the corporate vehicle structures to reveal their beneficial owners.

In addition to diversity in professional backgrounds and skills, we sought to achieve regional diversity among the experts we consulted both in terms of the jurisdictions where the investigators were located and the jurisdictions in which they had experience conducting investigations.

5.2 Methodology

Information from investigators was gathered chiefly by means of a confidential questionnaire. (See Figure B.2) An initial draft questionnaire was sent to various experienced investigators for their feedback. Based on their input, the questionnaire was finalized and sent by e-mail to nearly 200 prospective respondents in 51 jurisdictions from March to June, 2010. In total, 42 responses were received from 25 jurisdictions. The questionnaire sought to obtain insights of investigators on the obstacles they face, as well as the tools and sources of information they find most useful in identifying the beneficial owners of corporate vehicles involved in grand corruption and other financial crimes. It also asked investigators for their "wish lists" and the good practices they employ to unravel the beneficial ownership of involved corporate vehicles.

Although individual investigators completed the questionnaires, a number of investigators had sought and incorporated the insights of colleagues in their respective agencies. Some respondents indicated that they had received specialized training in investigating corporate vehicle misuse, whereas others responded that their training had been "on the job." Most of the respondents possessed between one and two decades of experience, with a few respondents having had three decades of experience or more in the field, thus providing the benefit of a historical perspective on this issue.

In addition, two regional roundtable discussion meetings were organized in Washington, D.C. (April 2010) and in Miami, Florida (May 2010) with law enforcement investigators. These meetings included investigators from Brazil, the British Virgin

Islands, Canada, Colombia, Costa Rica, Guatemala, Jamaica, the Netherlands, Panama, the United Kingdom, the United States, and Uruguay. A third meeting was held in Mauritius (March 2010) with civil practitioner members, on the margins of a meeting of the International Chamber of Commerce's (ICC) FraudNet, a private network of top law firms from around the world working in the area of financial crimes.[101] These civil practitioners were drawn from both civil and common law jurisdictions (the Bahamas, Brazil, Canada, France, Germany, Israel, Liechtenstein, Luxembourg, Mauritius, Nigeria, Switzerland, the United Kingdom, the United States, and Ukraine) and possessed direct experience in working on grand corruption cases involving corporate vehicle misuse, having been retained by affected governments or other victims. During January to June 2010, the study researchers also undertook in-person meetings and teleconferences with investigators and other experts to test early findings from the completed questionnaires and the roundtable discussion meetings. In total, more than 77 investigators and experts from 33 jurisdictions were consulted.

---

101. FraudNet is a private organization of the Paris-based International Chamber of Commerce's Commercial Crime Services. Membership in the group is by invitation and is limited to only those law firms that represent victims of fraud or other financial crimes. Additional information about ICC FraudNet may be accessed at http://www.icc-ccs.org/index.php?option=com.content&view=article&id=1&Itemid=11.

Confidentiality Pledge: Please be assured that your participation and your responses will be kept strictly confidential.

PRELIMINARY MATTERS

Please fill in the following:

Name: _____

Title: _____

Organization: _____

Address: _____

Telephone: _____

E-Mail: _____

Number of years worked as an investigator or prosecutor: _____

Please describe your experiences and training on investigating corporate vehicles involved in grand corruption (or other financial crimes) cases:

Glossary for the Questionnaire:	
Grand Corruption	A broad range of offenses, including bribery, embezzlement, trading in influence, misappropriation of state funds, illicit enrichment, and abuse of office committed by high-level public officials or senior officers of state-owned entities.
Corporate Vehicles	A broad concept that refers to all forms of legal entities and legal arrangements (*examples:* corporations, trusts, partnerships, foundations, etc.)
Beneficial Owner	The natural person who ultimately owns or controls the Corporate Vehicle or benefits from its assets, and/or the person on whose

(continued)

	behalf a transaction is being conducted. It also encompasses those persons who exercise ultimate effective control over a legal person or arrangement.
Designated Non-Financial Businesses and Professions	Includes real estate agents and lawyers, notaries, other independent legal professionals and accountants.
Trust and Company Service Providers	Any person or business that provides any of the following services to third parties: acting as a formation agent of legal persons; acting as (or arranging for another person to act as) a director or secretary of a company, a partner of a partnership, or a similar position in relation to other legal persons; providing a registered office, business address or accommodation, correspondence or administrative address for a company, a partnership, or any other legal person or arrangements; acting as (or arranging for another person to act as) a trustee of an express trust; acting as (or arranging for another person to act as) a nominee shareholder for another person.

INSTRUCTIONS: PLEASE ANSWER THE QUESTIONNAIRE BASED ON YOUR EXPERIENCES OF THE PAST 10 YEARS IN INVESTIGATING GRAND CORRUPTION CASES INVOLVING THE MISUSE OF CORPORATE VEHICLES.

SECTION I. IDENTIFYING THE BENEFICIAL OWNERS OF CORPORATE VEHICLES

1. How often have you encountered obstacles in identifying the beneficial owners of involved corporate vehicles? Please check the box that best applies:

Infrequently	Sometimes	Frequently	Almost Always/ Always

2. Which three types of corporate vehicles have been the **most challenging** for you in terms of identifying their beneficial owners? Please describe:

	Jurisdiction (of CV Incorporation or Establishment)	CV Type (Exact legal form, if known)	Obstacle(s) Encountered
	(example: Delaware)	*LLC*	*No director and shareholder information filed with corporate registry*
1.			
2.			
3.			

(continued)

SECTION II: OBSTACLES TO IDENTIFYING THE BENEFICIAL OWNERS OF CORPORATE VEHICLES

3. Please review the following characteristics that may be used for obscuring the beneficial ownership of corporate vehicles, and please specify:

   a. How frequently you have encountered such a characteristic,
   b. To what degree it constituted an obstacle,
   c. Whether you were able to overcome the obstacle, and
   d. How you were able or unable to overcome the obstacle.

Characteristics of Corporate Vehicles	Frequency of Obstacle NA = not encountered/not applicable; 1 = least; 5 = most	Degree of Obstacle	Able to be Overcome? (Yes/No)	Please specify how you were able or unable to overcome the obstacle(s)
Bearer Shares				
Nominee Shareholders				
Nominee Directors				
Corporate Directors				
Shares Held by Trust				
Power of Attorney				
Use of Intermediaries to Establish, Own or Manage				
Use of Multiple Jurisdictions (*e.g.,* Corporate Ownership, Management or Control/Registration in Jurisdiction Different from the Jurisdiction of Incorporation)				

4. **OTHER OBSTACLES:** Please tell us about the most vexing and recurrent obstacles you have encountered that are not listed in Q3, the reason(s) why they were an obstacle, and explain how you were able or unable to overcome them:

Obstacle	Please explain why it was an obstacle	Please specify how you were able or unable to overcome the obstacle(s)
(e.g., claim of legal privilege)	*Located and interviewed the TCSP that established the CV but the TCSP had sold the CV to a law firm, which invoked a claim of legal privilege in withholding the beneficial owner's name.*	
1.		
2.		
3.		

(continued)

5. **TRUSTS AND FOUNDATIONS:** Please tell us about the obstacles you have encountered that were particular to identifying the natural persons who were related to the involved trusts and foundations, including their beneficial owners. Please explain why they were obstacles, and specify how you were able or unable to overcome them:

Obstacle(s) particular to:	Please explain why it was an obstacle	Please specify how you were able or unable to overcome the obstacle(s)
Trusts: 1. 2.		
Foundations: 1. 2.		

SECTION III: TOOLS AND SOURCES FOR IDENTIFYING BENEFICIAL OWNERSHIP

6. Based on your investigations on identifying the beneficial owners of corporate vehicles, please rate each of the following Tools and Sources of Information on how **useful** you found them and the **timeliness** of your access to them:

Tools and Sources	Useful	Timely Access
	(NA = not used/not available; 1 = least useful/timely; 5 = most useful/timely)	
Corporate Registries		
Public Registries (not including corporate registries) (e.g., land registries, licensing, etc.)		
Personal Inspection and/or Observation (e.g., site visit to address given for a corporate vehicle on its incorporation form)		
Law Enforcement Databases		
Information Sharing among domestic law enforcement agencies, including financial intelligence units and tax authorities		
Law Enforcement Compulsory Powers (e.g., seizure of business records and interview of Trust and Company Service Providers)		
Undercover Informants		
Wire Taps/Surveillance		
Regional and International Law Enforcement Organizations (e.g., Egmont, Interpol)		

(continued)

Foreign Law Enforcement Agencies—via informal channels		
Foreign Law Enforcement Agencies—via legal channels *(e.g., Mutual Legal Assistance Treaty, Memorandum of Understanding, Letters Rogatory)*		

7. **BEST TOOLS AND SOURCES:** Please tell us about the tools and sources (*for example, specifying the particular public registry or compulsory power*) that you consider the most useful and provide the timeliest access in identifying the beneficial owners of corporate vehicles, and specify the reason(s):

	Tools and/or Sources	Reason
1.		
2.		
3.		

8. Based on your experience, how can the following be better sources of information that are *more useful and provide you with timelier access* to assist in identifying the beneficial owners of corporate vehicles?

Source of Information	Please specify how the source can be made more useful and provide you with timelier access
Corporate Registries	
Trust and Company Service Providers	
Designated Non-Financial Businesses and Professions	

MUTUAL LEGAL ASSISTANCE TREATY

9. What legal or practical obstacles, if any, have you encountered in seeking and/or obtaining assistance from foreign law enforcement agencies through the Mutual Legal Assistance Treaty (MLAT)?

10. What types of international assistance resulted in your obtaining the most useful information in identifying the beneficial owners of the involved corporate vehicles?

SECTION IV: BANK ACCOUNTS OF INVOLVED CORPORATE VEHICLES

11. Please tell us of three jurisdictions that have been the **most challenging** for you in locating the bank accounts of involved corporate vehicles and in identifying

(continued)

the accounts' beneficial owners. Please list the jurisdiction, describe the obstacles you encountered, and explain how you were able or unable to overcome them:

	Jurisdiction	Obstacles	Please specify how you were able or unable to overcome the obstacle(s)
	(e.g., Panama)	*The Bank where the account was established did not have information on its ultimate beneficial owner because the Bank was not legally required to collect it as part of its customer due diligence.*	*Was able to obtain information about the signatory to the bank account who turned out to be the BO*
1.			
2.			
3.			

12. What obstacles, if any, did you encounter when the bank accounts were established in a jurisdiction different from the jurisdiction where the corporate vehicle was incorporated or established? How were you able or unable to overcome these obstacles?

13. Please tell us which jurisdictions' banks held the most useful and provided the timeliest access to the information on the involved bank accounts' beneficial owners, and explain:

14. Based on your experience, what can be done to make banks become better sources of useful and timelier information regarding the beneficial ownership of bank accounts?

SECTION V: "WISH LIST" AND GOOD PRACTICES FOR IDENTIFYING THE BENEFICIAL OWNERS OF CORPORATE VEHICLES

15. **"WISH LIST" OF TOOLS AND SOURCES OF INFORMATION:** Based on your experience, please tell us your wish list of tools and sources of information to assist you in identifying the beneficial owners of corporate vehicles, drawing from the following categories or others:
    a. Tools
    b. Sources of information
    c. Modifications to domestic or international legal/regulatory framework or standards

(continued)

   d. Training

   e. Methods of information sharing (domestic, regional and international)

	"Wish List" Item	Reason(s)
1.		
2.		
3.		

16. **GOOD PRACTICES:** Please tell us about the good practices that you have used (or seen used by other investigators) in identifying the beneficial owners of involved corporate vehicles in grand corruption (or other financial crimes) cases:

	Good Practice	Explanation
1.		
2.		
3.		

CLOSING MATTERS

17. Would you be interested in participating in any follow-up efforts related to this questionnaire, including helping to review its preliminary findings or being interviewed by the study's researchers?

   ___ Yes

   ___ No

   ___ Please contact me at _____ to discuss.

18. Would you be willing to share with us the names of other experienced investigators of grand corruption (or financial crimes) cases involving corporate vehicle misuse, in order that we may invite them to participate in this questionnaire?

   ___ Yes, their names and contact information are: _____.

   ___ No

   ___ Please contact me at _____ to discuss.

Thank you for your participation. Please return the questionnaire via e-mail.

5.3 Summary of Findings

The findings of the Investigator Project are summarized below. The responses cover four main areas of interest: (1) obstacles frequently encountered; (2) sources of information; (3) tools and good practices; and (4) recommendations.

5.3.1 Obstacles Frequently Encountered

Investigators frequently encountered obstacles identifying the beneficial owners of involved corporate vehicles.

- *Jurisdictions of corporate vehicles cited as most challenging*
  These jurisdictions encompassed both "tax haven" and non-tax haven jurisdictions, the challenge arising from the fact that the involved corporate vehicle had been formed outside of the investigator's jurisdiction. An exception to this was in the responses by U.S. investigators, who listed those corporate entities formed in U.S. states for which the beneficial ownership information is not collected at the time of incorporation. The lack of availability of beneficial ownership information in a given jurisdiction was a common underlying challenge for investigators. Investigators also cited as challenging a jurisdiction's stringent bank secrecy or other anonymity laws that impeded, or prevented altogether, their access to beneficial ownership information that may be held by banks, corporate service providers, or other third parties.

- *Types of corporate vehicles cited as most challenging*
  Coupled with a legal and regulatory environment that provides for opacity in beneficial ownership information, investigators pointed out certain types of corporate vehicles as particularly challenging. They included corporate entities such as IBCs, which are not required to have a physical presence in the jurisdiction of their formation, and Limited Liability Corporations whose simple structures allow for formation with as few as one member. Investigators also pointed to the private nature of trusts that make it particularly challenging to ascertain their existence and to locate the trust deed or document to establish the identities of their settlors, beneficiaries, or trustees.

- *Obstacles in identifying beneficial ownership of corporate vehicles*
  A chief obstacle cited by investigators was the lack of availability of beneficial ownership information in the first place because it is not required to be collected and maintained by the corporate registry or a corporate service provider, or because it was required but not collected because of negligence or willful blindness by, for example, the bank or service provider. At other times, the challenge is being able to access persons with direct knowledge or third parties who may hold beneficial ownership information.

- *Characteristics used for obscuring beneficial ownership*
  Where bearer shares are still permitted, investigators found them to be one of the most challenging obstacles to overcome. The use of nominee shareholders and

nominee directors were obstacles that investigators could overcome as they involve natural persons. The use of corporate directors, while more challenging as it involves another layer of corporate vehicle, was not necessarily an insurmountable obstacle for investigators. If the corporate director was located in a jurisdiction that was different than the original involved corporate vehicle, then the ability to overcome this obstacle depended on the availability of and access to the beneficial ownership information in that jurisdiction, including being able to have the assistance of the law enforcement counterparts in the foreign jurisdiction. Use of intermediaries to form corporate vehicles can range from informal strawmen, such as family members or close associates, to formal nominees, including professional intermediaries who may be innocent agents in the scheme. Intermediaries sometimes possess beneficial ownership information and disclose it to investigators. But investigators also pointed out that an intermediary can be a low-level associate who can only provide nonuseful information such as a mobile number or e-mail address that has been changed. Even if these persons have an incentive to cooperate with the investigation, they can provide little assistance in reaching the beneficial owner.

- *Layering of corporate vehicles and use of multiple jurisdictions*
  Similar to the use of corporate directors, layering and multiple jurisdictions were cited as among the most challenging obstacles to overcome. Time and resources needed to peel away the layers of concealment are two main factors. In addition, when corporate vehicles span multiple jurisdictions, investigators must rely on the assistance and cooperation of their foreign counterparts, which may not always be available on a timely basis, if at all. This lack of cooperation may be due to a lack of legal basis for cooperation or practical barriers such as shortages in the staff power needed to carry out the requested assistance.

- *Lack of harmonization of international standards*
  Lack of harmonization of international standards regarding covered entities under domestic AML regimes was a gap that criminals would be able to take advantage of simply by moving to jurisdictions that afforded lax customer due diligence (CDD) and recordkeeping requirements, or by working with professionals that were not covered. The use of attorney-client privilege and lack of reporting requirements on monies transferred through attorney-client trust accounts were frequently cited as roadblocks or even insurmountable walls in an investigation.

5.3.2 Sources of Information

Investigators have access to, and utilize, a wide range of sources of information, including publicly available information, law enforcement databases, information held by Financial Intelligence Units, and information derived from individuals with knowledge of the corporate vehicles in question. To the extent possible, investigators also access information held by covered entities, such as TCSPs and financial intermediaries, as well as banks and other financial institutions.

- *Banks as sources of information*

  The jurisdictions with the most useful information tended to be those jurisdictions with significant Know-Your-Customer requirements that were strictly enforced; jurisdictions where obstacles were most frequently encountered included those with stringent bank secrecy laws or lack of recordkeeping.

- *Company registries as sources of information*

  Company registries are often the starting point for investigations, although it is important to recognize the inherent limitations of the fact that virtually all company registry information is unverified information. Online access would enable investigators to access information in a quicker and more direct manner, as would the availability of more information—such as the names of directors and shareholders, and the ability to search by the names of directors or shareholders rather than just the name of the corporate entity. A longer period of retention of records would also be helpful. In addition, some investigators remarked that beneficial ownership information, along with a copy of government-issued ID, while not deterring abuse, might help to prevent mass, bulk incorporations.

5.3.3 Tools and Good Practices

The most useful tools for investigators were their compulsory powers, such as subpoena powers, search and seizure and production orders, as well as "gag" or "nontipping off" orders to prevent information about the investigation being leaked. For civil practitioners, common law tools, such as *Norwich Pharmacal* and *Bankers Trust* disclosure orders, as well as *Anton Piller* search orders and insolvency proceedings against a corporate vehicle (which may enable the victim to step into the role of receiver/liquidator/trustee), were powerful aids.

- *Mutual Legal Assistance* (MLA)

  MLA was cited as the most useful—indeed, critical—tool in investigations of transnational corporate vehicle misuse schemes. In some instances, relevant information can be obtained through informal channels with foreign law enforcement counterparts, but if the information is to be used as evidence at trial, it must have been obtained through the MLA process. The lengthy delays or complete unresponsiveness of the requested jurisdiction were cited as obstacles, and investigators pointed to the need for an increased capacity of both the requesting and the requested states to enhance the effectiveness of the MLA process.

- *Good Practices*

  Many good practices were suggested by investigators, ranging from investigatory tips to ideas for systemic undertakings, such as the following: (1) the creation of interagency task forces, which would bring different perspectives and skills to the investigation; (2) greater cooperation among investigators from different jurisdictions, including greater informal contact and assistance to the extent permitted by domestic law and the embedding of formal liaisons within foreign law enforcement counterpart agencies; and (3) greater coordination of

multijurisdictional investigations, including joint investigations in which jurisdictions work together at the outset to divvy up responsibilities and work out
information-sharing arrangements.

5.3.4 Recommendations

Finally, a number of recommendations were made by the investigators, including:

- Overcoming the adherence by some banks, corporate service providers and others to a rigid definition of the concept of beneficial owner, and combating their
  insistence that CDD obligations have been met when owners of a certain minimum threshold percentage ownership have been identified, without a real attempt
  to understand the corporate vehicle and its ownership or control.
- Encouraging greater information-sharing among domestic law enforcement
  and regulatory agencies, including eliminating legal and practical barriers to
  information-sharing.
- Setting up funds within investigative agencies to cover travel expenses of investigators because, as one investigator put it, transnational corporate vehicle misuse
  investigations are akin to putting together a jigsaw puzzle, with investigators in
  different jurisdictions each holding the pertinent pieces of the puzzle. Face-to-
  face meetings enable the exchange of information necessary to piece together the
  whole puzzle.
- Harmonizing international standards, and in particular, eliminating the current
  gap of certain professionals being subject to CDD and recordkeeping obligations
  in one country but not in another.
- Extending greater international assistance, including considering taking nonco-
  ercive measures even when the criterion of dual criminality is not fulfilled. Or in
  cases in which MLA assistance is not available, being flexible about finding
  another basis to provide requested assistance.
- Building the investigatory capacity—in both knowledge and manpower—
  that is needed to take on the increasingly complex corporate vehicle misuse
  investigations.

Appendix C. Short Description of Selected Corporate Vehicles

Legal Persons

Before the 20th century, most business or commercial activity was undertaken by sole proprietorships or partnerships. They remain a significant feature of the 21st century economic landscape.

The sole proprietorship is the legal recognition of an individual conducting economic activity, such as providing a service or product to a purchaser for remuneration, or investing to generate income, without the need to create a formal entity structure or to engage in legal arrangements such as a trust. A sole proprietorship represents the simplest way of conducting business—the individual has no formal registration requirements or filing fees, does not need to create an operating agreement or to be held accountable to anyone, and files taxes as a part of personal duties.

General Partnerships

General partnerships are formed when an association of more than one person agrees to come together to pursue a business activity. This agreement is usually the determining feature that dictates whether a court will acknowledge the existence of partnership. Many jurisdictions allow for the existence of a partnership to be (a) predicated on an expressed acknowledgment on the part of partners to enter into the joint undertaking or (b) based on inference derived from actions taken. This means that a partnership may be found to exist without any documentation or admission on the part of partners to confirm this. Global laws lack uniformity dictating what independent legal personality a partnership may have, distinct from its individual partners. From one jurisdiction to the next, or even between different types of partnerships in the same jurisdiction, any given statute-specific partnership form may be recognized in law as, variously, (a) a legal person, (b) a legal relationship between individuals, or (c) a hybrid of the two, that is, a legal relationship that allows possession of an "incomplete legal personality"—an incomplete set of those capacities that are usually reserved for legal persons (for example, the right to own property, to sue or be sued, and so on).[102]

---

102. Due to space limitations, readers are referred to a joint report by The Law Commission of England & Wales and The Scottish Law Commission (advocating an attempt at reconciling the contradictory partnership laws of their different jurisdictions) for the issues surrounding the legal makeup of partnerships, comprehensively approached in a practical and jurisdiction-specific context. The Law Commission and The Scottish Law Commission. (LAW COM No 283) (SCOT LAW COM No 192). *Partnership Law. Report*

FIGURE C.1 Composition of Economic Activity Undertaken in the United States as Ascertained by Internal Revenue Service Tax Data[a]

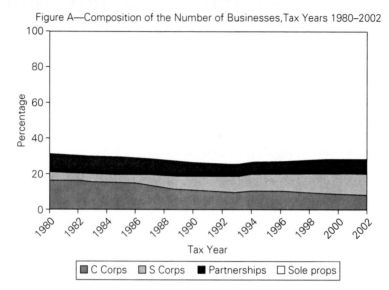

Figure A—Composition of the Number of Businesses, Tax Years 1980–2002

C Corps   S Corps   Partnerships   Sole props

Source: Graphic from Tom Petska, Michael Parisi, Kelly Luttrell, Lucy Davitian, and Matt Scoffic, *An Analysis of Business Organizational Structure and Activity from Tax Data,* U.S. Internal Revenue Service, http://www.irs.gov/pub/irs-soi/05petska.pdf (accessed on August 15, 2010).
Note: The "C corp" is a company that is taxed at the company level and again at the member level when distributions are made; the "S corp" is a company that has pass-through taxation, that is, only the member is taxed; the U.S. Internal Revenue Service does not formally acknowledge limited liability companies (LLCs), so they may be classed (at the discretion of the filer, subject to restriction) as either an "S corp" or a disregarded entity (In the case of single-member LLCs, the member files tax returns as would an individual in a sole proprietorship, while in multiple-member LLCs, the members each file tax returns as would partners in a partnership.)

These unincorporated forms of business activity necessarily vest both ownership and control of business assets in the partners, unless contracts with third parties (creditors) determine otherwise.[103] With respect to partnerships, a contract among the partners divides the relative rights of each partner to ownership and control. Partners, however, need not be physical persons. Common law countries do not require business partnerships to register with a government entity or court or to commit the governing contract to a written document. Civil law countries, by contrast, generally require both. Although a review of both partnership agreements and any contracts with third parties can help determine ownership and control among partners and creditors, in common law jurisdictions, these documents normally are not publicly

---

on a Reference under Section 3(1)(e) of the Law Commissions Act 1965. Presented to the Parliament of the United Kingdom by the Lord High Chancellor by Command of Her Majesty. Laid before the Scottish Parliament by the Scottish Ministers November 2003. http://www.lawcom.gov.uk/docs/lc283.pdf (accessed on August 1, 2010).

103. In most common law jurisdictions, partnerships, although not separate legal persons, are deemed to be separate "entities" in that they may hold assets and make contracts in their own name rather than in just the names of the partners themselves. This creates additional problems for determining ownership and control in that "ABC Partnership" may hold legal title to the assets, with the operation of law extending that ownership to the partners themselves.

available, if they exist at all. Historically, these forms of business did not limit the liability of proprietors or partners to the business's creditors, which created a disincentive to investment. In response, the original French Commercial Code of 1807 created a new form of partnership that allowed for a general partner (with general liability to creditors) and limited partners (whose liability was limited to the amount of their investment). The code, however, significantly restricted the control rights of limited partners. In most cases of modern limited partnerships, the general partner is a company with few attachable assets as a protection against any creditor litigation. Because of the liability issues inherent to sole proprietorships or partnerships, many persons engaged in business sought to establish companies.

Limited Partnerships

Limited partnerships (LPs) are partnerships in which limited liability is granted to certain partners and not others. This statutory partnership form, which can only be brought into existence through a formal process that includes the creation of a written partnership agreement, is most useful as a way to encourage silent investment partners (those persons who contribute capital to an endeavor but do not meaningfully act in its management or operations). This limited liability is conditional, as limited partners who take too active a role in the partnership business can be found to have breached their limited status and be held jointly and severally liable, along with the general partners, to settle creditor obligations occasioned by criminal, tort, or other civil actions. In most jurisdictions, limited liability partnerships (LLPs) convey limited liability status on all partners.[104] Unlike general partnerships, for which nations have little consistency as to whether a distinct legal entity is created, LPs and LLPs have complete independent legal personality from their owners. The attractiveness of this liability shield comes at the cost of anonymity, however; these partnerships are subject to registration and supervisory regimes that are quite similar in scope to those for companies. In the Grand Corruption Database Project (see appendix B), these partnership forms were not found to have been used specifically achieve opacity of beneficial ownership.

Companies

Companies are the primary engine of economic activity in the world. Every jurisdiction in the world provides for one or more domestic company types in one form or another. As mentioned as a key consideration in the design of the Trust and Company Service Providers (TCSP) Project (see appendix C), companies exist in numbers of an order of magnitude greater than all other forms of legal persons. Panama's estimated 26,000 foundations (already almost the largest number of that entity type in any given jurisdiction) pale before its 320,000 total active companies. Legal arrangements such as trusts

---

104. Arthur O' Sullivan and Steven M. Sheffrin, *Economics: Principles in Action* (Upper Saddle River, NJ: Pearson Prentice Hall, 2003), p. 190.

may be as prevalent as companies, but because virtually no country in the world registers those, we do not have a precise way to determine their total number.

Companies were originally envisioned with the intention of protecting investors and creditors. The legal separation of the individual from the assets vested to a company was a means to achieve this protection. In the twenty-first century, this separation of asset from individual has become an end in itself, sought after not for protection of interest but for camouflage. Companies are the most significantly misused vehicle documented within this study. Because so much can be said about their misuse, those issues that deal with companies have been divided into two categories: one dealing with public companies and the other dealing with private companies. For the purposes of this report, the limited liability company (LLC) will be included in that latter category. In its report of 2001, the Organisation for Economic Co-operation and Development (OECD)[105] dismissed LLCs with a brief mention that they were at the time of writing a recent, spreading phenomenon, presenting the potential for misuse in the furtherance of anonymity. Now, 10 years later, the significant presence of LLCs in the database of grand corruption schemes confirms this potential (see appendix B).

Although different jurisdictions have different company laws (and related securities laws), they share a number of similar key elements with respect to ownership and control.

All jurisdictions require companies to register with a government agency or court. In general, basic company law separates ownership (through shares) and control (through a board of directors). Jurisdictions typically require a certain minimum number of directors. Shares come in two basic types: those that carry votes and those that do not. Voting shares may be split into different categories, with shares in different categories carrying different voting rights. Generally, voting shareholders elect directors to serve for a fixed period, typically between one and three years. The directors set general policies for the company and select company officers, who manage the day-to-day operations of the company. Although shareholders may serve as directors and officers, in many common law jurisdictions, controlling shareholders may not, because this would breach the separation of ownership and control. Certain key decisions—typically including mergers, divisions, windings-up, and sometimes dividend payments—must be ratified by a majority of shareholder votes. In the vast majority of jurisdictions, companies are required to keep a share register so that they may consult shareholders when required and so that they may know to whom to pay dividends when declared. In some cases, pure bearer shares are allowed (that is, in cases in which they do not need to be "immobilized" in the hands of a custodian); here, shareholders must approach the company to exercise any shareholder rights. Most company laws require that shares be freely transferable, meaning that shareholders may not form agreements that would deny free

---

105. See Organisation for Economic Co-operation and Development (OECD), *Behind the Corporate Veil: Using Corporate Entities for Illicit Purposes* (Paris: OECD, 2001), p. 23.

transferability. Laws also require that certain information, such as the names of board members and officers, be made available to shareholders.

Civil law jurisdictions typically divide companies into two types: (a) those that are public, usually defined as exceeding a minimum number of shareholders, and (b) those that are private. For public companies, certain additional rules apply, the most important of which are securities laws and stock exchange rules that are designed to protect the interests of the investing public. Among these are requirements that shareholders voluntarily disclose when they control a certain percentage of the total voting rights of the company or when they make tender offers (offers to buy all shares) to any remaining shareholders. Common law countries do not typically distinguish between public or private at the company level, but rather they do so based on whether share offerings are made to the general public.

In most jurisdictions (those that do not allow pure bearer shares), it is easy to determine if any single shareholder of record has sufficient votes to control board elections and to approve (or veto) major company decisions, as well as to determine board and officer composition, by inspection of share registers and board or officer lists. Such examination, however, will not identify who the ultimate physical person is who controls the vote of voting shares because the vast majority of company shares are held by other legal persons or arrangements, including other companies, trusts, and foundations. As a result, it is impossible for any company to know for certain who the ultimate physical persons are who control the voting shares of the company unless shareholders have so informed the company. Even if one were to identify the physical person who commands a voting share majority, shareholders, directors, and officers may be severely constrained in their decision-making power. Companies may cede much of their authority to third parties via contract. A typical example involves company finance: Loan covenants often restrict what companies may do to guarantee debt repayment. Therefore, to determine the extent of control of a shareholder, director, or officer, it is necessary to determine whether any such covenants cede control to a third party. Such documentation is not normally available to shareholders because it is deemed to constitute matters of "control" rather than "ownership."

In all jurisdictions, the ownership of company assets belongs to the company as a separate legal person. Persons with claims on the company (such as creditors) have first claim to those assets up to the amount of the claim: If a creditor has a security interest, its claim comes before the claims of other creditors (often with some public policy exceptions for the government or employees). Directors may make payments to shareholders in the form of dividends or share repurchases, although some jurisdictions restrict such payments to accumulated profits or those profits plus a percentage of unimpaired (that is, unsecured) property. Different categories of shareholders may have different rights to payment of profits or other property. In the event of dissolution or winding-up, most jurisdictions require that creditors be paid before any residual property is distributed to shareholders.

Limited Liability Company

The LLC is rapidly replacing partnerships and LPs. The typical LLC adopts the basic rule of partnerships—ownership and control rights are determined by a contract, often referred to as the operating agreement—with limited liability for equity investors, who are known as members. Unlike typical common law partnerships, however, LLCs must be registered with a government agency and are separate legal persons from their members. As with partnerships, members may be physical or legal persons.

An LLC can be organized as either member managed (the members jointly operate the LLC, as in a typical partnership) or manager managed (the members select managers similar to the way company shareholders select boards of directors). The most important feature of the LLC is that it is a creature of contract. That contract—the operating agreement—defines the rights and responsibilities of its members. This has given the members of an LLC extraordinary latitude in determining how the LLC should divide ownership and control among them. Operating agreements may be brief or may be hundreds of pages long; they may make simple distinctions regarding ownership and control or may define such relationships in exquisite detail. Of course, ownership and control matters may be further complicated by third-party creditor agreements that are not a part of the operating agreement.

LLCs are used for many legitimate purposes. In addition to organizing a business that has limited liability but retains flexibility with respect to management and benefits, LLCs are often used to effectuate particular business transactions and reorganizations. LLCs are also used to, in effect, extend limited liability to individuals. For example, physicians in tort-plaintiff-friendly jurisdictions in the United States often use LLCs to protect their assets from satisfaction of tort judgments beyond what is provided by liability insurance. In effect, they transfer assets that would normally be held directly (for example, residence, investments) to the LLC. In general, U.S. laws restrict such transfers once a tort has occurred and the legal process has begun, but they do not restrict transfer earlier.

The U.S. state of Delaware is rapidly becoming the most important jurisdiction in the United States for forming LLCs. The general rules regarding the centrality of the operating agreement are the same in Delaware as in most jurisdictions. It is, however, especially inexpensive and easy to create and maintain an LLC in Delaware. The initial fee is $90 with a $250 annual fee, and registration can be completed online with approval granted in less than 24 hours. Although Delaware requires the disclosure of an agent for service of process, it does not require the disclosure of member or manager names. In fact, Delaware law specifically states that the names of members or managers may be included in LLC registration, but they are not required.[106] In addition, agents are not required to keep any information on the members or beneficial owners of an LLC, and Delaware does not require that the beneficial owner's identity be disclosed to the agent.

---

106. Delaware Limited Liability Company Act, sections 18–102.

Foundations

A foundation (based on the Roman law *universitas rerum*) is the civil law equivalent to a common law trust, in that it may be used for similar purposes. A foundation traditionally requires property from a donor dedicated to a particular purpose or purposes for an undetermined period of time. Typically, the income derived from the principal assets (as opposed to the assets themselves) is used to fulfill the statutory purpose. A foundation is a legal entity and, as such, may engage in and conduct business. It is controlled by a board of directors and has no owners. In most jurisdictions, a foundation's purpose must be public. In certain jurisdictions, however, foundations may be created for private purposes. Different legal definitions reflect either common law traditions with an emphasis on trusteeship, or civil law traditions and the distinction between membership and non-membership-based entities (see box C.1 and C.2 for examples in Liechtenstein and Panama).

Legal Arrangements

The term "corporate vehicles" in this report is used to refer to all possible legal constructs that can engage in business, that is, in Financial Action Task Force on Money Laundering (FATF) terms, "legal arrangements" and "legal persons":

> "Legal arrangements" refers to express trusts or other similar legal arrangements . . . including *fiducie, treuhand* and *fideicommiso*. "Legal persons" refers to bodies corporate, foundations, *Anstalten*, partnerships, or associations, or any similar bodies that can establish a permanent customer relationship with a financial institution or otherwise own property.[107]

The distinctive difference between the two is the fact that the legal person can engage in business on its own behalf and be the holder of rights and obligations, whereas a legal arrangement, as the term suggests, is rather a relationship between different people, the essential characteristic being that one person holds the legal title while another holds a beneficial title. A *fideicommiso*, for instance, is an arrangement of Roman law extraction used, in testate law, to leave an estate to one person, entrusting him to pass it on to another person. A *usufruct* achieves something similar, often used to allow a surviving spouse the full benefit of an estate, while the title rests with the children. The most typical and certainly most discussed legal arrangement when it comes to the use of corporate vehicles for illicit purposes is the trust.

The Trusts

The trust relationship was originally created by the English Court of Equity. In a typical trust, a grantor or settlor transfers the legal title to property (the right to control

---

107. See *Methodology for Assessing Compliance with the FATF 40 Recommendations* and the *FATF 9 Special Recommendations*, p. 67, available at http://www.fatf-gafi.org/dataoecd/16/54/40339628.pdf.

The *Anstalt* (Establishment) is a flexible corporate form particular to Liechtenstein, where it is closely related to the trust enterprise (*Treuunternehmen*) but distinct from a foundation (*Stiftung*) or trust (*Treuhanderschaft*). Unusual for a civil law jurisdiction, it has a relatively long history in the Principality dating back to 1928.

Unlike a trust, an *Anstalt* has a legal personality like a company or foundation. Its capital may be divided into shares; however, because this incurs a withholding tax liability, it is rare. An *Anstalt* can be formed in three to five days when the founder, who may be a legal or natural person, transfers rights to assets to a board of directors by an act of assignment. Capital of at least either CHF 30,000 or US$30,000 must be paid up, with the *Anstalt* created by entry into the Public Register. The board, which may only have one member, administers the *Anstalt*, subject to the bylaws of the *Anstalt*. The bylaws do not have to be registered, and they may be revoked or modified by the founder, who is also the beneficiary unless the bylaws specify otherwise. Historically, *Anstalten* could be used for either commercial or noncommercial purposes, although recently the former purpose has been restricted. Since 1980, *Anstalten* pursuing commercial activity have had to lodge annual audited accounts. Those used like a holding company must also have a local representative in Liechtenstein, who usually is the board member, although the representative may be a local company. Often an individual from the TCSP creating the *Anstalt* will be both the sole board member and representative. TCSPs charge in the order of CHF5,000 to form an *Anstalt*, plus CHF3,000 annually for administration. The *Anstalt* is taxed annually at 0.1 percent of capital, or CHF1,000, whichever is the greater.

Source: Adapted from *ATU Allgemeines Treuunternehmen* (international trust company) specialist brochure, "Forms of companies in the Principality of Liechtenstein" (Liechtenstein, 2010) and Caroline Doggart, *Tax Havens and Their Uses* (London: Economic Intelligence Unit, 2002).

The Panamanian Foundation (formally the Panama Private Interest Foundation) was established by legislation in 1995, being jointly modeled on the Liechtenstein foundation, the Panamanian corporation, and the common law trust. Rather than commercial operations, Foundations are designed for use in estate planning, holding shares and property, asset protection, or charitable purposes. A foundation is established when the founder transfers assets to the foundation, which becomes the legal owner of these assets. The founder specifies the purposes of the foundation in a charter (a public document) or in bylaws (which are private). A foundation council carries out administration of the assets. The charter or bylaws specify one or more beneficiaries, which may include the founder. In

(continued next page)

BOX C.2   *(continued)*

its founder-foundation-council-beneficiary structure, the foundation resembles a common law trust, with its settler-trustee-beneficiary arrangement. Unlike trusts, however, foundations are, like companies, legal persons.

While separating the founder from legal ownership of the assets transferred to the foundation, this vehicle also combines a high level of practical control with tight confidentiality. Founders, foundation council members, and beneficiaries may be corporate entities from any jurisdiction, any of which may be controlled by the founder. Furthermore, it is common to use nominee founders (usually a law firm in Panama, which must act as the registered agent), so that the identity of the original founder, which would otherwise be included in the public charter document, remains unregistered. Aside from setting the rules governing the foundation through the charter and bylaws, the founder may be a member of the foundation council, or a beneficiary, or a protector, the latter who may be empowered to veto certain decisions of the foundation council. The foundation pays no tax in Panama and is specifically not covered by foreign inheritance laws.

the property) to a trustee, and the equitable title (the right to enjoy the benefits of the property) to beneficiaries. The terms of such transfer are set out in the trust instrument. If the trustee and beneficiary are the same, legal and equitable title are said to merge and the trust ceases to exist. As a general rule (but see below, discussion on some exceptions), the separation of legal and beneficial interests prevents creditors of the beneficiary from seizing trust assets in satisfaction of claims.

Trustees owe beneficiaries a duty of loyalty, meaning that with respect to the trust relationship, they must prefer the interests of the beneficiary over their own interests. A trust relationship may be created involuntarily in instances in which someone has a claim to property or its benefits but in which transfer of legal title is impossible for some reason. This is called a constructive trust. In most jurisdictions, the grantor may select the law that governs the operation of the trust. Although the trust is the product of the English Court of Equity, some civil law jurisdictions have adopted specific trust statutes. Most common law jurisdictions have modified trust law by statute.

Many jurisdictions have added to the role of trustee a type of "super" trustee known as the trust protector. In many cases, grantors choose professional managers as trustees, and the trust protector is a close friend or attorney of the trustee. Although not managing the day-to-day operations of the trust, the protector acts as a kind of overseer of the trust, and is often given the right to replace the trustee or to change the trust's governing law.

Trusts and similar legal arrangements (as a general rule) are distinguishable from other corporate vehicles in that they usually will not possess a separate legal personality like a company or a civil law foundation. This means, among other things, that a trust cannot own property, engage in business, or be a party to contracts.

The vast majority of trusts are used for legitimate purposes, such as family estate planning, managing charitable donations, and various corporate functions (for example, a trust may be used to isolate the funding of an employee pension plans from the attachable assets of a business). Settlor, trustee, beneficiary, and assets may be companies or other corporate vehicles. Although many jurisdictions have moved toward greater levels of transparency in the arena of government (and often public) access to information on legal persons like corporations and LLCs, trusts have always been granted confidentiality. With one or two exceptions, no jurisdiction in the world currently requires trusts to register in a publicly accessible register. Many jurisdictions have enacted strict confidentiality laws, prohibiting the disclosure of any information regarding trusts. In Panama, for example, if a trustee, government agent, or any person transacting with the trust discloses information about the trust, except as required by law, then that person will be sanctioned with a penalty of up to six months in jail and a fine of up to US$50,000.[108]

Trust relationships are also used to protect an individual's assets from creditors. For example, many physicians have chosen to place their personal assets (for example, homes, investments) into a trust so that patients who receive a malpractice judgment that exceeds insurance cannot directly attach those assets in satisfaction of that judgment. Some trusts have been set up primarily to hold company stock with the specific intention of retaining control over a company either after the grantor has died or, if still alive, simultaneously to act as an asset protection trust. In jurisdictions that follow English law, this has created some difficulty. The duty to manage assets for the benefit of the beneficiary would suggest the sale of stock, for example, if the company were losing money, or voting the voting stock in ways that may be contrary to the wishes of the grantor, who may be the company director. In the United States, this is not a problem, because the courts follow the terms of the trust instrument over general fiduciary duty rules, which can require retention of stock or forbid voting the stock contrary to the grantor's wishes. A number of Commonwealth offshore centers (including many that are British dependencies or overseas territories) have adopted a similar rule by statute, creating the so-called Virgin Islands Special Trust Act (VISTA) trust (see box C.3).

Although the confidentiality of trusts serves many legitimate functions, it has led to a popular perception of trusts and similar legal arrangements as particularly useful instruments for illicit activities.[109] Broadly speaking, trusts can be used to assist in

---

108. Panama Law No. 1, Art. 37.

109. "[T]rusts which hide the identity of the grantors and the beneficiaries have become a standard part of money laundering arrangements." Jack A. Blum, Esq., Prof. Michael Levi, Prof. R. Thomas Naylor and Prof. Phil Williams, *Financial Havens, Banking Secrecy and Money Laundering*, United Nations Office for Drug Control and Crime Prevention, Global Programme Against Money Laundering (1998), p. 95. See also European Commission and Transcrime, University of Trento (Italy), *Euroshore: Protecting the EU financial system from the exploitation of financial centres and off-shore facilities by organized crime*, January 2000, p. 46 ("Trusts can be easily exploited for money laundering purposes, considering the rules

Trusts established under the British Virgin Islands Special Trust Act of 2003 (referred to as VISTA trusts) provide a recent example of a sophisticated corporate structure. The main purpose of the VISTA trust is to provide the advantages of a conventional trust (such as asset protection and succession planning), while allowing the settlors more control over the business activities carried on within the structure than is possible within the bounds of a conventional trust.

A VISTA trust structure must consist of at least two basic elements: (a) the trust itself, and (b) an underlying British Virgin Islands (BVI) company whose shares are owned entirely by the trust. The trustee of the VISTA trust must be a licensed service provider in the BVI. This service provider is responsible for collecting and retaining customer due diligence records. The settlors typically act as directors of the underlying company. These settlors retain business control, because the trustees are excused from the normal fiduciary duty to monitor the performance of the company owned by the trust, and the responsibility of maximizing the value of the company's shares (the "Prudent Man of Business" Rule). Trustees are thus disengaged from the actual management of the company, and the operational conduct of its business, even to the point of being prevented from changing company directors. Aside from their role as directors of the underlying company, settlors may retain control through appointing a protector, who may be able to veto certain decisions by the trustees, or even replace them.

Ownership of the underlying company remains vested with the trust, however, and the company is protected against attacks on its assets. These attacks might come in the form of a disputed inheritance or a commercial dispute with creditors. VISTA trusts might be particularly useful for the head of a family business who wants to plan ahead for succession while retaining practical control of operational activities in the meantime. They may be devoted to charitable purposes, in which case no beneficiary is named. VISTA trusts may be part of an overarching, more complex structure. For example, the underlying company owned by the VISTA trust may be a Private Trust Company that acts as trustee over one or more other normal, non-VISTA trusts, which in turn might hold the shares of other operational companies.

laundering the proceeds of corruption (or other crimes) in two main ways: (a) through camouflaging the existence of assets, and (b) through creating barriers to the recovery of these assets. By acknowledging the nature of a trust deed as a private document, allowing corporate vehicles to be parties to all aspects of trusts, and further having

governing them, such as those which do not require the disclosure of the identity of the beneficiary or of the settlor, those which do not require any governmental license to operate and those which allow for flee clauses pursuant to which a trustee is able to move the trust to a different jurisdiction in the event of a criminal investigation."). See also the FATF typologies report on the Misuse of Corporate Vehicles including Trust and Company Service Providers, October 13, 2006, p. 61: "Responses to the questionnaires [sent out for the purposes of this study] support the conclusion that Trusts and Private companies are the vehicles that are most susceptible to abuse."

often eschewed implementation of any requirement to register trust particulars, it often is difficult for a jurisdiction (and investigators in particular) to determine whether a trust exists at all, let alone the "who" and "what" with which it is concerned.[110] In such a situation, the assets are camouflaged, in that they appear to be the unqualified property of a trustee, who cannot volunteer the information that he is a trustee for any particular party, with no readily ascertainable link to the providers or enjoyers of the assets. In terms of creating barriers to asset recovery, once the trust has been formed, the trust assets legally do not belong to the settlor or to beneficiary parties, although the trustee has a fiduciary duty to manage the assets on behalf of another. Having split legal and beneficial ownership, it is difficult for other private or public parties to enforce claims against these assets, unless it can be shown that the trust was specifically set up to defeat legitimate claimants (for example, creditors).

Asset protection trusts do not always prevent action against the settlor or beneficiary. For example, courts may order the trustee to release assets to creditors if they find that the transfer of assets to the trust breached a specific statute or was otherwise a fraudulent attempt by the transferor to escape liability. To do so, however, the court must have jurisdiction over the trustee (or the protector, if he or she has such powers) to enforce asset release under threat of punishment for contempt of court. To guard against such possibilities, many trusts were created with specific flee clauses: In the event of litigation against the trust or trustee (typically on behalf of a creditor), a trustee is required to transfer those assets to another jurisdiction. Once such a transfer was made, the litigant would have to bring an action in the new location with jurisdiction over the new trustee. The development of the *Mareva* injunction (and similar techniques in the United States) made such flee clauses less effective. The *Mareva* injunction, whereby a court can order the trustees not to transfer or otherwise move assets, or the more recent "*Mareva* by letter," whereby a creditor puts the trustee on notice that they will seek court action declaring that a constructive trust in favor of creditors exists by automatic operation of law, has made flee clauses less effective. These injunctions can prevent asset transfer before legal requirements are completed. In many cases, flee clauses have been replaced with Protector Resettlement Clauses, which give the protector power to move assets in a manner that can be implemented more easily and quickly, and may make it easier to defeat *Mareva* actions.

---

110. Some qualifications to this statement are addressed more comprehensively in Part 4 of this study.

Appendix D. Grand Corruption: 10 Case Studies

Case Study 1: Bruce Rappaport and IHI Debt Settlement

Overview

In 1990, the Government of Antigua and Barbuda (GOAB), under former Prime Minister Lester Bird, issued to GOAB Ambassador Bruce Rappaport[111] the authority to renegotiate the GOAB's debt with the Japanese company Ishikawajima-Harima Heavy Industries Co., Ltd. (hereinafter referred to as IHI).[112] According to the civil complaint filed in Florida, the United States, by the GOAB, Rappaport manipulated the debt settlement numbers so that the GOAB in effect agreed to make periodic over-payments to IHI Debt Settlement Company Ltd. (IHI Debt Settlement)—a company beneficially owned by Rappaport and that purportedly was used to administer the terms of the debt.[113] The IHI debt required monthly payments of only US$199,740.25 to IHI for 25 years; Rappaport had allegedly manipulated the numbers so that the GOAB instead was to pay US$403,334 on a monthly basis for 25 years.[114] The GOAB actually began making the payments on December 31, 1996, eight months before Rappaport claimed to have reached an agreement with IHI.[115] As a result of this scheme, the GOAB was deceived into making payments in excess of US$14 million.[116] As will be described later, in further detail the GOAB eventually was able to recoup the majority of the US$14 million through a settlement with IHI Debt Settlement and Bruce Rappaport.[117]

---

111. As stated in the second amended civil complaint filed in Florida by the Government of Antigua and Barbuda, "'World-Check,' a leading provider of intelligence to the financial community, which tracks the identities of known heightened-risk financial customers, including money launderers, fraudsters, terrorists, PEPs, [and] organized criminals . . . reports that Rappaport is linked to various financial controversies over the last 25 years, including an investigation into his relationship with the Bank of New York and Inter-Maritime Bank." Second Amended Complaint at 12-13, Antigua and Barbuda v. Rappaport, No. 06-03560 CA 25 (11th Fla. Cir. Ct. March 21, 2006).
112. Ibid.
113. Ibid., p. 15.
114. Ibid., pp. 15, 17.
115. Ibid., p. 16.
116. Ibid., p. 3.
117. Press Release, Government of Antigua and Barbuda, "Government of Antigua and Barbuda Recoups US$12 million in case against former government officials and others" (February 10, 2009), http://www.ab.gov.ag/gov_v2/government/pressreleases/pressreleases2009/prelease_2009Feb10_1.html (accessed July 3, 2010).

From December 1996 to October 2003, the monthly payments were made into IHI Debt Settlement's bank account at Bank of N.T. Butterfield in Bermuda.[118] After the money was moved into the account of IHI Debt Settlement, court documents show that Rappaport then funneled the stolen overpayments to a web of various other corporate vehicles (CVs) beneficially owned by him and a number of other government officials, allegedly including Bird's Chief of Staff Asot Michael and his mother Josette Michael.[119] Among those CVs named in the complaint were a Cayman Islands corporation, Giddie Ltd. Co., and a Panamanian corporation, Bellwood Services S.A. (Bellwood).[120]

This scheme was predicated on the misuse of CVs. As a result of Rappaport's status as ambassador and the alleged involvement of various other influential government officials like Bird and Michael, the success of the scheme was wholly reliant on maintaining complete anonymity.[121] Hiding behind the shield of entities, the officials were able to transfer funds from one CV to the next without any of the Politically Exposed Person's (PEP's) names appearing on the transfers.[122] Two notable issues from this case were the choice of jurisdictions employed in the scheme and the use of shelf companies.

Choice of Jurisdictions: From Hong Kong SAR, China, to Florida, United States

IHI Debt Settlement, the corporate predecessor to Rappaport's Debt Settlement Administration LLC (discussed in the section "Use of Shelf Companies") was set up in Hong Kong SAR, China, by Bruce Rappaport or his wife Ruth Rappaport.[123] Although both were listed as directors on the company's 2006 annual return, only Ruth Rappaport's signature appeared on the return.[124] According to the annual return, IHI Debt Settlement issued Hong Kong SAR, China dollars (HKD) $200 worth of shares, with two other companies—Dredson Limited (Dredson) and Gregson Limited (Gregson)—listed as the principal shareholders.[125] IHI Debt Settlement, Dredson, and Gregson all shared the same registered office and corporate secretary in Hong Kong SAR, China.[126]

In late 2003, the banking component of the scheme moved from Bermuda to Florida.[127] On September 24, 2003, Debt Settlement Administrators LLC (DSA) was formed in

118. Complaint at 22, Antigua and Barbuda v. Rappaport, No. 06-03560 CA 25 (11th Fla. Cir. Ct. March 21, 2006).
119. Ibid., pp. 6, 22-24.
120. Ibid., pp. 9–10.
121. Ibid., p. 4.
122. Ibid., pp. 22–25.
123. Ibid., pp. 9, 12.
124. IHI Debt Settlement Co. Ltd., Annual Return (Form AR1), p. 9 (May 29, 2006) (H.K.)
125. Ibid., p. 3.
126. Ibid., p. 1. *See also* Dredson Ltd, Annual Return (Form AR1), p. 1 (July 31, 2006) (H.K.). *See also* Gregson Ltd. Annual Return (Form AR1), p. 1 (July 31, 2006) (H.K.).
127. Complaint at 22, Antigua and Barbuda v. Bruce Rappaport, No. 06-03560 CA 25 (11th Fla. Cir. Ct. March 21, 2006).

Florida.[128] The GOAB alleged that DSA was created for the sole purpose of facilitating and administering the fraud of the GOAB. In October 2003, IHI Debt Settlement wire transferred US$569,767.92 from its Bermuda bank account to the Florida bank account of DSA. One month later, the GOAB began making payments directly to DSA's bank account. Essentially, DSA was taking over IHI Debt Settlement's role in the scheme, whereby DSA would transfer the US$199,740.25 payments to IHI.[129]

The broad protection against creditors and civil court judgments provided under the homestead exemption of the Florida Constitution may make the state an attractive destination for incorporators seeking asset protection.[130]

Use of Shelf Companies

IHI Debt Settlement, Dredson, and Gregson were all shelf companies. IHI Debt Settlement was incorporated under the name Offshore Services Limited in 1970.[131] It was not until September 1997 that the company changed its name to IHI Debt Settlement.[132] The other two companies—Dredson and Gregson—were both incorporated in 1972, 17 years before being named as IHI Debt Settlement's principal shareholders.[133]

People may choose to use shelf companies for a variety of reasons. One such reason may be to create the appearance of legitimacy that comes with longevity. Another reason might be to circumvent information requirements required at incorporation. According to then–senior counsel for the U.S. Department of Justice, Jennifer Shasky,

> criminals can easily throw investigators off the trail by purchasing shelf companies and then never officially transferring the ownerships. In such cases the investigation often leads to a formation agent who has long ago sold the company with no records of the purchaser and no obligation to note the ownership change.[134]

Investigation and Asset Recovery

A potential obstacle in this case dealing with the Hong Kong SAR, China, entities was the corporate ownership structure. The listing of Gregson and Dredson as the principal

---

128. Debt Settlement Adm'rs LLC, Electronic Articles of Organization (September 24, 2003).

129. Complaint at 22, Antigua and Barbuda v. Rappaport, No. 06-03560 CA 25 (11th Fla. Cir. Ct. March 21, 2006).

130. Fla. Constitution §4 (1968), http://www.flsenate.gov/Statutes/index.cfm?Mode=Constitution&Submenu=3&Tab=Statutes#A10S04 (accessed July 3, 2010).

131. Offshore Services Ltd., Certificate of Incorporation (May 29, 1970) (H.K.).

132. Offshore Services Ltd., Certificate of Incorporation on Change of Name (September 24, 1997) (H.K.).

133. *Supra* note 126. *See also* Dredson Ltd, Certificate of Incorporation (July 21, 1972) (H.K.). See also Gregson Ltd., Certificate of Incorporation (July 21, 1972) (H.K.).

134. Business Formation and Financial Crime: Finding a Legislative Solution Before the Comm. on Homeland Sec. and Gov't Affairs for the U.S. Senate (2009) (statement of Jennifer Shasky, then–Senior Counsel to the Deputy Attorney General for the U.S. Department of Justice).

shareholders to IHI Debt Settlement, created a further layer of anonymity, potentially allowing the Rappaports to further separate their ownership from the CV.[135]

Another potential obstacle to investigators was the fact that,[136] for both corporations and limited liability corporations (LLCs) formed in Florida, ownership information does not need to be disclosed upon incorporation, and it does not need to be disclosed in annual reports filed with the state.[137] Legal ownership information is required to be kept only with the corporation or the LLC.[138] Information on ownership structure is critical to learning who ultimately is controlling the scheme—or, at least, the particular CV. When such information is not publicly available, the only remaining option is to obtain it from the company through legal procedure.

Fortunately for the GOAB, they were able to recover some of the stolen assets despite these obstacles. In March 2006, GOAB Attorney General Justin Simon filed a civil claim concerning the IHI matter in the High Court of Antigua and Barbuda for special damages in the sum of US$14,414,904 plus interest, as well as general damages and exemplary damages for fraudulent misrepresentation and misfeasance in public office.[139] The GOAB also brought a similar suit in the Eleventh Judicial Circuit Court in Miami-Dade Country, Florida, to recover assets there.[140] Along with Rappaport and IHI Debt Settlement, the other defendants in the claim were Bird, Asot Michael, Bellwood, and DSA.[141] The GOAB secured the services of forensic investigator Mr. Robert Lindquist to prepare an investigative report on the matter.[142] The collaboration between the GOAB and Lindquist proved essential in reaching a settlement with Rappaport.

On February 10, 2009, Bruce Rappaport agreed to settle the civil claim against himself and IHI Debt Settlement by paying to the GOAB US$12 million.[143] The settlement was the result of months of hard negotiations between the GOAB and the Rappaports

---

135. *Supra* note 126.
136. Fla. Stat. § 607.0202.
137. Ibid. Fla. Stat. §607.1622 (2009), http://www.leg.state.fl.us/statutes/index.cfm?App_mode=Display_Statute&Search_String=&URL=Ch0607/SEC1622.HTM&Title=->2009->Ch0607->Section%201622#0607.1622 (accessed July 3, 2010). Fla. Stat. § 608.407 (2009), http://www.leg.state.fl.us/statutes/index.cfm?App_mode=Display_Statute&Search_String=&URL=Ch0608/SEC407.HTM&Title=->2009->Ch0608->Section%20407#0608.407 (accessed July 3, 2010). Fla. Stat. § 608.4511 (2009), http://www.leg.state.fl.us/statutes/index.cfm?App_mode=Display_Statute&Search_String=&URL=Ch0608/SEC4511.HTM&Title=->2009->Ch0608->Section%204511#0608.4511 (accessed July 3, 2010).
138. Fla. Stat. §608.4101 (2009), http://www.leg.state.fl.us/statutes/index.cfm?App_mode=Display_Statute&Search_String=&URL=Ch0608/SEC4101.HTM&Title=->2009->Ch0608->Section%204101#0608.4101 (accessed July 3, 2010).
139. Press Release, *supra* note 117.
140. Second Amended Complaint at 12-13, Antigua and Barbuda v. Rappaport, No. 06-03560 CA 25 (11th Fla. Cir. Ct. March 21, 2006)
141. Press Release, *supra* note 117.
142. Ibid.
143. Ibid.

based on information provided in Mr. Lindquist's report.[144] A Notice of Discontinuance was filed in the High Court of the GOAB with respect to the two defendants; the effect of the notice was to inform the court and seek the court's permission to discontinue the civil claim against the two defendants, but to continue the civil claim against the other defendants.[145] A similar notice was filed in the Miami, Florida, court.[146] At the time of writing, litigation against Bird and Michael and the other named defendants is pending.[147]

Case Study 2: Charles Warwick Reid

Overview

Charles Warwick Reid, a lawyer from New Zealand, arrived in Hong Kong SAR, China,[148] to join the Attorney General's Chambers in 1975 and eventually worked his way up to principal crown counsel and the head of Hong Kong SAR, China's Commercial Crime Unit.[149] By 1989, he had acquired control of assets amounting to roughly HK$12.4 million.[150] In October 1989, Reid was suspended from duty and arrested by Hong Kong SAR, China's then–Independent Counsel Against Corruption (ICAC) on suspicion of corruption.[151] Reid jumped bail two months later, fleeing through Macau[152] and China before being apprehended in and deported from the Philippines.[153] Accepting a deal with Hong Kong SAR, China prosecutors, Reid pled guilty to a single count of unexplainable possession of pecuniary resources and property disproportionate to his present and past official emoluments. He testified in the trials of several barristers and solicitors who had participated in his corrupt activities that the funds were in fact bribes received for obstructing prosecutions of certain criminals.[154] He served four-and-a-half years of his eight-year sentence, and then was deported to New Zealand, arriving November 30, 1994.[155] Despite being stripped of his status and reputation, Reid became embroiled in another bribery scandal shortly upon his return to New Zealand.[156]

---

144. Mr. Robert Lindquist was also instrumental in the forensic investigation of the Piarco International Airport scandal in Trinidad and Tobago. Ibid.
145. Ibid.
146. Plaintiff's Notice of Dropping Certain Parties. Antigua and Barbuda v. Rappaport, No. 06-03560 CA 25 (11th Fla. Cir. Ct. February 20, 2009).
147. Press Release, *supra* note 117.
148. Now Hong Kong SAR, China.
149. *In re* Reid, [1993] No. CACV149/1993, ¶4 (H.K.).
150. Att'y Gen. for H.K. v. Reid, [1994] 1 A.C. 324 (P.C.) (appeal taken from N.Z.) (N.Z.).
151. *In re* Reid, [1993] No. CACV149/1993, ¶5 (H.K.). The Independent Counsel Against Corruption was the precursor to the current Hong Kong Independent Commission Against Corruption.
152. Now Macao SAR, China.
153. Ibid., ¶¶6-9.
154. Ibid., ¶11, ¶¶13-14.
155. Ch'ngPoh v. Chief Executive of the HKSAR, [2002] No. HCAL182/2002, ¶74 (H.K.).
156. Ibid.

Although dated, the case of Charles Warwick Reid is informative because of the note-worthy strategies that he employed to maintain anonymity through the use of corporate vehicles (CVs) to keep distance from the laundering of the bribery funds, namely, his misuse of legal arrangements. Additionally, the challenges encountered in recovering the ill-gotten gains and Reid's ostensible cooperation with the recovery process provide valuable insight as well.

Misuse of Legal Arrangements

The evidence presented in the various trials involving Reid show the frequent use of trust arrangements on his part to obscure the ownership and control of his illegal assets. Reid held money in trust in the trust accounts of his local solicitors,[157] and his family lived in a home that was legally registered to Solicitor Marc Molloy, who served as trustee.[158] Following his deportation from Hong Kong to New Zealand, Reid was alleged to have received an additional bribe payment to help derail another trial, with a trust being created by Reid's accountant; the bribe giver acted as settlor, the accountant as trustee, and Reid and his family as beneficiaries. The trust money was transferred to and managed from a foreign bank account.[159]

A short time passed between Reid's release from incarceration in Hong Kong SAR, China, to his setting up of a new trust. In a period of just over a week, Reid was again in possession of corrupt assets that flowed from a foreign jurisdiction into New Zealand and back out to another foreign jurisdiction.[160] Circumstances in New Zealand have certainly changed since Reid operated.[161] However, the risks of money laundering from tactics employed by Reid (transferring assets into and out of the jurisdiction's financial institutions through trusts and similar arrangements, especially by utilizing agents, lawyers, and straw persons) still exist.[162] As in a number of countries throughout the world, New Zealand faces a dangerous absence of regulatory and due diligence safeguards specifically designed to detect and mitigate the risks of these abuses.[163]

---

157. Att'y Gen. for H.K. v. Reid, [1992] Appeal No: 44 of 1992, at 10-27 (C.A.) (reasons for judgment of Penlington J) (N.Z.).
158. Ibid.
159. Ch'ng Poh v. Chief Executive of the HKSAR, [2002] No. HCAL182/2002, ¶74 (H.K.).
160. Ibid.
161. In 1996 the Financial Transactions Reporting Act (FTRA) came into effect, however the 2009 FATF New Zealand Mutual Evaluation Report reported specific deficiencies with the New Zealand's AML regime: "Even though it is not explicitly stated, the application of the FTRA prevents financial institutions from keeping anonymous accounts or accounts in fictitious names, but the CDD [customer due diligence] requirements of the FTRA do not apply to accounts opened before the FTRA entered into force in 1996. In addition, clarification is needed of the verification requirements to ensure that the documents being used are reliable and from an independent source." *Financial Action Task Force & Asia-Pacific Group, Mutual Evaluation Report*, Executive Summary ¶18 (2009).
162. Ibid., Table 1.
163. According to the MER, "[m]ost money laundering occurs through the financial system; however, the complexity usually depends on the sophistication of the offenders involved. There appears to be a higher degree of sophistication in laundering the proceeds of crime now than in previous years. Since 2007, the

Development of the Constructive Trust Doctrine

As a result of Reid's crime, the attorney general of Hong Kong was forced to fight a precedent-setting battle through New Zealand's lower courts all the way up to the Judicial Committee of the Privy Council in London. These steps were necessary to recover the portions of approximately HK$12.4 million of bribe money that had been converted into property after passing through various CVs and legal owners in New Zealand on Reid's behalf.[164]

The issue at stake was that the Government of Hong Kong maintained it held a caveat-able interest in the Reid-owned properties in New Zealand, as they represented the proceeds of bribery, while Reid was in dereliction of his fiduciary duties as a civil servant. The Privy Council judgment took for granted that the New Zealand properties were purchased with Reid's bribe money, and that neither Mrs. Reid nor Mr. Molloy was a bona fide purchaser of a legal estate without notice.[165]

The Privy Council judgment was based on the principle of equity, which considers "as done that which ought to have been done." The Council determined that the assets received by Reid as bribe payments should have been "paid or transferred instead to the person who suffered from the breach of duty."[166] This point is of great consequence to the legal relationship held between the bribe-receiving fiduciary and the party whose trust has been betrayed; it provides a means of redress.[167] Due to the Privy Council ruling, English common law (and many other legal systems) now recognizes that property acquired—either innocently or criminally—in breach of trust belongs in equity to the *cestui que* trust; in other words, persons holding such property do so on constructive trust for the true owner.[168] Although not without its controversies, the Constructive Trust Doctrine is now a useful tool for those who seek to prevent the dispersal of corrupt funds and recover the proceeds of corrupt activities, such as bribery.

---

purchase of real estate, the use of professional services and foreign exchange dealers have been popular means to launder funds." Ibid., ¶4. According to the MER's Ratings of Compliance with FATF Recommendations, New Zealand, while found to have a "quite robust" AML/CFT measures in place, was rated Non-Compliant with Recommendations 5, 6, 9, 12, 34. Ibid., Table 1. For explanation of these relevant recommendations, please see FATF 40+9 Recommendations.

164. *In re* Reid, [1993] No. CACV149/1993, ¶4 (H.K.).

165. Att'y Gen. for H.K. v. Reid, [1994] 1 A.C. 324 (P.C.) (appeal taken from N.Z.) (N.Z.).

166. Ibid.

167. Had the precedent on the treatment of bribes not been overturned by the Reid case, the absence of such a proprietary remedy would mean that the government of Hong Kong, would first have to procure a personal restitutionary order and see it enforced in order to recover assets. This would have meant that the government's only option would have been to pursue a claim in personam against the fiduciary. Additionally, if the fiduciary in breach is bankrupt, the injured party (*i.e.,* the owner of a debt) would be required to compete with any other unsecured creditors for what assets are available. Att'y Gen. for H.K. v. Reid, [1992] Appeal No: 44 of 1992, pp. 50-51 (C.A.) (reasons for judgment of Penlington J) (N.Z.).

168. Att'y Gen. for H.K. v. Reid, [1994] 1 A.C. 324 (P.C.) (appeal taken from N.Z.) (N.Z.).

Investigation

The bribery schemes involving Reid used several CVs, agents, straw persons, and a combination of foreign and domestic bank accounts to evade detection. He kept his name from being attached to the bribe money, as the funds were transferred into secretive trusts and portions converted into real property purchases. These several methods created investigative obstacles and were employed across a range of jurisdictions; the persons, accounts, and properties stretched across Hong Kong, SAR, China; Singapore; Vanuatu; and New Zealand.

An additional investigative obstacle was caused by Reid's dual foreign and domestic status. Reid took advantage of the fact that while his residence was in Hong Kong, SAR, China, during his tenure as a civil servant, he remained a citizen of New Zealand.[169] As noted, his bribe money stayed out of his name and out of Hong Kong, SAR, China, in Hong Kong, SAR, China, it appeared as though he had not been accruing such assets at all. Had things gone as planned, the assets would have been waiting for him upon retiring to his homeland.[170]

Proving every instance of bribery would have been a challenging task for the prosecution. ICAC was able to rely on an "illicit enrichment" provision of the Prevention of Bribery Ordinance of the Hong Kong Legal Code to investigate and arrest Reid.[171] Illicit enrichment laws, although not embraced by all nations,[172] are listed in the United Nations Convention against Corruption (UNCAC).[173] By convicting Reid on the illicit enrichment charge, ICAC was able to leverage an offer of immunity from further prosecution into getting a detailed account of Reid's misdeeds and money laundering[174] while still getting a sentence of eight years imprisonment and an order of restitution in the amount of HK$12,415,900.72.[175]

---

169. Att'y Gen. for H.K. v. Reid, [1992] Appeal No: 44 of 1992, at 16 (C.A.) (reasons for judgment of Penlington J) (N.Z.).

170. Reid admitted to receiving official emoluments of HK$4,795,123.77 over his 14 years of service in Hong Kong and had expended nearly the entire amount of those licit funds on living expenses for himself and his family. Ibid. p. 27.

171. Ibid. p. 34.

172. The United States and Canada have refused to adopt illicit enrichment provisions, on the basis that such provisions would be incompatible with their constitutional principles and legal systems. United States, B-58: Inter-American Convention against Corruption, http://www.oea.org/juridico/english/sigs/b-58 .html (accessed July 1, 2010).

173. According to the United Nations Convention against Corruption, "Subject to its constitution and the fundamental principles of its legal system, each State Party shall consider adopting such legislative and other measures as may be necessary to establish as a criminal offence, when committed intentionally, illicit enrichment, that is, a significant increase in the assets of a public official that he or she cannot reasonably explain in relation to his or her lawful income." G.A. Res. 58/4, Art.20, U.N. Doc. A/RES/58/4 (October 31, 2003).

174. Att'y Gen. for H.K. v. Reid, [1992] Appeal No: 44 of 1992, p. 26 (C.A.) (reasons for judgment of Penlington J) (N.Z.).

175. Ibid. p. 19.

Asset Recovery

In May 1990, the Government of Hong Kong SAR, China, lodged caveats in New Zealand, claiming an estate or interest in the properties listed as belonging to Reid, his wife, and his solicitor. The caveats were accepted and registered by the Assistant Land Registrar.[176] In December 1990 and February 1991, Reid and the others tried to register instruments of mortgage on the caveated properties; such an application has the effect of causing the caveats to lapse unless the caveator gets an order from the High Court of New Zealand.[177] In the summer of 1991, the High Court of New Zealand judged in favor of Reid,[178] although he acknowledged the strength of the attorney general of Hong Kong SAR, China's, claims that the bribe money Reid had received had been funneled into the properties and that the nominal owners had knowledge of these facts.[179] This ruling was later upheld by the Court of Appeal in December 1991.[180] Upon final appeal to the Privy Council, however, a favorable judgment for the attorney general was reached on November 1, 1993, restoring the Crown's claim of beneficial ownership interest in the Reid properties.[181] In this manner, through the civil legal process, asset recovery was effected.[182]

Case Study 3: Diepreye Alamieyeseigha

Overview

Diepreye S. P. Alamieyeseigha was arrested at Heathrow Airport in September 2005 by the London Metropolitan Police on suspicion of money laundering offences.[183] A search of "his" apartment (it was registered in the name of a company) revealed nearly a million pounds' worth of British, European, and U.S. currency.[184] After his arrest, he fled the United Kingdom and returned to Nigeria where he was impeached and dismissed from his position as governor of Bayelsa State.[185] During Alamieyeseigha's initial two terms of public office in Nigeria, from 1999 to 2005, the Federal Republic of

---

176. Att'y Gen. for H.K. v. Reid, [1992] Appeal No: 44 of 1992, ¶7 (C.A.) (case for the respondents) (N.Z.).
177. Ibid., ¶8.
178. Ibid., ¶12.
179. Ibid., ¶14.
180. Ibid., ¶1.
181. Att'y Gen. for H.K. v. Reid, [1994] 1 A.C. 324 (P.C.) (appeal taken from N.Z.) (N.Z.).
182. It should be noted that none of the money in the accounts at the time of Reid's flight from Hong Kong was ever recovered. *Supra* note 149. Speculating as to the reasons for Reid's prolonged legal efforts to prevent asset forfeiture, Lord Templeton bluntly stated in his judgment that: "Since an unfulfilled order has been made against Mr. Reid in the courts of Hong Kong to pay HK$12.4m, his purpose in opposing the relief sought by [the government of Hong Kong at the time] in New Zealand must reflect the hope that the properties, in the absence of a caveat, can be sold and the proceeds whisked away to some Shangri La which hides bribes and other corrupt monies in numbered bank accounts." Ibid.
183. Nigeria v. Santolina Inv. Corp., [2007] EWHC (Ch) 3053, ¶6 (Eng.).
184. Ibid.
185. Ibid.

Nigeria alleged that by participating in corrupt activities, he had enriched himself by tens of millions of dollars worth of internationally held monetary assets and property holdings, often registered in the name of corporate vehicles (CVs).[186]

Alamieyeseigha created at least five CVs that separated his name and beneficial interest from the legal ownership and control of various financial and real estate assets. Following typical trends of misusing CVs, the majority were private limited companies in a variety of jurisdictions (acquired and managed through a variety of banking and administration trust and company service providers[TCSPs]): Santolina Investment Corporation (incorporated in the Seychelles), Solomon & Peters Limited (incorporated in the British Virgin Islands), Falcon Flights Inc. (incorporated in the Bahamas), and Royal Albatross Properties 67 (Pty) Limited (incorporated in South Africa).[187] The ownership and control of Falcon Flights, Inc. was held by a Bahamas trust that he established, as settlor, for the benefit of his wife and children.[188] As will be described in the section "Misuse of Trusts to Obscure Beneficial Ownership of CVs and Assets," the misuse of this trust to obscure his beneficial ownership of these CVs and assets was an essential part of his scheme.

Misuse of Trusts to Obscure Beneficial Ownership of CVs and Assets

In May 2001, upon the advice of Alamieyeseigha's bank, UBS AG,[189] Alamieyeseigha settled "the Salo Trust" for the benefit of his wife and children.[190] Alamieyeseigha later acknowledged that he was a beneficiary of the trust, but he maintained that he was initially unaware that he was himself listed as a beneficiary along with his wife and children.[191] The trustees of the Salo Trust either purchased or incorporated Falcon Flights, Inc. pursuant to the terms of the trust agreement.[192]

In the first claim made against Alamieyeseigha and his companies in early 2007, the England and Wales High Court (Chancery Division) held that it was either common-ground or incontrovertibly established by documentation that in September 1999 Alamieyeseigha opened a U.S. dollar account with UBS in London (No. 323940.01) with an initial deposit of US$35,000 and a balance in December 2005 of US$535,812 attributable to various sources. The originator often was recorded simply as "Foreign Money Deposit."[193] Alamieyeseigha stated that the UBS account funds amounted to "contributions from friends and political associates towards the education of my

---

186. Nigeria v. Santolina Inv. Corp., [2007] EWHC (Ch) 437, ¶1 (Eng.).
187. Nigeria v. Santolina Inv. Corp., [2007] EWHC (Ch) 3053, ¶6 (Eng.).
188. Ibid. at ¶34. Nigeria v. Santolina Inv. Corp., [2007] EWHC (Ch) 437, ¶¶4, 13, 39 (Eng.).
189. UBS AG, a Swiss bank, was named as the 9th defendant in the civil case in London. Nigeria v. Santolina Inv. Corp., [2007] EWHC (Ch) 437, ¶1 (Eng.).
190. Defence of the Third Defendant [10.1]. Nigeria v. Santolina Inv. Corp., [2007] EWHC (Ch) 437, ¶1 (Eng.).
191. Defence of the Third Defendant, ¶37.
192. Defence of the Third Defendant, ¶10.2.
193. Nigeria v. Santolina Inv. Corp., [2007] EWHC (Ch) 437, ¶6, ¶38 (Eng.).

children," a claim that the court would later find dubious in light of the governor's inconsistent and changing explanations as to why money entered the account.[194] Alamieyeseigha's defense further stated that the UBS account's status as a trustee-account led him to not list the account on the declaration-of-assets form that is required for all Nigerian governors.[195]

The net effect of the preceding evidence was that Alamieyeseigha represented himself as or admitted to being, in various capacities, (a) the settlor, though claiming the true economic settlements came from "friends" whom he could not specifically recall; (b) the trustee, insofar as the UBS account legally opened and controlled in his own name was held out to be a trust account; and (c) a beneficiary, a concession made by his defense. The existence of this trust separated Alamieyeseigha from the legal and beneficial ownership and control of the assets contained therein, and added another layer of complexity to those who would have tried to discover that he did indeed hold such assets.

In addition, this account received funds in the amount of approximately US$1.5 million, through two deposits made in 2001 by one Aliyu Abubakar (described elsewhere in the judgment as the "moving spirit" behind a company called A Group Property that received contracts with Bayelsa state either in 2001 or 2002.)[196] Abubakar, a state contractor, made the acquaintance of Alamieyeseigha just one year earlier in 2000.[197] These deposits were immediately converted into bonds, which were then transferred to the portfolio holdings of Falcon Flights, Inc. (the private company procured by the trust) in January of 2002, effectively burying Alamieyeseigha's claim over the assets within a nested CV structure.[198]

Investigation

As mentioned earlier, the London Metropolitan Police arrested Alamieyeseigha in the United Kingdom on September 15, 2005, for suspicion of money laundering and fled the country while on bail. On December 9, 2005, immediately following his impeachment—which stripped him of government immunity—Alamieyeseigha was arrested by the Economic and Financial Crimes Commission (EFCC) of Nigeria. Charged along with him were the following private companies: Solomon & Peters Limited, Santolina Investment Corporation, Pesal Nigeria Limited, Salomein & Associated (Nig) Limited, Kpedefa Nigeria Limited, Jetty Property Limited, and Herbage Global Services Limited.[199]

---

194. Nigeria v. Santolina Inv. Corp., [2007] EWHC (Ch) 3053, ¶70 (Eng.).
195. Nigeria v. Santolina Inv. Corp., [2007] EWHC (Ch) 437, ¶39 (Eng.). As stated earlier, Alamieyeseigha's defense to the charge was that he was unaware that he was the beneficiary of the trust, despite the fact the UBS account was opened under his name. Defence of the Third Defendant, ¶¶10.1, 37.
196. Nigeria v. Santolina Inv. Corp., [2007] EWHC (Ch) 437, ¶¶14, 40 (Eng.).
197. Ibid.
198. Ibid., ¶¶26, 28, 38.
199. Nigeria v. Santolina Inv. Corp., [2006] No. CA/L/01/2006, pp. 1-2 (Nig.).

Concurrent with the criminal proceedings in Nigeria, the federal government of Nigeria went abroad to seize suspect assets in a number of jurisdictions. The most significant attempt was a petition for summary judgment filed in a civil asset recovery case in the U.K. High Courts to claim various identified monetary and real estate properties in that country.[200] The hearing took place on February 27, 2007, and judgment was delivered on March 7, 2007.[201] While conceding that the Federal Republic of Nigeria had presented a strong case for such a ruling, the court concluded that by presenting only inferential arguments, relying on suspect witness testimony, and lacking a criminal conviction from the home jurisdiction, any move to deprive the defendants of the right to a trial by seizing his assets would have been ill-advised.[202]

In July 2007, Alamieyeseigha pleaded guilty before a Nigerian High Court to six charges of making false declaration of assets and caused his companies to plead guilty to 23 charges of money laundering. Alamieyeseigha was sentenced to two years in prison and the court ordered the seizure of assets in Nigeria. He also pled guilty on behalf of Solomon & Peters Limited and Santolina Investment Corporation, two of the CVs he had employed as part of his money laundering scheme (the governor's signing of the guilty plea for each company being a sign of control that was noted as significant in mid-2007).[203] All of the companies charged were found guilty and subsequently wound up and had their assets forfeited to the government.[204] This change in circumstances destroyed any possibility that Alamieyeseigha would had been able to mount a reasonable defense against the suit and, accordingly, the Chancery Division allowed a second hearing for summary judgment, which was granted on behalf of Nigeria.[205] Claims were initiated against Alamieyeseigha's real estate in South Africa.

Asset Recovery

Nigeria was able to reclaim a sizable amount of Alamieyeseigha's tainted assets that had been dispersed among CVs and bank accounts around the world. US$2 million belonging to Alamieyeseigha was also returned to Nigeria by the British government.[206] The Lagos High Court ruling of 2007 contained an explicit seizure order for the government

---

200. Nigeria v. Santolina Inv. Corp., [2007] EWHC (Ch) 437, ¶1 (Eng.).

201. The basis of summary judgment is to save the time and expense of going to a whole trial in those instances where the defendant has no real prospect of successfully defending the issue, and must be decided on such grounds, if such a matter can be decided without conducting a "mini-trial" to determine the reasonableness of the defense. Ibid.

202. Nigeria v. Santolina Inv. Corp., [2007] EWHC (Ch) 437, ¶¶72-74 (Eng.).

203. Nigeria v. Santolina Inv. Corp., [2007] No. FHC/L/328C/05, at 3-4 (Nig.). Nigeria v. Santolina Inv. Corp., [2007] EWHC (Ch) 3053, ¶¶3-5 (Eng.).

204. Nigeria v. Santolina Inv. Corp., [2007] No. FHC/L/328C/05, at 6 (Nig.).

205. Nigeria v. Santolina Inv. Corp., [2007] EWHC (Ch) 3053, ¶¶52-54 (Eng.).

206. Damilola Oyedele culled from *This Day Newspapers*, posted on the website of the Economic and Financial Crimes Commission, "UK to Return £40m Stolen Funds to Nigeria" (June 2, 2008), at http://efccnigeria.org/index.php?option=com_content&task=view&id=102&Itemid=34 (accessed March 23, 2011).

to take control of millions of pounds of assets of the various CVs involved in Alamieye-seigha's misdeeds, as well as 10 properties held in Nigeria and abroad.[207] As a result of the civil suit in London, the government recovered three residential properties in London (registered to Solomon & Peters) and assets held at the Royal Bank of Scotland PLC (in the accounts of Santolina Investment Corp).[208]

This recovery process culminated in a July 2009 ceremony whereby the current head of the EFCC participated in a handover ceremony in which the federal government remitted to Bayelsa state the misappropriated funds. The funds totaled 3,128,230,294.83 Nigerian Naira (₦), US$441,000, €7,000, and £2,000.[209] Additionally, control of two unsold real properties (valued respectively at ₦2.8 billion and ₦210 million) was transferred to Bayelsa. In May 2011, U.S. Assistant Attorney General Lanny Breuer announced that the U.S. Department of Justice's Kleptocracy Asset Recovery Initiative had filed, in March and April 2011, two civil asset forfeiture actions to recover more than $1 million in Alamieyeseigha's alleged illicit proceeds in the United States. According to Mr. Breuer's May speech, in the state of Maryland, the Department of Justice was seeking forfeiture of a private residence worth more than US$600,000 and in Massachusetts, the forfeiture of close to US$400,000 in a brokerage account.[210]

Case Study 4: Frederick Chiluba

Overview

Dr. Frederick Jacob Titus Chiluba was the President of the Republic of Zambia from 1991 to 2001.[211] In 2007, the attorney general of Zambia brought a private civil action in the United Kingdom on behalf of the Republic of Zambia to recover funds that had been transferred from Zambia's Ministry of Finance for the private use of then-President Chiluba and various other co-conspirators.[212] Although the U.K. case was composed of three different sets of allegations, this study's focus is limited to the Zamtrop conspiracy and the BK conspiracy.[213] Both schemes were complex, involving dozens of persons, corporate vehicles (CVs), and intermediaries as tens of millions of dollars were siphoned out of the Zambian treasury. Charges were brought

---

207. Nigeria v. Santolina Inv. Corp., [2007] No. FHC/L/328C/05, pp. 6-8 (Nig.).

208. Nigeria v. Santolina Inv. Corp., [2007] EWHC (Ch) 3053, ¶¶7-8, ¶¶52-54 (Eng.).

209. Press Release, Economic and Financial Crimes Commission, "Remarks by the Executive Chairman, Mrs. Farida Waziri, AIG (RTD), at the Handover Ceremony of Chelsea" (July 14, 2009), http://efccnigeria .org/index.php?option=com_content&task=view&id=667&Itemid=34 (accessed July 1, 2010).

210. U.S. Department of Justice, "Assistant Attorney General Lanny Breuer of the Criminal Division Speaks at the Fritz-Hermann Bruner Memorial Lecture at the World Bank," May 25, 2011, available at www.justice .gov/criminal/pr/speeches/2011/crm_speech_110525.html (accessed June 2, 2011).

211. Republic of Zambia v. Meer Care & Desai, [2007] EWHC (Ch) 952, ¶5 (Executive Summary) (Eng.).

212. Ibid. at ¶3.

213. The three separate components are individually known as 'The Zamtrop Conspiracy," "The BK conspiracy," and "The MOFED Claim." This case study does not delve in the claims of fiduciary breaches involved in the MOFED claim, as the presiding Justice dismissed it. Ibid., ¶¶3, 51.

against 18 defendants, and 76 other individuals and companies were implicated in the convoluted web of illicit activities in President Chiluba's misdeeds.[214]

The Zamtrop conspiracy centered around the alleged misuse of a significant portion of US$52 million of Zambian Ministry of Finance funds that had been transferred into a bank account (known as Zamtrop) at the Zambia National Commercial Bank Limited in the United Kingdom.[215] This account was opened in December 1995 by Xavier Franklin Chungu, a close associate of President Chiluba and the head of the Zambia Security Intelligence Service (ZSIS).[216] The account opening forms were filled out improperly and Chungu was, at various times over the life of the account, the sole signatory.[217] Funds originating in the Zambian Ministry of Finance entered the account from the official state budget as a result of the overpayment of debts originating in fraudulent contracts with Wilbain Technology, Inc., and Systems Innovations, Inc.—corporations based in Delaware and Virginia, United States, respectively.[218] The money was then routed through Access Financial Services Limited (AFSL), a Zambian non-bank financial institution, and into the control of the various other individuals and companies to make payments and purchases on behalf of the conspirators. Total misappropriations by the conspiracy were demonstrated to be US$25,754,316.[219]

The BK conspiracy was a similar scheme in which President Chiluba, Chungu, and others allegedly acted in breach of their fiduciary duties to the Republic of Zambia.[220] A fraudulent financing agreement involving a 10-year US$100 million loan for the purpose of purchasing military equipment for Zambia was entered into in 1999.[221] No evidence existed of any such deal and yet US$20,200,719 was paid into bank accounts in Belgium and Switzerland created for this purpose. The England and Wales High Court (Chancery Division) concluded that the money had been "dissipated away" in favor of the conspirators.[222]

A common theme in both of these schemes was the misuse of professional intermediaries, otherwise known as Designated Non-Financial Businesses and Professions (DNFBPs). Two other interesting aspects of the case were the misuse of a publicly tradable entity and the distance between the conspirators and the CVs.

---

214. Republic of Zambia v. Meer Care & Desai, [2007] EWHC (Ch) 952 (Dramatis Personae) (Eng.).
215. Republic of Zambia v. Meer Care & Desai, [2007] EWHC (Ch) 952, ¶2, ¶123 (Eng.).
216. Ibid., ¶127. Republic of Zambia v. Meer Care & Desai, [2007] EWHC (Ch) 952 (Dramatis Personae) (Eng.).
217. Republic of Zambia v. Meer Care & Desai, [2007] EWHC (Ch) 952, ¶¶127-128 (Eng.).
218. Ibid., ¶151. Republic of Zambia v. Meer Care & Desai, [2007] EWHC (Ch) 952 (Dramatis Personae) (Eng.).
219. Republic of Zambia v. Meer Care & Desai, [2007] EWHC (Ch) 952, ¶¶40-42 (Executive Summary) (Eng.).
220. Republic of Zambia v. Meer Care & Desai, [2007] EWHC (Ch) 952, ¶1054 (Eng.).
221. Ibid., ¶¶1056-1059.
222. Ibid., ¶¶1058, 1069.

Misconduct by DNFBP Intermediaries

Figuring prominently in both the Zamtrop and BK conspiracies were two firms of English solicitors: Meer Care & Desai (MCD) and Cave Malik & Co. (CM), as well as its Zambian offshoot, Cave Malik & Ndola, Zambia.[223] Both firms participated in the creation and operation of various corporate vehicles and their bank accounts for the benefit of the two conspiracies.[224]

Iqbal Meer, a partner of MCD, undertook an agreement with Chungu to act on behalf of AFSL in the receipt and disbursement of Republic funds for official ZSIS business.[225] MCD, through Meer, effectively "washed" the illicit government money through their client accounts.[226] Although Meer and MCD had made little or no money at all for their participation in these activities,[227] Chungu singled out Meer for this role because of his perceived susceptibility to the benefit of being associated with the politically powerful.[228]

In court, Meer maintained that he held himself to a higher professional ethical standard and received a character reference from Nelson Mandela, another client of his firm.[229] Nevertheless, the court found that Meer's professional responsibilities, as well as his international savvy, should have prevented him from carrying out the dubious transactions he unquestionably performed.[230] MCD and CM were both found liable for conspiracy and dishonest assistance with judgments entered against them for several (U.S.) million dollars each, although the ruling against MCD were later overturned on the grounds that the judge had made an inappropriate leap between negligence and dishonest assistance.[231]

Distance between the Primary Conspirators and the Corporate Vehicles

The attorney general of Zambia alleged that both conspiracies materially concerned President Chiluba and Chungu. They were, in the case of the Zamtrop conspiracy, its primary architects; in the BK matter, they breached their fiduciary duties to the Republic and knowingly received tainted money.[232] The court expressed a belief that the

---

223. Republic of Zambia v. Meer Care & Desai, [2007] EWHC (Ch) 952 (Dramatis Personae) (Eng.).

224. Ibid.

225. Republic of Zambia v. Meer Care & Desai, [2007] EWHC (Ch) 952, ¶544 (Eng.).

226. Ibid., ¶435.

227. Professional intermediaries, because of their knowledge, abilities, and the deference shown to them, can help parties to grand corruption smoothly navigate the world's financial systems. Justice Smith highlights this notion in his decision: "[t]he sad thing however is that there have been many cases in the courts where professionals have become embroiled in fraud for little or no personal benefit. They often commit the fraud out of a desire to please clients whom they wish to impress. They are sometimes flattered that famous or powerful people use them. Ibid., ¶¶556-561.

228. Ibid., ¶561.

229. Ibid., ¶543.

230. Ibid., ¶¶564-565.

231. Ibid., ¶¶128-129, ¶¶133-134.

232. Republic of Zambia v. Meer Care & Desai, [2007] EWHC (Ch) 952, ¶¶87, 1054 (Eng.).

secrecy surrounding Chungu and the ZSIS was used as "an engine of fraud at the expense of the Republic" to shield the conspirators' illicit activities from challenge or enquiry.[233] Chungu also recruited another primary figure to the conspiracy to act on his behalf: Faustin Kabwe, a friend since childhood.[234]

The primary conspirators sought to maintain as much distance as possible between themselves and the illegal activity by inserting friends and associates between themselves and the various transactions. In addition, they created further distance by using their prestige and the secrecy prerogative of the ZSIS to convince others to assist them without asking too many questions. As noted, to operate the various CVs and their bank accounts, Chungu sought out intermediaries from whom he maintained a degree of separation on a personal level.[235]

Misuse of a Publicly Tradable Entity

One of the 18 defendants in this matter was a Belgian company, Belsquare Residence N.V. (Belsquare).[236] Belsquare was part of a chain of CVs; it was a *naamloze vennootschap*, the equivalent of a public limited liability entity, and was wholly acquired by Jarban S.A., a Luxembourg company that in turn was owned by Harptree Holdings, a British Virgin Islands International Business Company with bearer shares.[237] Harptree Holdings and Jarban both were incorporated by Iqbal Meer of MCD for the benefit of Faustin Kabwe/ZSIS.[238]

Because publicly traded companies are usually subject to a number of disclosure regulations, reported cases of the misuse of these entities are rare. Through this chain of CVs, however, a person engaging in grand corruption, by holding a bearer share in his hand, was able to acquire control of a publicly held Belgian entity. This entity converted misappropriated Ministry of Finance funds into European real estate purchases.[239]

Investigation and Asset Recovery

President Chiluba stepped down in 2001 and Xavier Chungu retired in 2002 after the election of Levy Mwanawasa SC.[240] The schemes perpetrated by the two men and other conspirators began receiving widespread publicity after the Zambian newspaper

---

233. Ibid., ¶¶145, 150.
234. Ibid., ¶486.
235. Iqbal Meer had been friends with Faustin Kabwe for over 20 years, but was not shown to have any personal connection to Chungu. Ibid.
236. Ibid., ¶¶593-597. Republic of Zambia v. Meer Care & Desai, [2007] EWHC (Ch) 952 (Dramatis Personae) (Eng.).
237. Ibid.
238. Ibid.
239. Publicly held entities typically qualify for simplified due diligence measures by financial institutions (less oversight); the use of real estate for money laundering, while a common practice and known in theory, is also still not regarded as particularly high risk. Ibid.
240. Ibid., ¶¶222-224.

The Post ran an article that uncovered the Zamtrop account activities. Chiluba, Chungu, Kabwe, MCD, and CM were implicated as recipients of the Zamtrop funds.[241] Shortly thereafter, Chungu departed from Zambia.[242]

Zambia initiated criminal proceedings against Chiluba, Kabwe, and former AFSL executive director Aaron Chungu on October 11, 2004, centering on charges of theft and possession of stolen assets (by a public official in the case of Chiluba; by private citizens in the case of Kabwe and Chungu).[243] This trial would last just short of five years, with an eventual verdict being rendered that saw Chiluba acquitted on the grounds that the defense failed to prove beyond a reasonable doubt that any of the assets traced to Chiluba originated from the stolen money.[244] Kabwe and Aaron Chungu were found guilty of three theft-related charges.[245] The judge speculated that the undoing of the prosecution's case was their failure to produce Xavier Chungu, whose flight had precluded any opportunity to gather his testimony.[246]

Concurrent with these criminal proceedings, the attorney general of Zambia initiated a civil case in the United Kingdom. The trial opened on October 31, 2006, and the final judgment was rendered on April 5, 2007.[247] The full range of defendants involved in the Zamtrop and BK conspiracies and subconspiracies were found guilty and collectively held liable for the roughly US$25 million (from the Zamtrop conspiracy) and US$20 million (from the BK conspiracy); damages for fiduciary breaches and dishonest assistance were also awarded.[248] At the time of writing, the Supreme Court of Zambia is weighing whether the London judgment can be registered locally.

Case Study 5: Jack Abramoff

Overview

In 2006, Jack Abramoff pled guilty to charges of fraud, bribery, and tax evasion.[249] He was later ordered to pay more than US$23 million in restitution to his victims, with most of it going to the Native American gaming tribes he had defrauded through a

---

241. Ibid., ¶¶226-227.
242. Ibid., ¶75.
243. The People v. Chiluba (2009) No. SSP/124/2004, at 1 (Zambia).
244. Ibid., ¶178.
245. Ibid., ¶¶179-180.
246. Ibid., ¶178.
247. Republic of Zambia v. Meer Care & Desai, [2007] EWHC (Ch) 952, ¶49, ¶53 (Eng.).
248. Ibid. at ¶¶1119-1136. In the words of Justice Smith, "[t]he people of Zambia will know that whenever FJT [Chiluba] appears in public wearing a smart handmade suit of a pair of his 'signature' shoes that they were acquired by stealing money from the people—the vast majority of whom live at subsistence levels." Ibid.
249. Plea Agreement and Factual Basis for the Plea of Jack A. Abramoff, United States v. Abramoff, No. 06-cr-001-ESH, (D.D.C. January 6, 2006).

secret kickback scheme with his coconspirator, Michael Scanlon.[250] According to Abramoff's plea agreement, he and his associates "offered and provided a stream of things of value to (high) public officials"[251]—generally congressmen and their staffers—in exchange for official acts and influence favorable to Abramoff's objectives. The U.S. Senate Committee on Indian Affairs, which conducted a two-year investigation into the case, concluded that Abramoff and Scanlon's use of corporate entities and nonprofit organizations to "receive funds [and] conceal their destination" was a constant in their scheme.[252]

As of August 2009, 20 individuals connected to Abramoff had been convicted, pleaded guilty, or were awaiting trial.[253] They include Michael Scanlon, a former top aide to then–House Speaker Tom DeLay;[254] Congressman Robert Ney;[255] and senior administration officials, senior legislative aides, and lobbyists.[256] House Speaker Tom DeLay resigned from Congress three days after his top aide, Tony Rudy, pleaded guilty in connection with the Abramoff scandal in 2006.[257]

The Abramoff case raises two key issues relating to CV misuse: (a) the role of a Delaware, United States, nonprofit corporation in the scheme, and (b) the role of a tax advisor in facilitating Abramoff's misuse of a private charitable foundation.

Misuse of Sham Delaware Nonprofit Corporation

The U.S. Government Accountability Office, in a 2000 report examining the use of Delaware shell corporations by Russian Federation entities for possible money laundering activities, concluded that, "[i]t is relatively easy for foreign individuals or entities to hide their identities while forming shell corporations that can be used for the purpose of laundering money."[258]

---

250. United States v. Abramoff, No. 06-cr-001-ESH, (D.D.C. September 19, 2009) (order granting restitution).
251. Plea Agreement, p. 9, United States v. Abramoff, No. 06-cr-001-ESH, (D.D.C. January 3, 2006).
252. Ibid. *See also* Comm. on Indian Affairs, 109th Cong., "Gimme Five"—Investigation of Tribal Lobbying Matters (2006).
253. Press Release, U.S. Department of Justice, "Former Government Official Indicted on Public Corruption Charges Related to Ongoing Abramoff Investigation" (August 21, 2009). Abramoff himself pleaded guilty in January 2006 to charges of conspiracy to commit honest services fraud, honest services fraud and tax evasion, and was sentenced in September 2008 to 48 months in prison. Ibid.
254. Plea Agreement and Attachment A: Factual Basis for the Plea of Michael P.S. Scanlon, United States v. Scanlon, No. 05-cr-411-ESH, (D.D.C. November 11, 2005).
255. Plea Agreement and Attachment: Factual Basis for the Plea of Robert W. Ney, United States v. Ney, (D.D.C. September 13, 2006).
256. U.S. Department of Justice, Report to Congress of the Activities and Operations of the Public Integrity Section for 2009, pp. 22–23 (2009).
257. Plea Agreement and Information, United States v. Rudy, No. 06-cr-082, (D.D.C. March 31, 2006). See also Jonathan Weisman and Chris Cillizza, "DeLay to Resign from Congress," *Washington Post*, April 4, 2006.
258. U.S. Government Accountability Office (GAO), *Suspicious Banking Activities: Possible Money Laundering by U.S. Corporations Formed for Russian Entities* 11 (2000). In a later report, the GAO noted that Delaware ranked fourth in 2004 among all U.S. states for the most number of domestic corporations and

Although Abramoff and Scanlon employed a number of entities that they or their associates owned or controlled as part of their scheme, the U.S. Senate Committee on Indian Affairs (Senate Committee) investigating the scheme delved into the two men's use of the American International Center (AIC), a supposed think-tank based in Rehoboth Beach, Delaware. According to information retrieved from the Delaware corporate registry, AIC was formed on February 28, 2001, as a domestic nonprofit corporation. Its registered agent is listed as American International Center, Inc. at 53 Baltimore Avenue, Rehoboth Beach, Delaware 19971.[259]

According to the Senate Committee's 2006 investigative report, "With two of Scanlon's beach buddies sitting on its board, AIC's purpose was actually to collect fees associated with activities conducted by others and, in some cases, divert those fees to entities owned or controlled by Scanlon or Abramoff. In other words, AIC was a sham."[260] The Senate Report continues, "[e]arly in 2001, Scanlon called his long-time friend and fellow lifeguard David Grosh and asked him whether he wanted to serve as a director of an 'international corporation.' Grosh, who knew quite well that his background was unsuited for such a position, thought that this was a joke but finally agreed."[261] Grosh was paid $500 per month to serve as director of AIC.[262] The other "director" of AIC was Grosh's housemate, Brian Mann, a yoga instructor.[263]

For his part in making AIC appear to be a legitimate entity, on January 19, 2002, Abramoff e-mailed to Benjamin Mackler of MackDesign Studios: "Ben, I need to set up a website for the American International Center, which should have all sorts of goodies to make it look real."[264] The website set forth AIC's mission statement as "a Delaware-based corporation with the global minded purpose of enhancing the methods of empowerment for territories, commonwealths, and sovereign nations in possession of and within the United States."[265]

Limited Liability Corporations (LLCs) formed within its jurisdiction. *U.S. Government Accountability Office, Company Formations: Minimal Ownership Information Is Collected and Available 13 (2006).*

259. See https://delecorp.delaware.gov/tin/GINameSearch.jsp (type "American International Center" in "Entity Name"; follow "American International Center, Inc." hyperlink) (accessed July 3, 2010).

260. Comm. on Indian Affairs, 109th Cong., "Gimme Five," *supra* note 252, p. 12.

261. Ibid. p. 257.

262. Ibid.

263. Grosh told Senate investigators that, "Scanlon enticed Mann and [Grosh] to work for AIC by promising, among other things, that AIC would pay for both to go surfing at the island of St. Barts. Ibid. at 259. The Senate Report noted that between February and July 2001, "AIC had no office; AIC's business address was the beach house that [Grosh] and [yoga instructor Brian Mann] rented in Rehoboth Beach." Scanlon had a telephone installed that "he instructed Grosh never to answer." Ibid. at 258. Grosh and Mann told the Senate investigators that AIC had fewer than five meetings of its board, and that Scanlon "characterized these meetings as 'a paperwork formality.'" Ibid. at 260. They also testified before the Senate Committee to doing little to no work in their capacities as "directors," and that they were, to their knowledge, the only employees of AIC. Ibid. p. 261.

264. Ibid. p. 262.

265. Grosh and Mann told Senate investigators, "they had no idea what this meant." This is despite the fact that the AIC website stated that AIC was a "premiere international think tank" founded "under the high powered directorship of David A. Grosh and Brian Mann." Ibid. p. 264.

In actuality, AIC played three main roles in the Abramoff-Scanlon scheme: (a) as conduit for more than US$4 million in payments by Native American tribes to be passed to entities controlled by their one-time friend and business associate who performed grassroots lobbying work on behalf of the tribes but did not want to be associated publicly with the tribes;[266] (b) as a domestic entity cover, to receive payments from foreign government clients as a way to circumvent disclosure requirements under the Foreign Agents Registrations Act (FARA),[267] which would have had to be made to Congress regarding lobbying activities for foreign entities; and (c) as a means for Scanlon to funnel US$1.3 million in Native American tribe payments from AIC to his own company, Capitol Campaign Strategies, and then execute "shareholder draws" to use these funds for personal expenses, including the remodeling of his beach home.[268]

Role of Abramoff's Tax Advisor in Facilitating Misuse of a Foundation

The Senate Report also offered insights into the role played by Abramoff's tax advisor in the misuse of the Capital Athletic Foundation (CAF), the ostensibly private charitable foundation that Abramoff formed and managed. He and his wife were CAF's sole directors. CAF's stated mission was to promote "sportsmanship" among disadvantaged youth in the Washington, D.C. area, but the Senate Committee stated that "Abramoff treated CAF as his own personal slush fund, apparently using it to evade taxes, finance lobbying activities such as a golfing trip to Scotland, purchasing paramilitary equipment, and for other purposes inconsistent with CAF's tax exempt status and stated mission."[269]

For example, the third largest recipient of CAF funding in 2002 was "Kollel Ohel Tieferet, a purported educational institution in Israel; according to CAF's 2002 tax return, the grant was supposedly used for education, athletics, and security." Upon review, however, the Senate Committee found that "the Kollel Ohel Tieferet was nothing more than an entity established on paper to conceal the ultimate recipient of CAF grants: Shumel Ben Zvi," Abramoff's high-school friend, who had moved to Israel.[270] In fact, the Senate Report goes on to detail the role played by Gail Halpern, Abramoff's tax advisor, in helping to make the payments to Ben Zvifor a jeep and military equipment appear compatible with CAF's stated charitable mission.[271]

---

266. Ibid. p. 270. The friend and business associate was Ralph Reed, the politically influential first executive director of the Christian Coalition. The Reed-controlled entities were Century Strategies and Capitol Media. Ibid. p. 290.

267. Ibid., pp. 266-267. From 2001 through 2003, AIC was Abramoff's largest lobbying client, paying him and Greenberg Traurig about US$1.7 million in lobbying fees. In 2002 alone, AIC paid Greenberg Traurig US$840,000, making it the firm's fifth largest client that year. Ibid. p. 255.

268. Ibid.

269. Ibid. p. 278.

270. Ibid. p. 308.

271. Halpern had "labeled the purchases for Ben Zvi as 'spy equipment.'" Ibid. p. 309.

On November 11, 2002, Halpern wrote specifically about the payments to Ben Zvi: "[W]e need to work this into the tax exempt purpose of the foundation."[272] In response, Abramoff wrote to Ben Zvi, "if possible, it would be easier for me to get you funds through a kollel over there or something like that."[273] Ben Zvi replied, "Anyone can have a Kollel here."[274] A month later, Ben Zvi e-mailed Abramoff with wiring information for the "KOLLEL OHEL TIFERET (for: Shmuel Ben Zvi)."[275] When Abramoff informed Halpern, she stated "at the end of the year, he'll need to write us a letter on Kollel stationary [sic] thanking the Foundation for the money to promote their educational purpose."[276]

Although Halpern is the only person whose photograph is not shown in the firm's profiles of its principals, it is not known what consequences, if any, she faced for her role in assisting Abramoff in his misuse of the CAF.

Investigation

In February 2004, the *Washington Post*, which had been tipped off by a whistleblower close to the Native American tribe client-victims, published a front-page story delving into Abramoff's lobbying activities on behalf of the Native American gaming tribes and his ties to influential policy makers.[277] Soon after, the U.S. Senate Committee on Indian Affairs commenced its investigation, exercising its subpoena power to interview witnesses and holding five public hearings in 2004 and 2005.[278] Once the investigation was launched, the committee did not appear to face significant investigatory hurdles. Although it had been seemingly easy for Abramoff and Scanlon to form the entities involved in their scheme—in their work, home, or nearby state—it appears that the Senate Committee with its full investigatory resources and compulsory powers was able to unravel the veil of control and ownership of those entities and their illicit activities.

Abramoff and Scanlon invoked their constitutional privilege against self-incrimination and declined to testify, but many other witnesses did appear and testify. They included AIC nominee directors David Grosh and Brian Mann and Abramoff's tax advisor Gail

---

272. She subsequently wrote to Abramoff, "[B]ut let's try to figure it out in a way where we don't screw up the foundation. we [sic] need to get the money to a 501c3 [sic] or an educational institution, not directly to him. can [sic] you ask him if he can work something out w/ the kollel so the money goes from the kollel to him?" Ibid. pp. 310–311.
273. Kollel is a gathering or institute for advanced study of the Talmud. Ibid.
274. Ben Zvi also added, "If I set up the account name in the name of a Kollel and send you papers with a Kollel stationary [sic] would that work?" Ibid.
275. Ibid. p. 311.
276. Ibid. p. 312.
277. Susan Schmidt, "A Jackpot from Indian Gaming Tribes," *Washington Post*, February 22, 2004. Schmidt and fellow journalists from the *Washington Post* would go on to win the Pulitzer Prize, the top journalism award in the United States, for their reporting of the scandal. Ibid. p. 6.
278. Comm. on Indian Affairs, 108th Cong., Oversight Hearing Regarding Tribal Lobbying Matters, et al (2006). Michael Scanlon was "invited, but did not appear before the Committee on this date." Comm. on Indian Affairs, 109th Cong., "Gimme Five," *supra* note 252, p. xii.

Halpern.[279] At the same time, the U.S. Department of Justice Public Integrity Section commenced their probe. A number of U.S. law enforcement agencies were involved in the investigation: the Federal Bureau of Investigation, the Internal Revenue Service's (IRS) Criminal Investigation Division, the General Services Administration's Office of Inspector General, and the Department of the Interior's Office of the Inspector General. With testimonial and documentary evidence of corruption and fraud mounting against the conspirators, Scanlon entered a guilty plea in November 2005. Abramoff followed suit in January 2006.

Asset Recovery

In September 2008, Jack Abramoff was ordered to pay US$23,134,695 in restitution to his victims.[280] The Restitution Order noted that an amount of US$15,673,232 was uncompensated loss as of the date of the Order.[281] Abramoff was required to make restitution payments upon his release from prison.[282] Less than a year later, the U.S. government filed a Motion for Immediate Modification of Restitution Order, the day after being advised by Abramoff's counsel that Abramoff and his wife had received a refund from the U.S. IRS totaling US$520,189 and in two weeks prior to giving notice to the government, paid a total of US$422,000 to 10 nonrestitution creditors.[283] The government motioned the court to order Abramoff and his family to cease spending the remains of the IRS refund, to provide a complete accounting of how the refund had been spent, and to order Abramoff to provide notice to court of any debt or assets in excess of US$2,500 incurred or acquired by him or his family members.[284] In October 2009, the court ordered Abramoff to pay US$16,500 toward restitution in the present case, with the rest of the remaining tax refund authorized mainly for personal expenses.[285]

---

279. Comm. on Indian Affairs, 109th Cong., "Gimme Five," *supra* note 252, pp. xii–xiv.

280. United States v. Abramoff, No. 1:06-cr-0001-ESH (D.D.C. September 4, 2008) (order granting restitution Order). The order stated that when Scanlon was sentenced, that "both defendants will be jointly and severally liable" for the amount of losses incurred by the Indian tribes. Ibid. at 2. *See also* Press Release, U.S. Department of Justice, "Former Lobbyist Jack Abramoff Sentenced to 48 Months in Prison on Charges Involving Corruption, Fraud, Conspiracy and Tax Evasion" (September 4, 2008).

281. United States v. Abramoff, No. 1:06-cr-0001-ESH, 1 (D.D.C. September 4, 2008) (order granting restitution Order).

282. Abramoff was released from prison in June 2010. See "Jack Abramoff," New York Times, updated: June 24, 2010, available at http://topics.nytimes.com/top/reference/timestopics/people/a/jack_abramoff/index.html.

283. Motion for Immediate Modification of Restitution Order, United States v. Abramoff, No. 1:06-cr-0001-ESH (D.D.C. May 21, 2009). The non-restitution payments included payments for legal and accounting fees, back taxes owed to the State of Maryland, credit card debts and a US$87,000 loan from Abramoff's father. Ibid.

284. Ibid.

285. United States v. Abramoff, No. 1:06-cr-0001-ESH (order modifying restitution order) (D.D.C. October 19, 2009). The Order authorized Abramoff to pay up to US$35,000 for the repair of the roof of his house, US$16,500 to restitution creditors in his Florida case, and the remainder of the tax refund to cover his family's ordinary living expenses and professional services. The Court also ordered that "In the event that Mr. Abramoff receives, directly or indirectly, any sum or property valued in excess of $2,500 while incarcerated, Mr. Abramoff shall report the receipt of those funds or property" to the U.S. Department of

On February 17, 2011, Michael Scanlon was sentenced to a prison term of 20 months. He was ordered jointly and severally liable with his former coconspirator, Jack Abramoff, for the payment of US$20,191,537.31 in restitution to the Native American tribes that had been the victims of their fraud scheme.[286] A week later, Scanlon appealed his judgment to the U.S. Court of Appeals for the District of Columbia Circuit.[287]

Case Study 6: Joseph Estrada

Overview

Joseph Estrada was President of the Republic of the Philippines from June 1998 to January 2001. He stepped down during his Senate impeachment trial on charges of corruption and amid growing public protests against his presidency.[288] He was arrested in April 2001 and charged with violating the Anti-Plunder Law[289] for allegedly having amassed more thanUS$87 million in unlawful and unexplained wealth.[290]

Justice and the Court as soon as possible but not spend or distribute the funds or property before providing notice. He was precluded from spending or distributing the funds or property until the court issued an order authorizing such expenditure or distribution. Ibid.

286. United States v. Michael P.S. Scanlon, Case No. 05-cr-00411-ESH (D.D.C.), Restitution Order filed on February 11, 2011; Judgment in a Criminal Case filed on February 17, 2011; and Order Amending Judgment filed on March 7, 2011.

287. According to his February 23, 2011 Notice of Appeal, "Specifically, defendant Scanlon appeals the District Court's November 30, 2010 Memorandum Opinion and Order denying Defendant's Motion to Modify or Amend His Plea Agreement In Conformity With The Supreme Court's *Skilling* Decision." Notice of Appeal, United States v. Scanlon, Case No. 05-cr-411-ESH (D.D.C. February 23, 2011); Opinion, Skilling v. United States, No. 08-1394 (S.Ct. June 24, 2010).

288. People v. Estrada, No. 26558, at 14 (Sandiganbayan, Special Div., September 12, 2007) (decision for plunder) (Phil.)

289. Ibid. at 3–4. Anti-Plunder legislation was enacted "in the aftermath of the Marcos regime where charges of ill-gotten wealth were filed against former President Ferdinand Marcos and his cronies. Government prosecutors found no appropriate law to deal with he [*sic*] multitude and magnitude of the acts allegedly committed by the former President [Marcos] to acquire illegal wealth. They also found out that under the then existing laws such as the Anti-Graft and Corrupt Practices Act, the Revised Penal Code and other special laws, the acts involved different transactions, different time and different personalities. Every transaction constituted a separate crime and required a separate case and the over-all conspiracy had to be broken down into several criminal and graft charges. The preparation of multiple Informations was a legal nightmare but eventually, thirty-nine (39) separate and independent cases were filed against practically the same accused before the Sandiganbayan. R.A. No. 7080 or the Anti Plunder Law was enacted precisely to address this procedural problem." Ibid. at 293. For a conviction under the Anti-Plunder Law, all three of the following elements must be met: (a) the offender must be a public official who acting by himself or in conspiracy with others, (b) amassed or acquired ill-gotten wealth through a combination or series of criminal acts, and (c) the aggregate amount of the ill-gotten wealth is at least US$1,065,500 (PHP 50 million). Ibid. at 261. *See also* The Anti-Plunder Law, Rep. Act No. 7080 (July 12, 1991), http://www.oecd.org/dataoecd/37/19/46816908.pdf (accessed March 23, 2011).

290. People v. Estrada (decision for plunder), at 9-12. The total amount given in Pesos was 4,097,804,173.17. Ibid. Estrada had also been charged with Perjury for his allegedly false filings of his assets; he was tried and acquitted of this charge by a different Sandiganbayan court. People v. Estrada, No. 26905 (Sandiganbayan, Special Div., September 12, 2007) (decision for perjury).

On September 12, 2007, the *Sandiganbayan* (antigraft court) convicted Estrada of plunder,[291] holding that, from June 1998 to January 2001, Estrada had (a) conspired with Governor Luis Singson[292] and others, and had collected US$11.6 million in kickbacks from illegal *jueteng* gambling operators as protection money, of which US$4.26 million were found to have been concealed in the bank accounts of the Erap Muslim Youth Foundation, and (b) directed two government agencies to purchase shares in the Belle Corporation (Belle) and unjustly enriched himself by receiving US$4 million in commission for the sale which was held in a bank account under the fake name "Jose Velarde" of which he was the beneficial owner.[293]

As part of the plunder decision, the Sandiganbayan ordered the forfeiture of Estrada's illegally acquired assets from the *jueteng* collections and the commissions from the Belle Corporation shares.[294]

Two noteworthy issues in the Estrada case were the use of a foundation to conceal illicit proceeds and the involvement of a large number of individuals who acted in various capacities to help Estrada carry out his illicit schemes.

Misuse of Corporate Vehicles — Erap Muslim Youth Foundation

As part of its ruling in the plunder case, the Sandiganbayan held that the Erap Muslim Youth Foundation had been misused to conceal US$4.26 million of the illicit proceeds from the jueteng collection scheme.[295] The funds were deposited into the Foundation's accounts during April and May 2000.

"Erap" was Estrada's nickname, and also the acronym for Education, Research and Assistance Program.[296] President Estrada testified that he had asked his brother-in-law, Dr. Raul de Guzman, to form the Erap Muslim Youth Foundation to assist poor youth.[297] According to testimony at the plunder trial, the foundation did indeed carry out its

---

291. People v. Estrada (decision for plunder), p. 300.
292. Luis "Chavit" Crisologo Singson had been governor of the Ilocos Sur region, and Estrada's chief co-conspirator in the "jueteng" collections scheme. After a falling out, however, he publicly revealed the scheme and testified against Estrada at the Plunder trial. *Jueteng* is an illegal numbers game. Ibid. p. 22.
293. Estrada had also been charged with misappropriating, converting and misusing for his gain and benefit public funds in the amount of US$2.77 million (PF 130 million) from the PF 170 million tobacco excise tax share allocated for the Province of Ilocos Sur. The Court did not convict him of this charge, holding that "the paper trail in relation to the P130,000,000.00 diverted tobacco excise taxes began with Gov. Singson and ended with Atong Ang. This Court does not find the evidence sufficient to establish beyond reasonable doubt that Pres. Estrada or any member of his family had instigated and/or benefited from the diversion of said funds." Ibid. p. 193.
294. Ibid. p. 301.
295. Ibid. p. 158. Additional details on the bank paper trail for the sums deposited in the Foundation's account are provided in the Sandiganbayan decision. Ibid. p. 100–101.
296. Ibid. p. 121. "Erap" is also the Tagalog word "*Pare*" (friend) reversed.
297. Ibid. p. 122.

education mission.[298] The Sandiganbayan itself wrote that it was "not prepared to con-clusively rule [that] Erap is not a legitimate foundation or [that it was] set up purely to hide [Estrada's] illegally amassed wealth."[299]

Estrada publicized the foundation's activities and solicited donations on its behalf,[300] but he had no legal ties to it. Among its incorporators was attorney Edward S. Serapio, a codefendant in the plunder trial who was acquitted,[301] but Estrada was not among them. Estrada was considered the foundation's chairman emeritus, but he did not serve on its board of directors and he was not a signatory on its bank accounts. Based on this, the defense for Estrada argued that it was "impossible" for him to use the foundation for money laundering because "he was not a signatory . . . [and] its treasurer was the Chair-man of the bank who would not allow his name to be used in money laundering."[302] They further argued that when Estrada had learned from Serapio that Governor Sing-son had given US$4.26 million to the foundation, he ordered Serapio to return it to Singson because "his immediate reaction was that it was 'jueteng' money."[303]

Nonetheless, relying on the testimonial and documentary evidence of Singson, bank employees, and others, the Sandiganbayan held that the funds deposited in the founda-tion's account could be traced to the illegal *jueteng* collections, and ordered the money forfeited.[304] According to the court,

> [t]he paper trail of the [funds] deposited for the Erap Muslim Youth Foundation, Inc. incon-trovertibly established that the said sum of money came from jueteng collections through the cashier's/managers checks purchased by [Estrada's auditor Yolanda] Ricaforte using the deposits in the accounts that she opened in the different branches of [the bank].[305]

Use of Front Men and Others

As detailed in the Sandiganbayan's decision in the plunder trial, many individuals played major and minor roles in Estrada's schemes.[306] Luis Singson, then-governor of

---

298. According to the testimony given at the Plunder trial, Danilo Dela Rosa Reyes, Member of the Board of Trustees of the Erap Muslim Youth Foundation, stated that the Erap Muslim Youth Foundation's prede-cessor, "Erap Para sa Mahirap" foundation was duly established in 1988 and had 14,000 recipients of schol-arships as of the year 2000. Among the incorporators of the foundation was former President Estrada. The "Erap Para sa Mahirap" encountered financial constraints, however, and folded. The Erap Muslim Youth Foundation, Inc. came into existence in its place. Ibid. p. 135.
299. Ibid. p. 161.
300. Ibid. p. 122.
301. Ibid. p. 1. Other incorporators were prominent politicians, business people and academicians. Ibid.
302. Ibid. p. 124.
303. Ibid. p. 123.
304. Ibid. p. 301.
305. Ibid. p. 156.
306. It should be noted that Jinggoy Estrada, the former President's son who was a named co-defendant in the Plunder case, was acquitted of the charge by the Sandiganbayan which held that there was no evidence of his collecting or receiving the "*jueteng*" proceeds. Ibid. at 159. The Sandiganbayan also held that the

the Ilocos Sur region,[307] orchestrated the jueteng collection scheme for Estrada. He testified at the plunder trial to a long and close relationship with Estrada, and was even the baptismal godfather to Estrada's son. Estrada and Singson later had a falling out, and Singson publicly revealed the *jueteng* scheme and was a chief witness at Estrada's plunder trial. The Sandiganbayan wrote that Singson did not have the "purest motives in exposing the 'jueteng' collections," but nevertheless found him credible.[308] Singson, in turn, was aided by a number of his employees, including his assistant Emma Lim, Ma. Carmencita Itchon, and others.[309]

Charlie "Atong" Tiu Hay Sy Ang was also a key coconspirator in the scheme. Singson testified that Ang was the person who met with the *jueteng* operators and fixed the amount to be collected from each province.[310] In 2006, Ang was extradited from the United States, and in March 2007, he pleaded guilty to a lesser offense of Corruption of Public Officials.[311] Yolanda Ricaforte, mentioned earlier, was designated in April 1999 by Estrada as his auditor in the *jueteng* scheme.[312] She worked out of a building owned by Singson and testified that Estrada told him to pay her a monthly salary of US$1,705 (Philippine Peso ₱80,000),[313] and kept a detailed log of the twice-monthly collections (and expenses) in two sets of ledgers.[314] She opened numerous bank accounts and handled the transfers to and from the many accounts.[315]

The Belle Corporation shares sale scheme also involved Estrada friends and associates. Jaime Dichaves, a business associate of Estrada, was a director of Belle, a gaming company.[316] Estrada testified that Dichaves had spoken to him about the Belle shares, and he in turn mentioned it to Carlos A. Arellano, chairman of the Social Security System (SSS) and Federico Calimbas Pascual, president of the Government Service Insurance

---

government had not proved beyond a reasonable doubt that attorney Edward Serapio, who had been appointed in April 1999 by Estrada as Presidential Assistant for Political Affairs, had engaged in money laundering; he was also acquitted. Ibid.

307. Ibid. p. 24.

308. Ibid. p. 152.

309. Ibid. p. 32. Additional names are provided in the Sandiganbayan decision. Ibid. pp. 298–299.

310. Ibid. p. 31.

311. Ibid. pp. 20–21. Ang ultimately received probation.

312. Ibid. p. 32. Estrada admitted that he knew Ricaforte, whom he had appointed as director of Campo Carne. Estrada had appointed her husband Orestes Ricaforte as Undersecretary of Tourism and given him a black Lexus. Ibid. pp. 70, 120. Singson testified that Estrada had introduced Ricaforte to him and had appointed her as auditor because Estrada was "strict with money." Ibid. p. 120.

313. Ibid. p. 33.

314. The ledgers covered periods November 1998 to July 1999, and August 1999 to August 2000.

315. Ibid. p. 120.

316. Governor Singson had also testified that Dichaves had been a "front" for Estrada in Fontaine Bleau, Inc. "which was a casino owned by Pres. Estrada and built with the use of jueteng protection money. . . . According to Gov. Singson, the shares in the company were distributed as follows: five percent (5%) to Butch Tenerio, the President of the casino; twenty-five (25%) for Gov. Singson; seventy percent (70%) for Pres. Estrada which were placed in the names of Jaime Dichaves and his classmate Susie Pineda." Ibid. at 75. The Sandiganbayan did not make a finding about the ownership of Fontaine Bleau, which was dissolved in August 2000. Ibid. p. 72.

System (GSIS). Both Arellano, a childhood friend of Estrada, and Pascual had been appointed to their posts by Estrada.[317] They testified that they were uncomfortable with the pressure they received from Estrada to have their agencies purchase 329,855,000 and 351,878,000 shares respectively in Belle, which was involved in jai alai sporting and gambling and had a "speculative flavor."[318] Nevertheless, the two agencies spent nearly US$39.4 million in Belle shares.[319] Ocier, an owner of Belle and a cousin of Dichaves, testified that the commission check was made payable in cash and given to Dichaves, who deposited it in his account and then later transferred the money to the Jose Velarde accounts.[320] Although Dichaves testified that the Jose Velarde account belonged to him, the Sandiganbayan rejected his testimony and held that Estrada was the beneficial owner.[321] The Sandiganbayan relied on testimonial and documentary evidence in making its ruling, including the fact that Estrada's secretary, Lucena Baby Ortaliza, handled the transactions for the Velarde account.[322]

Investigation

Although Estrada was convicted of plunder, the approximate US$18.6 million the Sandiganbayan was able to trace to Estrada's illegal activities fell far short of the US$87 million that the government had charged him of illegally accumulating. The Sandiganbayan held that the government failed to offer sufficient evidence of the sources of the numerous deposits in the Joseph Velarde accounts, except for the Belle share commission and jueteng collections.[323]

One investigative obstacle in the case, as mentioned earlier, was that Estrada did not have legal ties to the foundation, that is, his name did not appear on the incorporation documents. Although Estrada had no legal ties to the foundation, the Sandiganbayan held him to be the beneficial owner of the funds deposited in its bank account that the Court traced to the illicit proceeds from the jueteng collection scheme. Estrada also had no legal ties to the Boracay Mansion in which his mistress lived.[324] The Sandiganbayan held that the funds used to purchase it could be traced to the Jose Velarde account, of which Estrada was the beneficial owner.

The Estrada case was prosecuted by the Office of the Ombudsman. It was tried over the course of six years by the Sandiganbayan, which noted that it had encountered and dealt with a number of novel issues, including a challenge by Estrada against the constitutionality of the plunder law. The Philippines Supreme Court's November 2001 decision

---

317. Ibid. p. 25.
318. Ibid. pp. 193, 245.
319. Ibid.
320. Ibid. p. 222.
321. Ibid. p. 234.
322. Ibid. pp. 235, 256–257.
323. Ibid. p. 297.
324. Ibid. p. 239. Boracay Mansion was owned by the St. Peter Holdings Corp., to which Estrada had no legal ties.

upholding the constitutionality of the plunder law allowed the Estrada case to proceed.[325]

Asset Recovery

At the conclusion of the plunder trial, the Sandiganbayan ordered the forfeiture of the (a) US$11.62 million with interest and income earned, inclusive of US$4.26 million deposited in the name and account of the Erap Muslim Youth Foundation; (b) US$4.02 million inclusive of interests and income earned, deposited in the "Jose Velarde" account; and (c) the Boracay Mansion.[326]

On October 25, 2007, then-President Gloria Macapagal-Arroyo granted Estrada a pardon, restoring his civil rights but maintaining the Sandiganbayan's forfeiture order.[327]

Case Study 7: Saudi Arabian Fighter Deals and BAE Systems

Overview

Beginning in the mid-1980s, BAE Systems plc (BAE) began serving as contractor to the government of the United Kingdom.[328] Under an arrangement known as the KSA Fighter Deals, BAE sold to the United Kingdom, which then sold to Saudi Arabia, military aircrafts, hardware, training, and services. Additional equipment, parts, and services have continued to be sold to Saudi Arabia since then.[329] Included in the agreements were "support services" that BAE provided to an unnamed KSA public official (Saudi official), who was in a position of influence regarding the sale of fighter jets and other defense materials.[330] The benefits were conferred through various means, including through the use of intermediaries and shell entities to conceal payments to those who assisted with the deals.[331]

BAE admitted it failed to undertake adequate review or verification of these benefits provided to the Saudi official, including inadequate review or verification of more than US$5 million in invoices submitted by a BAE employee from May 2001 to early 2002 to determine whether the listed expenses were in compliance with previous statements made by BAE to the U.S. government regarding its anticorruption compliance

325. Estrada v. Sandiganbayan (Third Division) and People of Philippines, G.R. No. 148560 (S.C. November 19, 2001) (Phil.), http://www.chanrobles.com/scdecisions/jurisprudence2001/nov2001/148560.php.
326. Ibid. p. 301.
327. Pardon by the President of the Philippines for Joseph Ejercito Estrada, Philippines Office of the Press Secretary (October 25, 2007), http://www.ops.gov.ph/records/pardon.pdf.
328. Plea Agreement, p. 11, United States v. BAE Sys's PLC., No. 1:10-cr-0035-JDB (D.D.C. February 2, 2010).
329. Ibid.
330. Press Release, U.S. Department of Justice, "BAE Systems PLC Pleads Guilty and Ordered to Pay $400 Million Criminal Fine." (March 1, 2010), http://www.justice.gov/opa/pr/2010/March/10-crm-209.html.
331. Plea Agreement, p. 13.

procedures.[332] In connection with these same defense deals, BAE also agreed to transfer more than British Pounds (£) 10 million, plus more than US$9 million, to a bank account in Switzerland controlled by an intermediary, being aware of the high probability that the intermediary would transfer part of these payments to the same KSA official.[333]

On March 1, 2010, BAE pled guilty to conspiring to defraud the United States by impairing and impeding its lawful government functions, to making false statements about its Foreign Corrupt Practices Act (FCPA) compliance program, and to violating the Arms Export Control Act and the International Traffic in Arms Regulations.[334] As a result, BAE was ordered to pay a US$400 million criminal fine, one of the largest criminal fines in the history of U.S. Department of Justice's effort to combat overseas corruption in international business and enforce U.S. export control laws.[335]

The following discussion highlights two interesting aspects of the case: (a) BAE's use of shell companies to conceal the role of its intermediaries and (b) the passive yet critical role of the Saudi official in the scheme.

BAE's Use of Shell Companies to Conceal Intermediary Relationships

BAE regularly retained what it referred to as "marketing advisors"[336] and intermediaries to assist in the soliciting, promoting, and securing of the Saudi Arabian Fighter Deals.[337] BAE made payments to these advisors through offshore shell companies—despite the fact they failed to perform the requisite due diligence under the FCPA.[338] Various offshore shell entities beneficially owned by BAE were used to pay some of these market advisors.[339] BAE also encouraged these advisors to establish their own offshore shell entities to receive payments to disguise the origins and recipients of such payments.[340]

One such entity, used by BAE to conceal the marketing advisor relationships, was established in the British Virgin Islands (BVI).[341] Under the *BVI Business Companies Act 2004*, incorporation of a legal entity in BVI requires minimal information at the time of registration, namely, only a registered office[342] and a registered agent.[343] The physical location of the place of business, legal ownership information, management information, or beneficial ownership information are not required to be filed in the central

---

332. Press Release, U.S. Department of Justice, "BAE Systems PLC Pleads Guilty," supra note 330.
333. Ibid.
334. Plea Agreement, p. 1.
335. Press Release, U.S. Department of Justice, "BAE Systems PLC Pleads Guilty," supra note 330.
336. Plea Agreement, p. 7.
337. Ibid. p. 13.
338. Ibid. p. 7.
339. Ibid.
340. Ibid.
341. Ibid. p. 8.
342. British Virgin Islands Bus. Co's Act § (9)(1)(c) (2004).
343. British Virgin Islands Bus. Co's Act § (9)(1)(d) (2004).

registry at any time. Both the register of members[344] and the register of directors[345] are required to be kept with the registered agent; however they are available only for inspection by directors and members of the company.[346] Incorporating in the BVI not only offered anonymity to conceal the identity of the agents, the intermediary relationships, and the stream of payments, but also inhibited the ability of authorities to penetrate the arrangements.[347]

The Role of the KSA Official

Like many cases of grand corruption, this case is exemplary of the often "passive" role of the Politically Exposed Person (PEP). Underlying the formal understanding and related framework between BAE, the United Kingdom, and the KSA were certain operational written agreements for specific component provisions of the KSA Fighter Deals.[348] The written agreements were divided into numerous Letters of Offer and Acceptance (LOAs) that were added and revised over the years; these LOAs identified the principal types of expenditures, work to be undertaken, services to be provided, and prices and terms.[349]

At least one of the LOAs identified "support services" that BAE considered it was obliged to provide to a Saudi public official who, as mentioned earlier, was in a position of influence regarding the Saudi Arabian Fighter Deals.[350] BAE provided these benefits through various payment mechanisms both in the territorial jurisdiction of the United States and elsewhere.[351] Additionally, BAE provided some of these "support services" to the Saudi official through travel agents retained by a BAE employee, who was also a trusted confidant of the Saudi official. These benefits included the purchase of travel, accommodations, security services, real estate, automobiles, and personal items.[352]

The role of the Saudi official and the degree of separation he maintained from the administration of the scheme is interesting. He did not function as the facilitator or intermediary behind the scheme; this role was fulfilled by BAE's marketing advisors. Although the Saudi official received money from the shell companies, his name appeared nowhere on the incorporation papers. He did not devise the scheme, but was merely—to no lesser fault—opportunistic. His role was limited to receiving the bribe payments in exchange for exerting his influence behind the scenes. It is often the case in grand corruption that the PEPs attempt to minimize their chances of getting caught by maintaining a more passive role in the scheme. Such was the case with the KSA official.

---

344. British Virgin Islands Bus. Co's Act § (41)(1)(d)(iv) (2004).
345. British Virgin Islands Bus. Co's Act § (96)(1)(c) (2004).
346. British Virgin Islands Bus. Co's Act §§ (100)(1)-(100)(2) (2004).
347. Plea Agreement at 8, United States v. BAE Sys's, No. 1:10-cr-0035-JDB (D.D.C. February 2, 2010).
348. Ibid. p. 12.
349. Ibid.
350. Ibid.
351. Ibid.
352. Ibid.

Investigation and Asset Recovery

An investigatory obstacle specifically cited in the plea agreement was BAE's establishment of the offshore entity in the BVI.[353] Penetrating an arrangement involving an incorporated BVI entity can be difficult because of the lack of information recorded on companies during registration; this difficulty, of course, does not apply only to entities incorporated in the BVI, but unfortunately, to numerous jurisdictions.

Another obstacle to the investigation may have been the inadequate information BAE maintained on its intermediary advisors, namely, who they were and what work they were doing to advance BAE's business interests. According to the plea agreement, BAE avoided communicating with the intermediaries in writing, obfuscating and failing to record the key reasons for the suitability of the advisor or any relevant document pertaining to work performed.[354] Often, the contracts[355] with these advisors were maintained by secretive legal trusts in offshore locations. This conduct thus served to conceal the existence of certain payments through the BAE advisors.[356]

According to the U.S. Department of Justice's press release, the BAE case was investigated by the Federal Bureau of Investigation's Washington Field Office's FCPA squad and special agents of the U.S. Immigration and Customs Enforcement's Counter Proliferation Unit. Investigative assistance was provided by the Department of Defense's Criminal Investigative Services, the General Services Administration's Office of Inspector General, and the Department of Justice's Criminal Division's Office of International Affairs. The press release stated that "[t]he Department of Justice acknowledges and expresses its appreciation of the significant assistance provided by the U.K.'s Serious Fraud Office, and further expresses its gratitude to that office for its ongoing partnership in the fight against overseas corruption."[357]

---

353. Ibid. p. 8.

354. Ibid. p. 8.

355. As described in detail in the sentencing memorandum, BAE has now replaced nearly all of its top leadership, including its Chief Executive Officer and Chairman of the Board. BAE also overhauled and expanded its Corporate Responsibility efforts. New positions include Chief Counsel, Compliance and Regulation (which carry global responsibility), and the Managing Director of Corporate Responsibility, who reports directly to the Chief Executive Officer. In addition, during the investigation, BAE imposed a moratorium on entering into new marketing advisor agreements or making payments under existing business marketing advisor agreements until a complete collection and review was undertaken of all such agreements. In 2007, BAE also initiated a review of all advisors with whom it had agreements, and terminated the majority of pre-existing agreements with advisors. In light of past problems, BAE enhanced its review procedures for marketing advisors and created an External Review Panel composed of U.S. and U.K. lawyers with experience in the FCPA and other anti-corruption laws. The new advisor review process requires any BAE employee who wishes to engage an advisor to formally propose the advisor to the Panel, which then examines corruption risk and potential reputational risk arising from hiring that advisor before making a recommendation to BAE's Group General Counsel. United States' Sentencing Memorandum at 11-12, United States v. BAE Sys's PLC, No. 1:10-cr-0035-JDB (D.D.C. February 22, 2010).

356. Plea Agreement p. 8.

357. Ibid.

Together, these agencies were able to overcome the various investigative obstacles. On March 1, 2010, BAE pleaded guilty in the U.S. District Court for the District of Columbia to conspiring to defraud the United States by impairing and impeding its lawful functions, to making false statements about its FCPA compliance program, and to violating the Arms Export Control Act (AECA) and International Traffic in Arms Regulations (ITAR). BAE was ordered to pay a $400 million fine for its criminal conduct—one of the largest criminal fines ever levied in the United States against a company for business-related violations.[358] As part of its guilty plea, BAE agreed to maintain a compliance program designed to detect and deter violations of the FCPA, other foreign bribery laws implementing the Organisation for Economic Co-operation and Development (OECD) Anti-Bribery Convention, and any applicable anticorruption laws designed to detect violations of U.S. export control laws, and to appoint a compliance monitor for three years.[359]

Case Study 8: Pavel Lazarenko

Overview

Pavel Lazarenko was prime minister of Ukraine from May 1996 to July 1997, when he left the position amid allegations of corruption.[360] He previously served as first vice prime minister of Ukraine and, before that, as governor and party official for the Dnepropetrovsk region. After being dismissed as prime minister, he formed and led the opposition Hromada Party.[361] As a Member of the Ukrainian Parliament, Lazarenko enjoyed immunity from prosecution. When the Ukrainian Parliament voted in February 1999 to lift his immunity, however, Lazarenko fled to the United States. He was arrested upon his arrival.

In 2000, the United States filed a 53-count indictment, accusing Lazarenko of involvement in five corruption schemes: (a) extortion of Peter Kiritchenko; (b) extortion of Alexei Alexandrovich Dityatkovsky and his company Dneproneft; (c) diversion of funds from accounts belonging to two state enterprises, Naukovy State Farm and Nikopolsky Metal Works factory; (d) receipt of US$97 million from Somolli, a company related to the United Energy Systems of Ukraine in exchange for official concessions; and (e) through GHP Corp. (a Panamanian company that Lazarenko and Kiritchenko allegedly controlled), sale of prefabricated homes to the Ukrainian Cabinet Ministers at an inflated price.[362]

---

358. Press Release, U.S. Department of Justice, "BAE Systems PLC Pleads Guilty," supra note 330.
359. Ibid.
360. United States v. Lazarenko, 564 F.3d 1026 (9th Cir. 2009).
361. Ibid.
362. United States v. Lazarenko, No. 00-cr-0284-01 CRB (N.D. Cal. February 4, 2010) (amended judgment in a criminal case).

Lazarenko was subsequently convicted of one count of conspiracy to commit money laundering and seven counts of money laundering.[363] He was sentenced to 97 months' imprisonment and fined US$9 million for his role in laundering $30 million in proceeds from extortion.[364] The U.S. conviction had been preceded by a 2000 conviction *in absentia* in Switzerland on charges of diverting US$72 million from a Ukrainian government contract, depositing US$43 million of it in Swiss accounts and then transferring them to accounts in Antigua and the Bahamas.[365] The Swiss court sentenced Lazarenko to an 18-month suspended prison term, and confiscated US$6.6 million from his Swiss accounts.

In a civil asset forfeiture claim filed in 2005, the U.S. alleged that Lazarenko misused his public office in amassing more than US$326 million in criminal proceeds that he laundered through a web of corporate vehicles and bank accounts all around the world.[366]

Two notable aspects of Lazarenko's money laundering scheme were the misuse of corporate vehicles (CVs) to shield his illicit assets and money laundering activities as well as the purchase and use of an offshore bank through which he further sought to conceal his assets. As described below, however, neither provided the bullet-proof protection from prosecution that Lazarenko may have sought.

Corporate Vehicle Misuse — Not a Bullet-Proof Shield

Although Lazarenko was convicted in the United States on only the eight counts related to the first scheme of extortion of Kiritchenko, his case still serves as proof that CVs are not a bullet-proof shield against prosecution.

---

363. Ibid.
364. Ibid. *See also* Press Release, U.S. Department of Justice, "Former Ukrainian Prime Minister Sentenced to 97 Months in Prison/Fined $9m for Role in Laundering $30m of Extortion Proceeds" (November 19, 2009).
365. The Swiss Federal Tribunal case decisions were 125 II 356 and 125 II 238. See also, David Chaikin & J. C. Sharman, *Corruption and Money Laundering: A Symbiotic Relationship* 138 (Palgrave Macmillan, 2009), pp. 137-39.
366. First Amended Verified Complaint for Forfeiture at 21-22, United States v. All Assets Held at Bank Julius Baer & Co., Ltd., No. 1:04-cv-00798-PLF (D.D.C. June 30, 2005). The amounts and entities listed in the civil asset forfeiture claim are (a) in 1996, at least US$84 million from Somolli Enterprises; (b) in 1996, at least US$65 million from United Energy International Limited; (c) between 1996 and 1997, at least US$42 million from L.I.T.A.T. Offshore, Limited; (d) between 1994 and 1998, at least US$30 million from businesses established by Kiritchenko, such as Agrosnasbnyt/ASS and GHP Corporation; (e) between 1996 and 1997, at least US$30 million from DAV Riga; (f) in 1996, at least US$25 million from ITERA Corporation and its affiliates; (g) in 1997, at least US$15 million from SB Corp.; (h) between 1993 and 1994, at least US$14 million from Naukovy State Farm; (i) in 1997, at least US$13 million from United Energy Systems of Ukraine; (j) between 1993 and 1996, at least US$5,886,000 from Ditiakovsky and Dneproneft; (k) between 1995 and 1997, at least US$2 million from Internova Trading Corp., and (l) in 1994, at least US$375,000 from Nakosta Metal Products, a business owned by Alex Kurkaev. Lazarenko officially reported his income as US$6,000 per year for 1996 and 1997. Ibid.

For example, two of the counts that Lazarenko was charged with involved the California corporate entity Dugsbery, Inc. (Dugsbery), which was used to funnel Lazarenko funds to purchase a US$6.745 million estate in Novato, California, United States.[367] Dugsbery was formed in California in 1994, was registered to an individual with ties to Kiritchenko, and its business address was a building that Kiritchenko owned. In other words, Lazarenko's name was not attached to any of the incorporation documents.[368] Lazarenko had no legal ties to Dugsbery, which normally might have proved an effective shield against criminal liability. What ultimately brought down the scheme was the change of heart by Lazarenko's advisor and coconspirator turned state-witness, Peter Kiritchenko.

Kiritchenko's relationship with Lazarenko dates back to 1992, when the Ukrainian businessman met with Lazarenko, because according to Kiritchenko, "to do any kind of serious trade one needed [Lazarenko's] agreement."[369] Lazarenko informed Kiritchenko that he did business with everyone "50-50." In 1993, Kiritchenko transferred a 50 percent interest in his company, Agronadsbyt, to Ekaterina Karova, a relative of Lazarenko. Over the years, he gave Lazarenko US$30 million in profits from his businesses.

At the same time, Kiritchenko also served as advisor and main coconspirator in Lazarenko's money laundering schemes.[370] Kiritchenko, who had moved to San Francisco in the mid-1990s, was arrested soon after Lazarenko. Kiritchenko pleaded guilty to a charge of receipt of property that had crossed a state or U.S. boundary after being stolen,[371] and became a main government witness in Lazarenko's trial. This change of heart by Kiritchenko penetrated the anonymity provided by the incorporation structure of Dugsbery. In convicting Lazarenko, the U.S. court held that the funds received by Dugsbery could be traced to Lazarenko's bank account in the Bahamas. These funds in turn were traced to Lazarenko's CARPO-53 Swiss account, where he had deposited proceeds from his extortion of Kiritchenko.[372]

Correspondent Banking Accounts—European Federal Credit Bank

As defined by the U.S. federal court in the Lazarenko case, a "correspondent account" is "an account established by a domestic banking institution to receive deposits from,

---

367. United States v. Lazarenko, 564 F.3d 1026 (9th Cir. 2009).

368. See http://kepler.sos.ca.gov/cbs.aspx (follow "Corporation Name" option and select; type "Dugsbery"; follow "Dugsbery Inc." hyperlink) (accessed July 3, 2010).

369. United States v. Lazarenko, 564 F.3d, p. 1030.

370. According to Lazarenko's indictment, Kiritchenko had been named in 1995 and 1996 as advisor to Lazarenko by Directive No. 568 and Directive 596, respectively, by the Ukrainian Cabinet of Ministers. Indictment at 2, United States v. Lazarenko, No. 3:00-cr-00284-CRB (May 18, 2000). The U.S. Federal Bureau of Investigation, acting on an MLAT request from Ukraine in late 1997, had been investigating Kiritchenko's ties to Lazarenko when the latter came to the United States in 1999. See Jason Felch, "To Catch an Oligarch," San Francisco Magazine (October 4, 2004).

371. Press Release, supra note 364. See also First Amended Verified Complaint for Forfeiture, United States v. All Assets Held at Bank Julius Baer & Co., Ltd., No. 1:04-cv-00798-PLF (D.D.C. June 30, 2005).

372. United States v. Lazarenko, 564 F. 3d, p. 1037.

make payments on behalf of, or handle other financial transactions for a foreign financial institution."[373] A February 2001 report by the U.S. Senate noted that "[c]orrespondent accounts in U.S. banks give the owners and clients of poorly regulated, poorly managed, sometimes corrupt, foreign banks with weak or no anti-money laundering controls direct access to the U.S. financial system and the freedom to move money within the United States and around the world."[374] In October 2001, the U.S. enacted the USA PATRIOT Act, which prohibited U.S. banks from having correspondent accounts with offshore shell banks like European Federal Credit Bank (EuroFed).[375]

In 1997, Lazarenko and Kiritchenko learned that the EuroFed was for sale. In August 1997, Lazarenko and Kiritchenko purchased a 67 percent majority share in the Antigua-domiciled bank for US$1.1 million.[376] Soon thereafter, EuroFed opened correspondent accounts with U.S. banks and investment firms, as well as with banks in Lithuania, Liechtenstein, Switzerland, and elsewhere.[377] According to the 2005 U.S. civil asset forfeiture claim, approximately US$85.5 million is alleged to have been formerly on deposit in accounts held for Lazarenko's benefit at EuroFed,[378] and in all, almost US$100 million was alleged to have been cycled through the various Lazarenko- and Kiritchenko-controlled accounts at EuroFed to launder the illicit proceeds. In addition to an account in his name, Lazarenko is alleged to have controlled accounts held at EuroFed in the following names: Lady Lake Investments Corporation, Fairmont Group, Ltd., Guardian Investment Group, Ltd., Firstar Securities, Ltd., Nemuro Industrial Group, and Orby International, Ltd.[379]

---

373. United States v. Lazarenko, 575 F. Supp. 2d 1139 (N.D. Cal, 2008).

374. Minority Staff of the Permanent Subcomm.on Investigations, "Report on Correspondent Banking: A Gateway for Money Laundering 1" (February 5, 2001). The report summarizes the problem as follows: "U.S. banks have too often failed to conduct careful due diligence reviews of their foreign bank clients, including obtaining information on the foreign bank's management, finances, reputation, regulatory environment, and anti-money laundering efforts. The frequency of U.S. correspondent relationships with high risk banks, as well as a host of troubling case histories uncovered by the Minority Staff investigation, belie banking industry assertions that existing policies and practices are sufficient to prevent money laundering in the correspondent banking field." Ibid. p. 2.

375. See generally U.S. Office of the Comptroller of the Currency, "Money Laundering: A Banker's Guide to Avoiding Problems" (December 2002).

376. United States v. Lazarenko, 564 F. 3d 1026. See also United States v. Lazarenko, 575 F. Supp. 2d, p. 1141.

377. Further information on these accounts is provided in the amended complaint for forfeiture. See also First Amended Verified Complaint for Forfeiture, United States v. All Assets Held at Bank Julius Baer & Co., Ltd., No. 1:04-cv-00798-PLF (D.D.C. June 30, 2005).

378. Ibid. In the fall of 1999, acting on a request by the Ukrainian authorities, the Government of Antigua and Barbuda began an investigation of EuroFed for alleged money laundering activities and froze its assets. In November 1999, EuroFed was put into receivership and liquidated. Ukraine and Antigua and Barbuda talk in London, Latest News: Issue No. 58 (October 2001), http://www.antigua-barbuda.com/news_archive/newsletter58.asp#s5 (accessed July 3, 2010).

379. First Amended Verified Complaint for Forfeiture at 6. No details are provided in the Amended Complaint about these entities, except their account numbers and transactions, therefore it is not certain whether they were corporate vehicles that were actually formed or existed in name only. It should be noted that these accounts are alleged to be only a part of the vast web of Lazarenko and Kiritchenko-controlled accounts in the names of other corporate entities, trusts and Stiftungs in several jurisdictions. Some of those other accounts allegedly include: (a) Accounts at Credit Suisse (Guernsey) Limited, in the name of

Investigation

Close cooperation and both formal and informal information sharing among motivated investigators in Antigua and Barbuda, Switzerland, Ukraine, the United States, and other jurisdictions resulted in two criminal convictions.

The Ukraine investigation was conducted by the prosecutor general's office. In the United States, the Federal Bureau of Investigation (FBI), the Department of Justice, and the Internal Revenue Service Criminal Investigation division were involved in the investigation and prosecution of the case.[380] The lead prosecutor Martha A. Boersch and the lead FBI investigator Bryan E. Earl were both fluent in Russian and both traveled to Kiev and other parts of the world to carry out their investigation. The Swiss investigation was led by Investigating Magistrate Laurent Kasper-Ansermet, who traveled to the United States under a mutual legal assistance agreement by the two countries to present the Swiss indictment to Lazarenko while he was in U.S. custody, thereby enabling the conviction in Switzerland to proceed. In the fall of 2009, the Government of Antigua and Barbuda began an investigation of EuroFed for alleged money laundering activities.[381] In October 2009, it froze the bank's assets and then put the bank in receivership and ordered its liquidation.

Asset Recovery

As part of the sentence in his U.S. criminal case, Lazarenko was ordered to pay a fine of US$9 million and forfeit US$22,851,000 and various specified assets resulting from his conviction.[382] He was ordered to pay restitution of US$19,473,309 to Peter Kiritchenko.[383] The U.S. Court of Appeals for the Ninth Circuit, however, reversed the lower court's ruling. The Court wrote "We hold that, in the absence of exceptional circumstances, a co-conspirator cannot recover restitution. Because no exceptional circumstances exist here, we reverse and vacate the order of restitution."[384]

In a civil asset forfeiture claim filed in 2005, the U.S. alleged that Lazarenko misused his public office in amassing more than US$326 million in criminal proceeds, which he laundered through a web of CVs and bank accounts around the world.[385] The United

---

Samante Limited as Trustee of the Balford Trust, valued at US$147,919,401.13; (b) Accounts at Credit Suisse (Geneva), Banque SCS Alliance S.A. (Geneva), and Vilniaus Bankas (Lithuania) in the name of European Federal Credit Bank Limited, totaling over US$34 million; and (c) Accounts formerly held in Liechtenstein in accounts in the names of Orilles Stiftung, Gruztam Stiftung, Lesja Stiftung, NRKTO 7541, which were valued at approximately US$7 million and were being held at banks in Liechtenstein in accounts in the name of Beranco Engineering Establishment, Ylorex Establishment, Tanas AG, and NRKTO 7541 or in the name of Pavlo Lazarenko. Ibid.

380. "To Catch an Oligarch," *supra* note 370.

381. United States v. Lazarenko, 575 F. Supp. 2d 1139, 1142 (N.D. Cal, 2008).

382. United States v. Lazarenko, No. CR00-cr-0284-01-CRB (N.D. Cal. February 4, 2009).

383. Ibid.

384. Decision, US (Plaintiff-Appellee) and Kiritchenko (Intervenor) v. Lazarenko, No. 08–10185 (9th cir. Nov 3, 2010).

385. First Amended Verified Complaint for Forfeiture, United States v. All Assets Held at Bank Julius Baer & Co., Ltd., et al., No. 1:04-cv-00798-PLF (D.D.C. June 30, 2005).

States is seeking to forfeit more than $250 million in property traceable to a series of corrupt acts and money laundering by Lazarenko and located in bank accounts in Antigua and Barbuda, Guernsey, Liechtenstein, Lithuania, and Switzerland.[386] At the time of writing, the case is ongoing.[387]

Case Study 9: Piarco International Airport Scandal

Overview

From 1996 through 2000, the government of Trinidad and Tobago conducted what was intended to be a competitive process to award and pay for various contracts in conjunction with the construction of the Piarco International Airport in Trinidad.[388] Birk Hillman Consultants, Inc. (BHC), a construction firm co-owned by Eduardo Hillman-Waller, was hired as designer, consultant, and project manager to oversee the airport construction project.[389] BHC and others, such as businessmen Raul Gutierrez and Armando Paz, were able to rig the bidding and selection process so that overpriced bids submitted by the companies they controlled, such as the Florida corporation Calmaquip Engineering Corp. (Calmaquip),[390] would be chosen to perform the contracts.[391] According to the civil complaint filed by Trinidad and Tobago against the conspirators, the influence of political appointees, which included chairman of the National Gas Company Steve Ferguson,[392] Minister of Finance Brian Kuei Tung,[393] and chairman of Tourism and Industrial Development Company of Trinidad and Tobago Ishwar Galbaransingh,[394] allowed BHC and the other conspirators to guarantee government approval for the projects.[395]

---

386. As part of his 2000 conviction, Switzerland seized US$6.6 million from Lazarenko-controlled accounts. David Chaikin & J.C. Sharman, *supra* note 365. *See also* "The Case against Pavlo Lazarenko," BBC News (August 25, 2006), http://news.bbc.co.uk/2/hi/europe/4780743.stm.

387. In 2008, the U.S. judge in the case denied Lazarenko's motion to dismiss for lack of subject matter jurisdiction and for failure to state a claim upon which relief can be granted. Ibid.

388. Indictment pp. 2, 4.United States v. Gutierrez, No. 05-20859 CR-HUCK (S.D. Fla. November 17, 2005), (entered in the U.S. District Court for the Southern District of Florida as Case 1:05-cr-20859-PCH).

389. Ibid. United States v. Hillman-Waller, No. 05-20859-CR-HUCK (judgment in a criminal case) (S.D. Fla. January 29, 2007).

390. Florida Department of State Division of Corporations, Details by Entity Name: Calmaquip Eng'g Corp., http://www.sunbiz.org/scripts/cordet.exe?action=DETFIL&inq_doc_number=228605&inq_came _from=NAMFWD&cor_web_names_seq_number=0001&names_name_ind=N&names_cor _number=&names_name_seq=&names_name_ind=&names_comp_name=CALMAQUIP&names _filing_type= (accessed July 3, 2010).

391. Indictment, p. 5. United States v. Gutierrez, No. 05-20859 CR-HUCK (S.D. Fla. November 17, 2005). *See also* United States v. Gutierrez, No. 05-20859-CR-HUCK (amended judgment in a criminal case) (S.D. Fla. March 19, 2007). *See also* United States v. Paz, No. 05-20859-CR-HUCK (judgment in a criminal case) (S.D. Fla. January 29, 2007). *See also* United States v. Calmaquip Eng'g Corp., No. 05-20859-CR-HUCK (judgment in a criminal case) (S.D. Fla. January 18, 2007).

392. Complaint at 7, Trinidad & Tobago v. Birk Hillman Consultants, No. 04-11813 CA 30 (11th Fla. Cir. Ct. April 13, 2007).

393. Ibid. p. 11.

394. Ibid. p. 24.

395. Ibid.

A contract designated CP-9 was approved for the building enclosure and interior construction of the airport.[396] Despite the fact that eight companies had prequalified to submit bids, only one company from Trinidad and Tobago, Northern Construction Limited (Northern), submitted a bid.[397] According to the indictment, Northern was owned by Galbaransingh. Despite the fact that Northern's bid was approximately US$10 million above the cost estimate, Northern was awarded the contract for CP-9.

The contract designated CP-13 was awarded to Calmaquip for miscellaneous specialty equipment, such as jetways, elevators, escalators, and x-ray machines. Despite the fact that 10 companies had been prequalified to invite bids for CP-13, only Calmaquip and SDC, an international construction firm, submitted bids. Neither Calmaquip nor SDC disclosed that SDC's subsidiary, SDCC, shared corporate officers, directors, and a business location with Calmaquip. Calmaqup won the bid, despite its bid being US$15 million higher than the estimated cost of CP-13. The proceeds of these fraudulently obtained contacts were then secreted into various offshore bank accounts connected to different shell companies.[398]

The misuse of corporate vehicles (CVs) was essential in this case. As will be discussed below, they were used not only to provide additional layers to the scheme, but also to give the scheme the appearance of legitimacy.

Misuse of CVs to Give Appearance of Legitimacy

CVs are often used to protect the anonymity of a Politically Exposed Person (PEP) in corruption schemes; they are further used to hide the names of those involved in the scheme altogether. Another reason CVs are used is to give a fraudulent scheme the appearance of legitimacy. Because of the large-scale nature of the Piarco airport construction project, the prominent role the government played in awarding the contracts, and the high-level PEPs allegedly involved, it would have been nearly impossible for those PEPs to remain completely anonymous throughout the duration of the scheme. In other words, the primary motivation for using CVs was probably not the protection of the anonymity of the PEPs. Instead, the conspirators likely employed CVs to convince the public that the bidding and the awarding of contracts was being performed legitimately.

According to the civil complaint, despite the fact that BHC had been pre-assured of the position of project manager before the bidding process even began, BHC was still asked to give a presentation to the selection committee.[399] This was to give the appearance that a legitimate competitive process was being carried out. Furthermore, the selection committee invited Scott and Associates, a company from Toronto,

---

396. Indictment p. 3, United States v. Gutierrez.
397. Ibid. pp. 2–4.
398. Ibid.
399. Complaint p. 27, Trinidad & Tobago v. Birk Hillman Consultants, No. 04-11813 CA 30 (11th Fla. Cir. Ct. April 13, 2007).

Canada, to make a presentation to purportedly compete with BHC for the project manager contract.[400] BHC's role as project manager was essential to the securing of future subcontracts, so providing a façade of legitimacy was critical to the scheme's success.

The fact that payments from Trinidad and Tobago for the CP-9 and CP-13 contracts were transferred to Northern and Calmaquip also gave the appearance of legitimacy. It seemed logical that those CVs would receive the payments, because those companies actually bid on and performed the work.[401] It is now clear that the companies were vastly overpaid for their work, but at the time, this fact was obscured by the rigged bidding process, which appeared legitimate to the public eye.

Layering of Corporate Vehicles

The Airports Authority of Trinidad and Tobago (AATT) was the government agency assigned overall responsibility for the construction of the airport.[402] From April to November 2000, AATT paid funds into Calmaquip's bank accounts at Dresdner Bank Lateinamerika, AG (Dresdner) in Miami, Florida, United States, for Calmaquip's work on CP-13.[403] Forty-five payments were made, ranging from US$20,461.95 to US$5,500,663.75, and amounting to more than US$29,095,477.[404]

After the money was deposited into Calmaquip's Dresdner account, the conspirators used a system of layering to create levels of separation. On May 11, 2000, Raul Gutierrez, president and director of Calmaquip,[405] wire transferred US$2,000,000 from Dresdner Bank to Bank Leu Ltd. on behalf of the company, AMA Investment Group (AMA).[406] According to the indictment, that same day, AMA wire transferred US$1,500,000 from its Bank Leu account to the Bank Leu account of Argentum International Marketing Services, S.A. (Argentum). Over the course of the next month, Steve Ferguson, on behalf of Argentum, allegedly wire transferred from Argentum's Bank Leu account to other bank accounts held in the name of various other CVs, such as Bocora Holding, Inc. (Bocora) and Maritime Securities Holdings Ltd. In August and September 2000, Gutierrez and Armando Paz, both directors for Calmaquip, also made numerous transfers on behalf of Calmaquip to the Banco Bilbao Vizcaya Argentaria accounts of Empresas Sudamericana S.A. (Empresas). Later, Empresas allegedly would wire transfer money from this account to Argentum's Bank Leu account. After sufficient layers had been created, the payouts were made into the bank accounts of the conspirators.[407]

---

400. Ibid.
401. Indictment, pp. 3–4, United States v. Gutierrez.
402. Ibid. p. 2.
403. Ibid. p. 8.
404. Ibid. p. 9.
405. Ibid. p. 1.
406. Ibid. pp. 9–12.
407. Ibid.

This tactic of moving money from the bank account of one CV to the next, known as layering, is often used to disguise the trail of money. Layering separates the illegally obtained funds from the crime by obscuring the trail of money through a complex web of financial transactions. Rather than having the money transfer directly to one of the conspirators, it is being diverted to a company, thus giving it the appearance of legitimacy. In this case, securing disassociation from the rigged bidding process through this process of layering was a key step for the conspirators before they could enjoy their payday.

Investigation and Asset Recovery

This case presented various investigative obstacles. As discussed, the tactic of layering can obscure the trail of funds. The fact that the layered CVs were created in different jurisdictions also created an additional obstacle. According to the civil complaint, CVs from a wide variety of jurisdictions including—but not limited to—the Bahamas; Florida, the United States; Panama; Portugal; and Trinidad and Tobago were employed in the scheme.[408] For a criminal, such a structure of international layering can be convenient for hiding the trail of money—but from the perspective of an investigator, it creates a number of other investigative issues. For one, layering makes an investigation exponentially more costly—as was the case here.[409] In addition, when investigations become international, one jurisdiction's law enforcement must rely on another jurisdiction's law enforcement, and must make mutual legal assistance requests.

A number of CVs involved or allegedly involved in the scheme were from Panama. The aforementioned CVs, Argentum,[410] Bocora,[411] and Empresas,[412] for example, were all incorporated in Panama. Like a number of other jurisdictions, the Panamanian company registry does not collect legal ownership information (or beneficial ownership information); for *sociedad anónimas*/corporations, legal ownership information does not need to be disclosed upon incorporation.[413] Furthermore, in Panama, updating requirements are not set forth in the legislation for the information that must be submitted

---

408. Complaint pp. 6–8, 17, 72, Trinidad & Tobago v. Birk Hillman Consultants, No. 04-11813 CA 30 (11th Fla. Cir. Ct. April 13, 2007).

409. According to an experienced investigator from the British Virgin Islands, the most effective way to resolve the cost issue from layering is by striking early against exposed assets and liquidating them to add to available resources.

410. See https://www.registro-publico.gob.pa/scripts/nwwisapi.dll/conweb/prinpage (follow "Mercentil"; then follow "Sociedad Anónimas"; then follow "Alfabéticamente"; then type "Argentum International Marketing Services" in "Indique Nombre de Sociedad"; follow "Argentum International Marketing" hyperlink) (accessed July 3, 2010).

411. See https://www.registro-publico.gob.pa/scripts/nwwisapi.dll/conweb/prinpage (follow "Mercentil"; then follow "Sociedad Anónimas" then follow "Alfabéticamente"; then type "Bocora Holdings" in "Indique Nombre de Sociedad"; follow "Bocora Holdings, Inc." hyperlink) (accessed July 3, 2010).

412. See https://www.registro-publico.gob.pa/scripts/nwwisapi.dll/conweb/prinpage (follow "Mercentil"; then follow "SociedadAnónimas"; then follow "Alfabéticamente"; then type "Empresas Sudamericana" in "Indique Nombre de Sociedad"; follow "Empresas Sudamericana, S.A." hyperlink) (accessed July 3, 2010).

413. Panama Corp. Law, Law 32, (1927) (Art. 2).

at incorporation.[414] In essence, no public source exists for this information; the only place to obtain this information from Panama is from the company.

In spite of these obstacles, successful asset recovery was effected, and as of the date of this writing, efforts to recover further assets are ongoing. On November 17, 2005, the United States brought a criminal suit against Raul Gutierrez, Rene Diaz de Villegas, Eduardo Hillman-Waller, Steve Ferguson, Armando Paz, Ishwar Galbaransingh, Richard Lacle, Leonardo Mora, Northern, and Calmaquip in the Southern District of Florida for their involvement in the scheme.[415] From that list, Gutierrez,[416] Diaz,[417] Hillman-Waller,[418] Paz,[419] Lacle,[420] Mora,[421] and Calmaquip[422] have all pleaded guilty. In total, the defendants were ordered to pay more than US$25 million in restitution for their admitted guilt in the CP-13 contract.

A civil suit was brought by the RTT against many of the same defendants in the Eleventh Judicial Circuit Court for Miami-Dade County, Florida. In addition to the aforementioned defendants, Ronald Birk, Brian Kui Tung, and various other CVs were

---

414. Ibid.

415. Indictment pp. 2, 4. United States v. Gutierrez, No. 05-20859-CR-HUCK (S.D. Fla. November 17, 2005).

416. On March 19, 2007, Gutierrez pleaded guilty to conspiracy to commit wire fraud and to transfer money obtained by fraud and bank fraud in the Southern District of Florida in a suit brought by the United States. Gutierrez was ordered to pay US$22,556,100 in restitution. United States v. Gutierrez, No. 05-20859-CR-HUCK (amended judgment in a criminal case) (S.D. Fla. March 19, 2007).

417. On December 17, 2007, Diaz pleaded guilty to conspiracy to commit wire fraud and to transfer money obtained by fraud in the Southern District of Florida in a suit brought by the United States. He was ordered to pay a fine of US$50,000. United States v. Diaz de Villegas, No. 05-20859-CR-HUCK (amended judgment in a criminal case) (S.D. Fla. December 17, 2007).

418. On December 17, 2007, Hillman Waller pleaded guilty to conspiracy to commit wire fraud and to transfer money obtained by fraud and bank fraud in the Southern District of Florida in a suit brought by the United States. Hillman Waller was ordered to pay US$2 million in restitution. United States v. Hillman-Waller, No. 05-20859-CR-HUCK (judgment in a criminal case) (S.D. Fla. January 29, 2007).

419. On January 29, 2007, Paz pleaded guilty to bank fraud in the Southern District of Florida in a suit brought by the United States. Paz was ordered to pay restitution of US$489,618.06. United States v. Paz, No. 05-20859-CR-HUCK (judgment in a criminal case) (S.D. Fla. January 29, 2007).

420. On January 17, 2007, Lacle pleaded guilty to conspiracy to structure financial transactions in the Southern District of Florida in a suit brought by the United States. Lacle was ordered to pay a fine of US$15,000. United States v. Lacle, No. 05-20859-CR-HUCK (judgment in a criminal case) (S.D. Fla. January 17, 2007).

421. On January 17, 2007, Mora pleaded guilty to conspiracy to commit offense against the United States, that is, transportation of money obtained by fraud in the Southern District of Florida in a suit brought by the United States. United States v. Mora-Rodriguez, No. 05-20859-CR-HUCK (judgment in a criminal case) (S.D. Fla. January 17, 2007). On April 27, 2007, Mora was ordered to pay restitution in the amount of US$80,000. United States v. Mora-Rodriguez, No. 05-20859-CR-HUCK (ordering setting restitution amount) (S.D. Fla. April 27, 2007).

422. On January 18, 2007, Calmaquip pleaded guilty to conspiracy to commit wire fraud and to transfer money obtained by fraud and bank fraud in the Southern District of Florida in a suit brought by the United States. It is unclear how much Calmaquip was ordered to pay in restitution. United States v. Calmaquip Eng'g Corp., No. 05-20859-CR-HUCK (judgment in a criminal case) (S.D. Fla. January 18, 2007).

sued.[423] The complaint alleged improper dealings with the contracts CP-3, CP-5, and CP-9.[424] According to various news outlets, Ronald Birk, another coowner of BHC, signed a plea deal with the RTT to give evidence against his alleged coconspirators.[425] At the time of writing, this suit was ongoing.

Case Study 10: Telecommunications D'Haiti

Overview

Between 2001 and 2005,[426] government officials at Haiti's state-owned national tele-communications company, Telecommunications D'Haiti (Haiti Teleco), accepted bribes and laundered funds through corporate vehicles (CVs). As the sole provider of local telephone service in Haiti, Haiti Teleco contracted with international telecommunications companies to allow customers of those companies to make calls to Haiti.[427] Representatives of three such telecommunications companies, based in the United States, paid bribes to Haiti Teleco officials in exchange for commercial advantages that included preferential and reduced telecommunications rates and credits toward amounts owed, thereby defrauding Haiti Teleco of revenue.[428]

The bribes originating from the U.S. telecommunications companies were funneled systematically and incrementally through wire transfers and check payments[429] to intermediary shell companies.[430] These payments were made to appear as being for consulting services, commissions,[431] and vendor payments, although no such services were ever rendered.[432] The funds were dispersed from the intermediary accounts for the benefit of Haiti Teleco officials and their relatives, including Haiti Teleco's Director of International Affairs, a position held by Robert Antoine and subsequently by Jean Rene Duperval during the period of the scheme.[433] In dispersing the funds, false notations,

---

423. Complaint at 7, Trinidad & Tobago v. Birk Hillman Consultants, No. 04-11813 CA 30 (11th Fla. Cir. Ct. April 13, 2007).

424. Ibid. p. 99.

425. Darren Bahaw, "Birk Signs Plea Deal with State," *Trinidad & Tobago Express* (March 5, 2010), http://www.trinidadexpress.com/index.pl/article_news?id=161603723 (accessed July 3, 2010).

426. Factual Agreement, United States v. Antoine, No. 09-cr-21010-JEM (S.D. Fla. March 12, 2010).

427. Information p. 2, United States v. Diaz, No. 09-cr-20346-MARTINEZ/BROWN (S.D. Fla. April 22, 2009).

428. Indictment p. 8, United States v. Esquenazi, No. 09-cr-21010 (S.D. Fla. December 4, 2009).

429. Information p. 6, United States v. Diaz.

430. Indictment p. 10, United States v. Esquenazi.

431. Ibid. p. 8.

432. Information p. 6, United States v. Diaz. *See also* Indictment p. 9, United States v. Esquenazi. Diaz admitted that he never provided, and never intended to provide, any legitimate goods or services from JD Locator. Press Release, U.S. Department of Justice, "Two Florida Businessmen Plead Guilty to Participating in a Conspiracy to Bribe Foreign Government Officials and Money Laundering" (May 15, 2009), http://www.usdog.gov/usao/fls.

433. Factual Agreement, United States v. Robert Antoine. It had been mentioned that bribes were also paid to the director general of Haiti Teleco, and on July 13, 2011, the U.S. handed down an indictment against former Haiti Teleco Director General Patrick Joseph. See note 467. Information p. 6, United States v. Diaz.

such as inscribing fabricated invoice reference numbers on the memo portions of the checks, routinely would be made to conceal the true nature of the payments.[434]

Two intriguing aspects of this case were (a) the system of corruption at Haiti Teleco that allowed for the corruption to take place, and (b) the use of family members to administer parts of the scheme.

A System of Corruption

This case exhibits a system of corruption that remained in place even after Jean Rene Duperval succeeded Robert Antoine as Haiti Teleco's director of international relations. While Antoine was the director, he received US$1,150,000 in bribes from three U.S. telecommunications companies through intermediary shell companies,[435] including the Florida-based JD Locator Services (JD Locator),[436] which was formed by a codefendant Juan Diaz.[437] As described earlier, the bribes were made to appear as payments for consulting services, through the writing of false memo notations on checks, and through deposits into and withdrawals from accounts of intermediary shell companies.[438] At Antoine's direction, funds would be disbursed from the JD Locator bank account by sending wire transfers to Antoine's bank account, issuing checks payable to Antoine, which then were deposited into that same account, withdrawing currency that was given to Antoine, and sending funds to Antoine's family members and others at his direction.[439] Incremental disbursements were also paid to another intermediary company, Fourcand Enterprises, Inc. (Fourcand Enterprises), which was a Florida-based company established by Jean Fourcand, who served as its president and director.[440] Funds that accumulated in the Fourcand Enterprises account were collectively used to purchase real property, which was subsequently sold, the proceeds of which were transferred to Antoine via Fourcand's personal bank account.[441]

Once Antoine completed his tenure as director at Haiti Teleco, he was employed by two of the three U.S. companies that had paid him bribes. From this position, he facilitated the same corruption scheme, as bribes continued to be paid from the telecommunications companies to Duperval, who had succeeded him as director. Funds would be

---

434. Ibid. p. 7.
435. Factual Agreement, United States v. Antoine.
436. At least two other Florida-based corporate vehicles were misused in the corruption scheme in a manner similar to JD Locator. Indictment at 10, United States v. Esquenazi, No. 09-21010 (S.D. Fla. December 4, 2009).
437. Diaz would cash checks typically in amounts no greater than US$10,000, thereby obviating his obligation to file Currency Transaction Reports pursuant to relevant banking regulations and U.S. law. Information p. 7, United States v. Diaz.
438. Factual Agreement, United States v. Antoine.
439. Indictment p. 9, United States v. Esquenazi.
440. Press Release, U.S. Department of Justice, "Florida Businessman Pleads Guilty to Money Laundering in Foreign Bribery Scheme" (February 19, 2010).
441. Indictment pp. 23–24, United States v. Esquenazi. *See also* Press Release, U.S. Department of Justice, "Florida Businessman Pleads Guilty to Money Laundering in Foreign Bribery Scheme" (February 19, 2010).

paid to intermediary shell companies, including Process Consulting, which was Antoine's company, and to Telecom Consulting Services Corp. (Telecom Consulting), a company set up by the president and director of one of the U.S. telecommunications companies, Joel Esquenazi, another codefendant.[442] Similar to the disbursements from JD Locator, funds from Telecom Consulting were disbursed at Duperval's direction by the issuing of checks payable to Duperval and his family members, cash withdrawals, and purchases with such funds for Duperval's benefit.[443] It is alleged that more than US$1 million was received in the accounts of JD Locator[444] in 29 separate transactions and disbursed in 22 separate transactions[445] for the benefit of Antoine, and that US$75,000 was received in the account of Telecom Consulting in seven separate transactions, more than half of which was disbursed in 12 separate transactions for the benefit of Duperval.[446]

The two schemes mirrored each other in many regards: Both schemes were administered from the same director position within the government, and both schemes utilized an intermediary shell company to receive wire transfers. Another common aspect of the two schemes was the use of family members.

Involvement of Family Members

The misuse of CVs in this case was carried out to a substantial extent by and through the use of family members of Antoine and Duperval. Whether knowingly or inadvertently, these family members helped to conceal the connection of Antoine and Duperval to the bribes.

Duperval made his sister, Marguerite Grandison, the sole officer and director of intermediary shell company Telecom Consulting.[447] Grandison opened a bank account in the name of Telecom Consulting for which she was the sole signatory, which received more than US$70,000 in bribe payments via wire transfers and intrabank transfers from a U.S. telecommunications company.[448] At her brother's direction, she disbursed the funds from the account by issuing checks from Telecom Consulting payable to her brother and to his relatives, by withdrawing currency for him from the account, and by making purchases with the funds for her brother's benefit.[449] By having a family member conduct the money transfers, Duperval and coconspirator Esquenazi were able to enhance their anonymity in connection with the bribery; that is, Duperval was the true

---

442. Jean Rene Duperval's sister, Marguerite Grandison, served as the president and sole officer of Telecom Consulting, as described below. Indictment p. 10, United States v. Esquenazi.
443. Ibid. p. 11.
444. Information p. 6, United States v. Diaz, No. 09-20346-CR-MARTINEZ/BROWN (S.D. Fla. April 22, 2009).
445. Ibid. pp. 7–10.
446. Indictment pp. 15–16, United States v. Esquenazi. *See also* Factual Agreement, United States v. Antoine, No. 09-21010-cr-JEM (S.D. Fla. March 12, 2010).
447. Indictment p. 10, United States v. Esquenazi.
448. Ibid.
449. Ibid. p. 11.

beneficial owner of Telecom Consulting, and Ezquenazi, who served as the president and director of one of the bribe-paying U.S. telecommunications companies, had been involved in establishing Telecom Consulting[450] for use in the scheme. The names of either Duperval or Esquenazi, however, did not appear on any official documents of Telecom Consulting (such as its articles of incorporation,[451] or documentation of money transfers into or out of Telecom Consulting's bank account).[452] The only name that appears on the articles of incorporation is Grandison's, and that of the general counsel of the U.S. telecommunications company, who was listed as the registered agent.[453] Similarly, it is only Grandison's name that appears on banking documentation for Telecom Consulting.

Family members were used to accept bribery payments intended for Antoine and Duperval. When funds were disbursed from the intermediary shell companies, in certain instances, they were distributed to relatives of Antoine[454] and Duperval.[455] Again, the use of family members added a layer of separation between the bribe-payers and the bribe-takers, thereby helping to conceal the connection of Antoine and Duperval to the bribery.

Investigation

The systematic way in which the CVs were misused presented obstacles to the investigation. On the face of it, and according to the records kept at both the U.S. telecommunications companies as well as the intermediary companies, the bribe payments appeared to be made for legitimate services rendered. Furthermore, because the amounts of the checks cashed by JD Locator were each typically at or under US$10,000, Currency Transaction Reports would not have been filed with the banks in connection with the transactions.[456] In addition, the use of shell companies as intermediaries superficially dissociated the individual bribe-givers from the bribe-takers, by preventing their names from appearing as direct counterparties in any transactions transferring bribe money.

The investigation was able to proceed successfully, at least in part because of effective cooperation between United States and Haitian authorities. U.S. authorities obtained

450. Ibid. p. 10.

451. Ibid. Telecom Consulting Servs Corp., Articles of Incorporation (October 16, 2003).

452. The laws of Florida, where Telecom Consulting was incorporated, impose no obligation for the identity of the legal or beneficial owners of the company to be disclosed to a public authority, whether upon incorporation or on any on-going basis. Fla. Stat. § 607.1622 (2009), http://www.leg.state.fl.us/statutes/index.cfm?App_mode=Display_Statute&Search_String=&URL=Ch0607/SEC1622.HTM&Title=->2009->Ch0607->Section%201622#0607.1622 (accessed July 3, 2010).

453. Telecom Consulting Servs. Corp., Articles of Incorporation (October 16, 2003). See also Indictment p. 10, United States v. Esquenazi.

454. Information p. 6, United States v. Perez, No. 09-20347-CR-MARTINEZ/BROWN (S.D. Fla. April 22, 2009). *See also* Information p. 6, United States v. Diaz, No. 09-20346-CR-MARTINEZ/BROWN (S.D. Fla. April 22, 2009). See also Indictment p. 9, United States v. Esquenazi.

455. Indictment p. 11, United States v. Esquenazi.

456. Information p. 7, United States v. Diaz.

evidence supporting the charges through formal requests made under the Inter-American Convention Against Corruption. Once the indictment was issued, Duperval, a non-U.S. citizen, was arrested by agents of Haiti's *Bureau des Affaires Financières et Economiques* on the basis of a U.S. arrest warrant and then expelled to the United States to face charges.[457]

Asset Recovery

In 2009 and 2010, the U.S. Department of Justice initiated criminal cases against eight individuals involved in the bribery scheme. Informations were issued against Juan Diaz, Jean Fourcand, and Antonio Perez, who had served as controller of a U.S. telecommunications company. An indictment was also issued against Joel Esquenazi, Robert Antoine, Jean Rene Duperval, Marguerite Grandison, and Carlos Rodriguez, who was executive vice president of a U.S. telecommunications company.[458] According to the indictment, if convicted, these five defendants collectively would be required to forfeit to the United States US$963,818 representing proceeds of the conspiracy and offenses, in addition to all money properties, and commissions paid in connection with, or used to facilitate, the offenses.[459] In addition to forfeiture provisions, the various criminal charges carry maximum penalties of between 5 and 20 years in prison, as well as maximum fines of between US$100,000 and US$500,000, or twice the value of the property or the proceeds in question, whichever is greater.[460]

Antoine pleaded guilty to money laundering conspiracy in connection with US$800,000 in bribes.[461] He was sentenced to four years in prison[462] and was ordered to pay US$1,852,209 in restitution and to forfeit US$1,580,771.[463] Perez pleaded guilty to conspiring to commit Foreign Corrupt Practices Act (FCPA) violations and money laundering,[464] involving approximately US$674,193 in bribes to an official at Haiti

---

457. Press Release, U.S. Department of State, "Haiti Arrests and Expels Former Haiti Telecommunications Official for US Corruption-Related Charges" (December 8, 2009), http://haiti.usembassy.gov/press_releases/haiti-arrests-and-expels-former-haiti-telecommunications-official-for-u.s.-corruption-related-charges-8-december-2009.

458. Although the FCPA does not provide for prosecution of non-U.S. officials who accept bribes, the U.S. Department of Justice charged the Haitian officials for money laundering offenses under other (non-FCPA) legal provisions. Esquenazi and Rodriguez were U.S. citizens, and Grandison was a permanent U.S. resident. Indictment, United States v. Esquenazi.

459. Ibid. pp. 27–28.

460. Press Release, U.S. Department of Justice, "Florida Businessman Pleads Guilty to Money Laundering in Foreign Bribery Scheme" (February 19, 2010).

461. Press Release, U.S. Department of Justice, "Former Haitian Government Official Pleads Guilty to Conspiracy to Commit Money Laundering in Foreign Bribery Scheme" (March 12, 2010).

462. He was also sentenced to three years of supervised release following the time in prison.

463. United States v. Antoine, No. 09-cr-21010-MARTINEZ (S.D. Fla. June 1, 2010) (order of forfeiture). *See also* Press Release, U.S. Department of Justice, "Former Haitian Government Official Sentenced to Prison for His Role in Money Laundering Conspiracy Related to Foreign Bribery Scheme" (June 2, 2010). *See also* Plea Agreement pp. 8-9, United States v. Antoine, No. 09-cr-21010 (S.D. Fla. February 19, 2010).

464. Press Release, U.S. Department of Justice, "Former Haitian Government Official Pleads Guilty to Conspiracy to Commit Money Laundering in Foreign Bribery Scheme" (March 12, 2010).

Teleco. He was sentenced to 24 months in prison and ordered to forfeit US$36,375.[465] Diaz pleaded guilty in connection with concealing US$1,028,851 in bribes while serving as an intermediary for three private telecommunications companies, and was sentenced to 57 months' imprisonment and ordered to pay US$73,824 in restitution and to forfeit US$1,028,851.[466] Fourcand entered into a plea agreement pursuant to which he agreed to forfeit US$18,500 to the United States[467] and was sentenced to six months in prison.[468]

As of end of July 2011, Esquenzi and Rodriguez's trial was ongoing.[469] Duperval and Grandison's trial was scheduled to commence on August 1, 2011.[470] On July 13, 2011, the United States also handed down a superseding indictment against new defendants, including former director general of Haiti Teleco Patrick Joseph and other companies and individuals, as well as additional charges against Duperval and Grandison.[471] At the time of writing, trial has not yet been set for the newly added defendants.[472]

---

465. Press Release, U.S. Department of Justice, "Former Comptroller of a Miami-Dade Telecommunications Company Sentenced to 24 Months in Prison for His Role in Foreign Bribery Scheme" (January 21, 2011).

466. Plea Agreement at 2, United States v. Diaz, No. 09-20346-Cr-JEM (April 21, 2010). Press Release, U.S. Department of Justice, "Florida Businessman Sentenced to 57 Months in Prison for Role in Foreign Bribery Scheme" (July 30, 2010).

467. Plea Agreement p. 8, United States v. Fourcand, No. 10-20062-cr-JEM (S.D. Fla. February 19, 2010).

468. Press Release, U.S. Department of Justice, "Former Haitian Government Official Sentenced to Prison for His Role in Money Laundering Conspiracy Related to Foreign Bribery Scheme" (June 2, 2010).

469. Court Docket Report as of July 27, 2011, U.S. v. Esquenazi, et al, No. 1:09-cr-21010-JEM-4 (S.D. Fla.)

470. Order Regarding the Sequence of Trials, U.S. v. Esquenazi, et al, No. 1:09-cr-21010-JEM-4 (S.D. Fla. May 27, 2011)

471. Superseding Indictment, U.S. v. Vaconez Cruz, et al., No. 1:09-cr-21010-JEM-4 (S.D. Fla. July 13, 2011).

472. Docket Report as of July 27, 2011, U.S. v. Esquenazi, et al, No. 1:09-cr-21010-JEM-4 (S.D. Fla.).

Appendix E.   An Overview of Corporate Vehicles in Selected Jurisdictions

TABLE E.1 Companies

Country	Information registered	Is there a residency requirement?	Bearer shares permitted?	Corporate directors permitted?	Nominee directors permitted?	Foreign companies registered?	References
Anguilla	Physical address ✓ Registered office ✓ Registered agent ✓ Managers/directors Legal owners Officers	No	No	✓	✓	✓	Companies Act 2000, §§1, 5(1), 7, 28(5), 99, 188
Antigua and Barbuda	Physical address ✓ Registered office Registered agent ✓ Managers/directors ✓ Legal owners Officers	✓	No	No	✓	✓	Companies Act 1995, §§4, 29(2), 62(2), 69, 99, 176, 340
Bahamas, The	Physical address Registered office ✓ Registered agent Managers/directors Legal owners Officers	No	No (Warrants permitted)	✓	✓	✓	Companies Act 1992, §§3, 6, 48, 118; Business Licenses Act 1980; International Business Companies Act 2000, §§181, 184, 185

Jurisdiction	Information maintained						Ownership restriction	Bearer shares				Legal references
Belize	Physical address ✓	Registered office	Registered agent ✓	Managers/directors	Legal owners	Officers	No	Immobilized (Warrants permitted)	✓	✓	✓	Regulations of June 2001; Companies Act, §§5, 38, 251
Bermuda	Physical address	Registered office ✓	Registered agent	Managers/directors	Legal owners	Officers	60% local ownership, unless declared an Exempt Company	No	No	✓	✓	Companies Act (CA)1981, §§6, 53, 62(1-2), 91(1-2), 98, 133; CA Amendment 2009, 3rd Schedule, Part I (§114)
British Virgin Islands (BVI)	Physical address ✓	Registered office	Registered agent ✓	Managers/directors	Legal owners	Officers	No	Immobilized	✓	✓	✓	Business Companies Act (BCA) 2004, §§5, 9; BCA Amendment 2005, §§2, 55, 67–77, 132; International BCA 2000, §§185, 186
Cayman Islands	Physical address ✓	Registered office	Registered agent	Managers/directors	Legal owners	Officers	No	Immobilized	✓	✓	✓	Companies Law (CL) (2009 Revision), §§26, 163, 179, 229(1), 230

TABLE E.1 Companies (continued)

Country	Information registered	Is there a residency requirement?	Bearer shares permitted?	Corporate directors permitted?	Nominee directors permitted?	Foreign companies registered?	References
Cook Islands	Physical address Registered office Registered agent ✓ Managers/directors Legal owners ✓ Officers	No	Immobilized (Warrants permitted)	✓	No	✓	International Companies Act (ICA) 1981–82, §§13, 35(1), 36, 83, 91, 201, 226A; ICA Amendment 2003, No. 5, §35A
Cyprus	✓ Physical address ✓ Registered office ✓ Registered agent ✓ Managers/directors ✓ Legal owners ✓ Officers	To be resident, company must be managed in Cyprus (not just incorporated)	No (Warrants permitted)	✓	✓	✓ Requires permit of the Central Bank of Cyprus	Companies Law, Ch. 113, §§14, 75, 81, 102, 192, 197, 347; Cyprus Income Tax Law, No. N118 (I), 2002
Czech Republic	Physical address Registered office Registered agent ✓ Managers/directors ✓ Legal owners ✓ Officers	No	Dematerialized (Warrants permitted)	No	✓	✓	Commercial Code (Act No. 513/1991 Coll.), §§24, 28, 62, 156, 175, 184(5), 194(5,7), 217a

Jurisdiction	Information						Legal reference
Delaware, United States	Physical address Registered office ✓ Registered agent ✓ Managers/directors Legal owners Officers	No	No	No	No	✓ ✓	Delaware Code, Title 8, Ch.1, §§101, 132, 141(a), 145, 158, 371
Dubai, United Arab Emirates	Physical address Registered office ✓ Registered agent Managers/directors ✓ Legal owners Officers	No	No	No	No	✓ ✓	Companies Law 2009, DIFC Law No. 2 of 2009, Art. 11, 38, 51, 115
Florida, United States	Physical address ✓ Registered office ✓ Registered agent ✓ Managers/directors ✓ Legal owners Officers ✓	No	No	No	No	✓ ✓	Florida Business Corp. Act, §607 (203, 723, 802, 850, 1401, 1501, 1503); OECD Tax Co-operation 2009, "Towards a Level Playing Field," p.122

(continued next page)

Country	Information registered	Is there a residency requirement?	Bearer shares permitted?	Corporate directors permitted?	Nominee directors permitted?	Foreign companies registered?	References
Gibraltar	Physical address ✓ Registered office Registered agent ✓ Managers/directors Legal owners Officers	No	No	✓	✓	✓	Companies Ordinance, §§14, 15, 63, 136, 289
Guernsey	Physical address ✓ Registered office ✓ Registered agent ✓ Managers/directors Legal owners Officers	No	No	✓	✓	✓	Companies (Guernsey) Law 2008 §§14, 15, 17, 75, 77(e), 132, 143; Bailiwick of Guernsey Law 2000
Hong Kong SAR, China	Physical address ✓ Registered office Registered agent ✓ Managers directors ✓ Legal owners ✓ Officers ✓	Company secretary must be resident	No (Warrants permitted)	✓	✓	✓	Hong Kong Companies Ordinance, §§14, 73, 153(B), 154, 333

Jurisdiction	Information held on						Legal basis
Isle of Man (1)	Physical address Registered office ✓ Registered agent ✓ Managers/directors Legal owners Officers	No	No	✓	✓	✓	Companies Act 1931, §§ 12, 64, 312
Isle of Man (2) *New Manx Vehicle (NMV)*	Physical address Registered office ✓ Registered agent ✓ Managers/directors Legal owners Officers	No	No	✓ Must be licensed	✓	✓	Companies Act 2006, §§ 2, 30, 74, 91, 112, 162
Jersey	Physical address Registered office ✓ Registered agent Managers/directors Legal owners Officers	No	No	No[a]	✓	–	Companies (Jersey) Law 1991, Art. 3, 7, 42, 73, 77
Liechtenstein	Physical address Registered office Registered agent Managers/directors ✓ Legal owners Officers	1 board member must be a citizen of an EEA state and have a permanent office in Liechtenstein	✓[b]	✓	✓	–	Personen- und Gesellschaftsrecht, Art. 180, 279, 291, 263; Ordinance of 11 Jan 2005 on Due Diligence Act, Art. 3; OECD Tax Co-operation 2009, "Towards a Level Playing Field," p.214

(continued next page)

TABLE E.1	Companies *(continued)*						
Country	Information registered	Is there a residency requirement?	Bearer shares permitted?	Corporate directors permitted?	Nominee directors permitted?	Foreign companies registered?	References
Luxembourg	Physical address ✓ Registered office Registered agent ✓ Managers/directors Legal owners Officers	No	✓ AML rules require ID of beneficial owner	✓	✓	✓	Loi concernant les Sociétés Commerciales 27, (10 August 1915), Art. 11, 27, 51; OECD Tax Co-operation 2009, "Towards a Level Playing Field," p.221, fn.3
Mauritius	Physical address ✓ Registered office ✓ Registered agent ✓ Managers/directors ✓ Legal owners Officers	No	No	No	✓	✓	Companies Act2001, §§23, 49, 88, 131, 133, 161, 276
Netherlands Antilles	✓ Physical address ✓ Registered office ✓ Registered agent ✓ Managers/directors Legal owners ✓ Officers	One resident managing director	✓c	✓	✓	–	Netherlands Antilles Commercial Code, Art. 33-155; Civil Code,Art. 19; National Decree of Dec. 22, 2009, implementation of Art. 20 of the Trade Register Ordinance (2009 Trade Register Decree), Art. 15

Jurisdiction	Information kept					Legal references
Nevada, United States	Physical address — No Registered office ✓ Registered agent ✓ Managers/directors ✓ Legal owners Officers	No	No	No	✓	–	Nevada Revised Statutes, §§78.030, 78.035, 78.235(1), 78.115, 77.310
Nevis	Physical address — No Registered office ✓ Registered agent Managers/directors ✓ Legal owners Officers	Immobilized	No ✓Corporate directors must have individuals as directors	✓	✓	Nevis Business Corporations Ordinance 1999, §25; Companies Act 1996 (No. 22 of 1996), §§4, 51, 72, 73, 195
Ontario, Canada	Physical address — No Registered office ✓ Registered agent Managers/directors ✓ Legal owners Officers	Dematerialized	No	✓	–	Business Corporations Act, §§5, 14, 100, 118, 119, 136; Securities Transfer Act 2006
Panama	Physical address — No Registered office Registered agent ✓ Managers/directors ✓ Legal owners Officers	✓d	No	✓	✓	Commercial Code Decree-Law No. 32 of 1927, Decree-Law No. 5 of 1997, Articles 1, 2, 6, 28, 49, 90

(continued next page)

Country	Information registered	Is there a residency requirement?	Bearer shares permitted?	Corporate directors permitted?	Nominee directors permitted?	Foreign companies registered?	References
Seychelles	Physical address ✓ Registered office Registered agent Managers/directors Legal owners Officers	No	No	No	✓	✓	Companies Ordinance 1972, §§3, 10, 21, 100, 164, 310
Singapore	✓ Physical address ✓ Registered office Registered agent ✓ Managers/directors Legal owners ✓ Officers	At least one director must be ordinarily resident	No	No	✓	✓	Companies Act, Ch. 50, §§19, 66, 126, 145, 171, 172, 367; Business Registration Act, Ch. 32, §6
South Africa (1) *Company*	✓ Physical address ✓ Registered office Registered agent ✓ Managers/directors Legal owners Officers	No	No	✓[e]	✓	✓	Companies Act 2008, §§14, 19, 23, 50, 51, 56, 66, 69, 78

Jurisdiction	Information required		Immobilized				Legal reference
St. Kitts	Physical address Registered office ✓ Registered agent ✓ Managers/directors Legal owners Officers ✓	No		✓ Must have individuals as directors	✓	✓	Companies Act 1996 (No. 22 of 1996), §§4, 8, 51, 72, 73, 195
St. Lucia	Physical address – Registered office Registered agent Managers/directors Legal owners Officers	–	–	–	–	–	*To conduct local business, incorporate under Companies Act No.19 of 1996. (Could not be obtained)*
St. Vincent and the Grenadines	Physical address Registered office ✓ Registered agent ✓ Managers/directors Legal owners Officers	No	No	✓	✓	✓	The Companies Act, No. 8 of 1994, §§4, 9, 29, 62, 69, 176, 340

(continued next page)

Country	Information registered	Is there a residency requirement?	Bearer shares permitted?	Corporate directors permitted?	Nominee directors permitted?	Foreign companies registered?	References
Switzerland	✓ Physical address Registered office ✓ Registered agent Managers/directors Legal owners Officers	Directors may be foreigners residing abroad. Someonewho can sign for the company (not necessarily a director) must be resident	✓f	No	–	–	Code of Obligations, Ordinanza sul registro di commercio del 17 ottobre 2007 (Stato 1° gennaio 2008), Art. 66–68
Turks and Caicos	✓ Physical address ✓ Registered office Registered agent Managers/directors Legal owners Officers	No	Immobilized	✓	✓	✓	Turks and Caicos, Companies Ordinance (CO) 1998, Ch.122,§§4, 32, 208; CO (Amendment), 2001: Business Names Ordinance, (5); CO 1981 (as amended), (6)
United Kingdom	✓ Physical address ✓ Registered office ✓ Registered agent ✓ Managers/directors Legal owners ✓ Officers	No	✓g	✓ *At least one director must be an individual*	✓	–	Companies Act 2006, Parts 2, 9, 12, 21 (783, 779), Part 10 (155, 232)

Uruguay	✓	Physical address	No	Dematerialized	–	–	–	Ley N° 16.060 Sociedades Comerciales, art. 13; Ley N° 17.904, art. 13, 16; OECD Tax Co-operation 2009, "Towards a Level Playing Field," (2009), p. 221
	✓	Registered office						
		Registered agent						
	✓	Managers/directors						
		Legal owners						
	✓	Officers						
Wyoming, United States		Physical address	No	No	No	✓	✓	Wyoming Business Corporation Act, §17-16-201, -202, -625, -723, -802, -803, -851, -1801; §17-17-102
	✓	Registered office						
	✓	Registered agent						
		Managers/directors						
		Legal owners						
		Officers						

Note: a. Unless the company is permitted under its registration under the Financial Services (Jersey) Law 1998 to act as, or fulfill the requirements of, a director; and the company has no director that is a company.
b. AML rules require that at least one person acting as director of an entity that does not conduct any business in its country of domicile is obliged to identify and record the beneficial owner.
c. AML rules also provide a mechanism to identify owners of companies: see OECD Tax Co-operation 2009, "Towards a Level Playing Field: 2009 Assessment by the Global forum on Transparency and Exchange of Information" (2009), p. 221, fn. 3.
d. AML regulations allow for identifying holders of bearer shares. OECD Tax Co-operation 2009, "Towards a Level Playing Field: 2009 Assessment by the Global forum on Transparency and Exchange of Information"(2009), p. 216: "Regulations are in place requiring financial institutions, including trust companies, and registered agents to identify their clients and thus to identify the holders of registered and bearer shares."
e. Corporate directors cannot be foreign companies or trusts: see Companies Act, 2008, s. 69 (7): A person is ineligible to be a director of a company if the person . . . is a juristic person (s. 1: a "juristic person" includes (a) a foreign company; and (b) a trust, irrespective of whether or not it was established within or outside the Republic).
f. OECD Tax Co-operation 2009, "Towards a Level Playing Field: 2009 Assessment by the Global forum on Transparency and Exchange of Information" (2009), p. 221, fn. 3.
g. OECD Tax Co-operation 2009, "Towards a Level Playing Field: 2009 Assessment by the Global forum on Transparency and Exchange of Information" (2009), p. 221, fn. 3.

TABLE E.2 Exempt/International Business Companies

Country	Information registered	Is there a residency requirement?	Local business permitted?	Bearer shares permitted?	Bearer share warrants permitted?	Corporate directors permitted?	Nominee directors permitted?	References
Anguilla	✓ Physical address ✓ Registered office Registered agent Managers/directors Legal owners Officers	No	No	Immobilized	✓	✓	✓	Custody of Bearer Shares Regulations, Revised Regulations of Anguilla: I20-3, §§2–3; International Business Companies Act 2000, §§7, 16(1)(a & g). 39, 56
Antigua and Barbuda	✓ Physical address ✓ Registered office ✓ Registered agent ✓ Managers/directors Legal owners Officers	No	No	Dematerialized	✓	✓	✓	International Business Corporations Act, §§5, 61, 97, 111(5),130(2);Companies Act, §344; Corporate Management and Service Providers Act
Bahamas, The	✓ Physical address ✓ Registered office ✓ Registered agent Managers/directors Legal owners Officers	No	Must be licensed	No	–	–	✓	International Business Companies Act 2000, §§4, 13, 10, 40, 58, 187; Business Licenses Act 1980

Jurisdiction	Information required to be held						Legal basis
Belize	Physical address / Registered office ✓ / Registered agent ✓ / Managers/directors / Legal owners / Officers	No	—	Yes (Must be kept with local TCSP)	✓	✓	✓	International Business Companies Act 1990, as amended in 2000, §§3, 9, 12, 47, 63; Regulations of June 2001
Bermuda	Physical address / Registered office ✓ / Registered agent / Managers/directors / Legal owners / Officers	At least 2 directors, or secretary and director, or a secretary and a resident representative	Must be licensed	—	—	—	Companies Act 1981, §§129, 130
British Virgin Islands (BVI)							
Cayman Islands	Physical address / Registered office ✓ / Registered agent / Managers/directors / Legal owners / Officers	No	No	No	No	✓	✓	Companies Law (2009 Revision), §§26, 163, 179, 229(1), 230; Companies Law (2009 Revision)

(continued next page)

TABLE E.2	Exempt/International Business Companies *(continued)*							
Country	Information registered	Is there a residency requirement?	Local business permitted?	Bearer shares permitted?	Bearer share warrants permitted?	Corporate directors permitted?	Nominee directors permitted?	References
Cook Islands								
Cyprus								
Czech Republic								
Delaware, United States								
Dubai, United Arab Emirates								
Florida, United States								
Gibraltar								
Guernsey								
Hong Kong SAR, China								
Isle of Man								
Jersey								
Liechtenstein								
Luxembourg								

	Physical address Registered office Registered agent Managers/directors Legal owners Officers	At least two directors must be a resident individual; Shareholders must be nonresident	May conduct specified activities within Mauritius					Financial Services Act 2007, as described in Circular Letter (CL201207) of 21 December 2007 entitled "New Conceptual Approach to Global Business"; Companies Act, §23
Mauritius (2) Global business *company category 1 (GBC1)*	Registered office ✓ Managers/directors ✓ Legal owners ✓	At least two directors must be a resident individual; Shareholders must be nonresident	—	—	—	—	—	Financial Services Act 2007, as described in Circular Letter (CL201207) of 21 December 2007 entitled "New Conceptual Approach to Global Business"; Companies Act, §23
Mauritius (3) Global business company category 2 (GBC2)	Physical address Registered office ✓ Registered agent ✓ Managers/directors ✓ Legal owners ✓ Officers	*Shareholders must be nonresident; at least one director must be a resident*	No	—	—	—	—	Financial Services Act 2007, as described in Circular Letter (CL201207) of 21 December 2007 entitled "New Conceptual Approach to Global Business"; Companies Act, §23
Netherlands Antilles								
Nevada, United States								

(continued next page)

TABLE E.2	Exempt/International Business Companies *(continued)*							
Country	Information registered	Is there a residency requirement?	Local business permitted?	Bearer shares permitted?	Bearer share warrants permitted?	Corporate directors permitted?	Nominee directors permitted?	References
Nevis	Physical address Registered office ✓ Registered agent Managers/directors Legal owners Officers	*No*	No	Immobilized	✓	✓	✓	Nevis Business Corporation Ordinance 1984, §§21, 31, 56, 123
Ontario, Canada								
Panama								
Seychelles	Physical address ✓ Registered office ✓ Registered agent Managers/directors Legal owners Officers	*No*	No	No	No	✓	✓	International Business Companies Act 1994, §§5, 12, 15, 41, 56, 82
Singapore								

Jurisdiction								Legal basis
South Africa								
St. Kitts	Physical address	*No*	–	–	–	–	–	Companies Act 1996 (No. 22 of 1996), §§195, 206
	Registered office	✓						
	Registered agent	✓						
	Managers/directors	✓						
	Legal owners							
	Officers	✓						
St. Lucia	Physical address	*No*	✓	✓	No	No	No	International Business Companies Act 1999, §§4, 7, 28, 42, 57
	Registered office	✓						
	Registered agent	✓						
	Managers/directors							
	Legal owners							
	Officers							
St. Vincent and the Grenadines	Physical address	*No*	✓	✓	✓	Immobilized	No	International Business Companies (Amendment and Consolidation) Act 2007, §§4–7, 11, 14, 29, 30, 84
	Registered office	✓						
	Registered agent	✓						
	Managers/directors							
	Legal owners							
	Officers							

(continued next page)

Exempt/International Business Companies *(continued)*

Country	Information registered	Is there a residency requirement?	Local business permitted?	Bearer shares permitted?	Bearer share warrants permitted?	Corporate directors permitted?	Nominee directors permitted?	References
Switzerland								
Turks and Caicos	✓ Physical address ✓ Registered office ✓ Registered agent Managers/directors Legal owners Officers	No	No	Immobilized	–	–	–	Companies Ordinance (CO) 1998, Ch.122. §§4, 32, 180, 192, 208; CO (Amendment) 2001; Business Names (Registration) Ordinance, §5
United Kingdom								
Uruguay								
Wyoming, United States								

Source: Authors' compilation.
Note: TCSP = trust and company service providers.

TABLE E.3	Limited Liability Companies				
Country	Entity registered?	Residency Requirement?	Corporate members permitted?	Nominee members permitted?	References
Anguilla	Physical address ✓ Registered office Registered agent ✓ Managers/directors Legal owners Officers	No	✓	—	Limited Liability Company Act, §28, 11
Antigua and Barbuda	Physical address Registered office Registered agent ✓ Managers/directors Legal owners Officers	No	✓	✓	Antigua and Barbuda International Limited Liability Companies Act 2007, §§12, 17
Bahamas, The					
Belize					
Bermuda					
British Virgin Islands (BVI)					The BVI Business Companies Act 2004, §244, permits the Executive Council to make regulations for the formation, management, and operation of LLCs
Cayman Islands					

(continued next page)

Country	Entity registered?	Residency Requirement?	Corporate members permitted?	Nominee members permitted?	References
Cook Islands	Physical address Registered office ✓ Registered agent ✓ Managers/directors Legal owners Officers	No	No	✓	Limited Liability Companies Act 2008, §§11, 12, 26
Cyprus					
Czech Republic	Physical address Registered office Registered agent Managers/directors ✓ Legal owners ✓ Officers ✓	No	No	No, but one individual may not be a member of more than 3 LLCs	Commercial Code (Act No. 513/1991 Coll.), §§24, 28, 62, 105
Delaware, United States	Physical address Registered office ✓ Registered agent ✓ Managers/directors Legal owners Officers	No	No	✓	Delaware Code, Title 6, Ch.18, §§ 18-301, 18-902.; Certificate of formation must be filed with Secretary of State; foreign LLC must be registered; LLC Act, Ch.II, s. 18-201(a)(2)

Jurisdiction	Information required				
Dubai, United Arab Emirates	Physical address ✓ Registered office Registered agent ✓ Managers/directors Legal owners Officers	No	No	✓	Companies Law 2009, DIFC Law No. 2 of 2009, Art. 11
Florida, United States	✓ Physical address ✓ Registered office ✓ Registered agent Managers/directors Legal owners Officers	No	✓	✓	Florida Limited Liability Company Act, §§608.407(1), 608.409, 608.501
Gibraltar					
Guernsey					
Hong Kong SAR, China					
Isle of Man	✓ Physical address ✓ Registered office ✓ Registered agent ✓ Managers/directors ✓ Legal owners Officers	No	✓	✓	Limited Liability Companies Act 1996, §§4–7
Jersey					

(continued next page)

TABLE E.3 Limited Liability Companies (continued)

Country	Entity registered?	Residency Requirement?	Corporate members permitted?	Nominee members permitted?	References
Liechtenstein					
Luxembourg	✓ Physical address Registered office Registered agent ✓ Managers/directors Legal owners Officers	No	–	–	Loi concernant les Sociétés Commerciales 27, (10 August 1915), §§11bis
Mauritius					
Netherlands Antilles					
Nevada, United States	✓ Physical address ✓ Registered office ✓ Registered agent ✓ Managers/directors Legal owners Officers	No	✓	✓	Nevada Revised Statutes, §§77, 86
Nevis	✓ Physical address ✓ Registered office ✓ Registered agent Managers/directors	No	✓	✓	Nevis Limited Liability Company Ordinance 1995, §§21, 26, 37, 47, 83

Jurisdiction	Information				Legal basis
Ontario, Canada	Legal owners	✓			
	Officers	✓			
Panama	Physical address		No	✓	Law No. 4 of 2009 (Replaced Law No. 24 of 1966), Art. 5, 38
	Registered office	✓			
	Registered agent	✓			
	Managers/directors	✓			
	Legal owners	✓			
	Officers				
Seychelles					
Singapore					
South Africa					
St. Kitts					
St. Lucia					
St. Vincent and the Grenadines	Physical address	✓	No	✓	Limited Liability Companies Act 2008, §§12, 34, 76
	Registered office	✓			
	Registered agent				
	Managers/directors	✓			
	Legal owners				
	Officers				
Switzerland	Physical address	✓	✓[a]	–	Art. 814 Code of Obligations; Ordinanza sul registro di commercio del 17 ottobre 2007 (Stato 1° gennaio 2008), Art. 73
	Registered office	✓	–		
	Registered agent	✓			

(continued next page)

TABLE E.3 Limited Liability Companies (continued)

Country	Entity registered?	Residency Requirement?	Corporate members permitted?	Nominee members permitted?	References
	✓ Managers/directors ✓ Legal owners Officers				
Turks and Caicos	Physical address ✓ Registered office Registered agent Managers/directors Legal owners Officers	No	✓	✓	Turks and Caicos, Companies Ordinance 1998
United Kingdom					
Uruguay					
Wyoming, United States	Physical address Registered office ✓ Registered agent ✓ Managers/directors Legal owners Officers	No	✓	✓	Wyoming Limited Liability Company Act, §§17-15-106; 17-15-107

Source: Authors' compilation.
Note: a. Managers can be foreigners residing abroad, though each Swiss AG (stock company) must have someone, not necessarily a director, resident in Switzerland who can sign or act for the company.

TABLE E.4	Partnerships				
Country	Entity registered?	Is there a residency requirement?	Nominee partners permitted?	Corporate partners permitted?	References
Anguilla					
Antigua and Barbuda	No	No	✓	✓	Governed by the Partnership Act, which does not discuss restrictions on partners
Bahamas, The	No	No	✓	✓	Partnership Act, §3
Belize					
Bermuda	✓	No	✓	✓	Partnership Act 1902 (1989 Revision)
British Virgin Islands (BVI)					
Cayman Islands	No	No	✓	✓	Partnership Law (1995 Revision), §47
Cook Islands					
Cyprus	✓	No	✓	✓	Partnership and Business Names Law, §§50, 53
Czech Republic	✓	No	✓	No	Commercial Code (Act No. 513/1991 Coll.), §§24, 62
Delaware, United States	No	No	✓	✓	The Delaware Code, Title 6, Ch.15 §15-202
Dubai, United Arab Emirates	✓	No	✓	✓	Dubai General Partnership Law 2004, Art. 12, 13
Florida, United States					
Gibraltar	No	No	✓	✓	Partnership Act

(continued next page)

TABLE E.4 Partnerships *(continued)*

Country	Entity registered?	Is there a residency requirement?	Nominee partners permitted?	Corporate partners permitted?	References
Guernsey	No	No	✓	✓	The Partnership (Guernsey) Law 1995
Hong Kong SAR, China	No	No	✓	✓	Partnership Ordinance
Isle of Man	No	No	✓	✓	Partnership Act 1909, Part I
Jersey	✓	No	✓	✓	Limited Partnership (Jersey) Law 1994, Art. 4
Liechtenstein					
Luxembourg	✓ List of partners to be kept at registry	No	–	–	Loi concernant les Sociétés Commerciales 27, (10 August 1915); Loi du 19 decembre 2002 concernant le registre de commerce et des sociétés…. Art. 6
Mauritius					
Netherlands Antilles	✓	–	–	–	
Nevada, United States	No	No	✓	✓	Nevada Revised Statutes, §87.4322
Nevis					
Ontario, Canada	No	No	✓	✓	Partnership Act, §3
Panama	No	No	✓	✓	
Seychelles					
Singapore	No	No	✓	✓	Partnership Act 1994, Ch. 391, §2

Jurisdiction					
South Africa					
St. Kitts					
St. Lucia	Optional	No	✓	✓	Limited Partnerships Act 1996, §4
St. Vincent and the Grenadines					
Switzerland	✓	–	–	–	
Turks and Caicos					
United Kingdom	No	No	✓	✓	Partnership Act 1890, §2
Uruguay	–	No	–	–	
Wyoming, United States	No	No	✓	✓	Wyoming Uniform Partnership Act, §17-21-202

Source: Authors' compilation.

TABLE E.5   Limited Partnerships

Country	Entity registered?	Is there a residency requirement?	Nominee partners permitted?	Corporate partners permitted?	References
Anguilla	✓	✓	–	–	Limited Partnership Act 2000
Antigua and Barbuda					
Bahamas, The					
Belize					
Bermuda	✓	No	✓	✓	The Limited Partnership Amendment Act 2009
British Virgin Islands (BVI)	✓	No	–	–	The Partnership Act 1996, §§53, 84
Cayman Islands					
Cook Islands	✓	One partner must be a foreign company, international company or a TCSP and each partner must be nonresident	✓	✓	International Partnerships Act 1984, §55
Cyprus	✓	No	✓	✓	Partnership and Business Names Law, §§50, 53
Czech Republic	✓	No	✓	✓	Commercial Code (Act No. 513/1991 Coll.), §§24, 62
Delaware, United States	✓	No	✓	✓	Delaware Code, Title 6, Ch.17 §§17-401, 17-902

Jurisdiction					Law
Dubai, United Arab Emirates	✓	No	✓	✓	Dubai Limited Partnership Law, DIFC Law No. 4 of 2006, Art. 11, 12, 45
Florida, United States	✓	No	✓	✓	Florida Revised Uniform Limited Partnership Act of 2005, §§620.1201, 620.9102
Gibraltar	✓	No	✓	✓	Limited Partnership Act
Guernsey	✓	No	✓	✓	Limited Partnerships (Guernsey) Law 1995
Hong Kong SAR, China	✓	No	✓	✓	Limited Partnerships Ordinance
Isle of Man	✓	No	✓	✓	Partnership Act 1909, Part II, §48
Jersey					
Liechtenstein					
Luxembourg	✓ List of partners to be kept at registry	No	–	–	Loi concernant les Sociétés Commerciales 27, (10 August 1915); Loi du 19 decembre 2002 concernant le registre de commerce et des sociétés...., Art. 6
Mauritius	–	At least one member must be resident	–	✓	Limited Partnerships Bill 2009
Netherlands Antilles	✓				
Nevada, United States	✓ Filing with the Secretary of State required	No	✓	✓	Nevada Revised Statutes, §88.350
Nevis	✓	No	✓	✓	Limited Partnerships Act 1996, §§3, 4

An Overview of Corporate Vehicles in Selected Jurisdictions | 249

TABLE E.5 Limited Partnerships *(continued)*

Country	Entity registered?	Is there a residency requirement?	Nominee partners permitted?	Corporate partners permitted?	References
Ontario, Canada	✓	No	✓	✓	Limited Partnership Act, §3
Panama					
Seychelles	✓	At least one general partner must be resident (or a local company, local partnership or IBC)	✓	✓	Limited Partnership Act 2003, §§4, 5
Singapore	✓	*Where all partners are nonresident, registrar may appoint a local manager*	✓	✓	Limited Partnerships Act, Ch. 163B, 2009, §§10, 28
South Africa					
St. Kitts					
St. Lucia	Optional	No	✓	✓	International Partnership Act 2006, §§4, 14
St. Vincent and the Grenadines					
Switzerland	✓	–	–	–	

Jurisdiction			At least one general partner must be resident or incorporated in the Islands or if the partner is a partnership then at least one of the partners of the partnership must be resident or incorporated in the Islands		
Turks and Caicos	✓	✓		✓	Turks and Caicos, Limited Partnership Ordinance 1992, Ch.126, §§ 4, 7, 15
United Kingdom	✓	✓	No	✓	Limited Partnerships Act 1907, §§4, 5
Uruguay					
Wyoming, United States	✓	✓	No	✓	Limited Partnership Act, §§17-14-301, -1002

Source: Authors' compilation.
Note: IBC = international business corporation; TCSP = trust and company service providers.

TABLE E.6 Trusts

Country	Entity registered?	Is there a residency requirement?	Flee clauses prohibited?	Settlor can be other parties in the trust?	References
Anguilla	Optional	Where beneficiary is resident, and no trustee is resident, beneficiary may apply for resident trustee to be appointed	No	Settlor may be the trustee, beneficiary, or protector	Trusts Act 2000, §§8, 66
Antigua and Barbuda					
Bahamas, The	No	No	No	Settlor may be beneficiary, cotrustee, or protector	Trustee Act1998, §§3, 94; Registration of Records Act, Ch.187
Belize	Optional	No	No	Settlor may be beneficiary, trustee, or protector	Trusts Act 2000, §§4 (3–6), 9, 13, 20, 63
Bermuda	No	No	No	Settlor may retain certain rights and powers, trustee may be beneficiary	Trusts (Special Provisions) Act 1989, §§2, 12
British Virgin Islands (BVI) (2)	No	At least one trustee must be a BVI TCSP	Not allowed following court order, criminal proceedings or investigations	Settlor not prohibited from being a cotrustee, protector, or beneficiary	Trustee (Amendment) Act 2003, §11; BVI Trustee Act 1961, §§2, 81, 86

BVI (2) – Virgin Islands Special Trust (VISTA)	No	Trust deed must provide appointment of enforcer and at least one trustee must be a "designated person" (essentially a BVI licensed trustee)	No	No restrictions on settlor's role	Virgin Islands Special Trusts Act 2003
Cayman Islands	No	No	No	Settlor may be cotrustee, protector, or beneficiary	Trusts Law (2009 Revision), §§13, 14, 89; Tasarruf Meduati Sigorta Fonu v. Merrill Lynch Bank and Trust Company (Cayman) Ltd of 9 Sept 2009, provided confirmation that 'reserved powers' legislation is upheld in its home jurisdictions
Cook Islands	No	Only used by local residents	–	–	–
Cyprus	No	Either the settlor or any of the beneficiaries is a Cypriot	–	–	Companies Law, Ch.113, §112; Cyprus Trustees Law, Ch. 193
Czech Republic					

(continued next page)

Country	Entity registered?	Is there a residency requirement?	Flee clauses prohibited?	Settlor can be other parties in the trust?	References
Delaware (1) Common Law Trust	No	No	—	Settlor can create an irrevocable trust, where the settlor is a beneficiary, while retaining various interests in, and powers over, the trust	Delaware Code, Title 12, Ch. 35, §3556; Qualified Dispositions in Trust Act, 12 Del. C. §3570 et seq. (1997)
Delaware (2) Statutory Trust	Certificate of Trust must be filed with Secretary of State	One trustee must be resident in Delaware	No	Settlor may be beneficiary; any person may be manager of trust	Delaware Code, Title 12, Ch. 38 §§3801, 3802, 3806–7, 3807, 3852
Dubai, United Arab Emirates Trust (cont.)	No	No	No	No restrictions on settlor's role	DIFC Trust Law of 2005, Articles 23, 24, 29, 68
Country	Entity registered?	Is there a residency requirement?	Flee clauses prohibited?	Settlor can be other parties in the trust?	References
Florida, United States	No	No	No	No restrictions on settlor's role	Florida Trust Code, §§736.0401, 736.0409
Gibraltar	No, unless settlor wants to use special asset protection under bankruptcy ordinance	No	No	No restrictions on settlor's role	Registered Trust Act, §§3, 8; Trustee Act of Gibraltar. The Registered Trust Ordinance 1999

Jurisdiction					
Guernsey	No	No	No	Settlor may revoke or amend the terms of a trust; give trustees directions in relation to investments or remove a trustee, beneficiary or enforcer; settlor or trustee of a trust may also be a beneficiary	The Trusts (Guernsey) Law 2007, §§8, 15(1), 38
Hong Kong SAR, China	No, but any interest in land, which is in writing, must be registered with the Land Registry	No	No	No restrictions on settlor's role	Hong Kong Trustee Ordinance, Ch. 29; Recognition of Trusts Ordinance, Ch. 76
Isle of Man (1)	No	No	No	No restrictions on settlor's role	Recognition of Trusts Act 1988; In Re Heginbotham's Petition 1999
Isle of Man (2) *Purpose Trust*	No	Must use at least one Isle of Man trustee	No	–	Purpose Trusts Act 1996
Jersey	No	No	No	Settlors may maintain control and a beneficial interest in the trust	Trusts (Jersey) Law 1984, Articles 7, 9, 12
Liechtenstein (1) *Private Trust*	✓ If created for longer than 12 months must be registered in the Public Register	At least one trustee must be an European Economic Area (EEA) Member State TCSP	No	Beneficiary may be trustee, but not if sole beneficiary; settlor may be beneficiary, but not if sole beneficiary	Law on Persons and Companies (PGR), LGBl 4/1/1926, Art. 897–932, 900, 902; Law on Trust Enterprises, LGBl 6/1928, PGR Art. 932a

(continued next page)

TABLE E.6 Trusts (continued)

Country	Entity registered?	Is there a residency requirement?	Flee clauses prohibited?	Settlor can be other parties in the trust?	References
Liechtenstein (2) – *Trust Enterprise*	✓	One of the trustees must be a Liechtenstein TCSP	No	Settlor may reserve rights in the trust instrument	Law on Persons and Companies (PGR), Art.932a, §§1, 7, 49
Luxembourg					
Mauritius	No	Must have local TCSP serving as a trustee; nonresident Settlors and beneficiaries may apply for GBC1 or GBC2 license	No	Settlor may also be a trustee, a beneficiary, a protector or an enforcer, but shall not be the sole beneficiary of a trust of which he is a settlor	Trusts Act 2001, §§4, 8, 19, 23, 27; Registration Duty Act, 1982 and the Transcription and Registration Act 1982
Netherlands Antilles					
Nevada, United States	Business trusts must be filed with Secretary of State	No	No	Settlor may maintain power to amend trust	Nevada Revised Statutes, Ch. 88 (Business Trusts); Nevada Revised Statutes, §63.160
Nevis	All International Trusts and qualified foreign Trusts must be registered with the Registrar of International Trusts	No	No	*Settlor may be a protector, trustee, or beneficiary*	International Exempt Trust Ordinance 1994, §§9, 37, 47

Ontario, Canada	No					
			No		No restrictions on settlor's role	Trustee Act
Panama	No, only trusts holding property in Panama must be registered	No	Agent must be Panamanian lawyer	No	Settlor can be a beneficiary of the trust but cannot administer any of its assets; settlor cannot be the trustee	Law No. 1 of 1984
Seychelles	Must file a brief declaration by the licensed resident trustee with the Government Registry	No	Settlor may not be a Seychelles resident (under international trust)	No	*Settlor may be the enforcer; can also be a beneficiary under the international trust (but not a sole beneficiary)*	International Trust Act 1994, §§4, 13, 14, 17, 75, 76
Singapore *(foreign trust)*	No	No	Every settlor and beneficiary must be either (a) individuals who are neither citizens nor residents of Singapore or (b) foreign companies, including unit trusts beneficially owned wholly by such individuals or foreign companies	No	*Trustee may delegate power to settlor (not to beneficiaries).*	The Trustees (Amendment) Act 2004 and The Trust Companies Act 2005

(continued next page)

TABLE E.6 Trusts (continued)

Country	Entity registered?	Is there a residency requirement?	Flee clauses prohibited?	Settlor can be other parties in the trust?	References
South Africa	✓	No	No		Trust Property Control Act 57 of 1988, §4
St. Kitts	✓	One trustee must be resident	No	Settlor may retain control; settlor or beneficiary may be protector	Trusts Act 1996, §§4, 19, 25, 95
St. Lucia (International Trust)	No, but if registered must be by a local TCSP	No	No	Settlor may retain control[a] and be a beneficiary	International Trusts Act 1999, §§3, 7, 9, 19, 22
St. Vincent and the Grenadines (International Trust)	No (optional)	Neither the settlor or any beneficiary may be resident	No	Settlor is permitted to retain substantive control or have "reserve powers" over the trust; settlor may be beneficiary or the sole beneficiary; settlor may not be trustee; settlor may be a protector	The Companies Act, No. 8 of 1994, §186; The International Trust Act 1996, §§9, 12, 36, 52

Jurisdiction					
Switzerland					Ratified The Hague Convention on the international recognition of trusts; as financial intermediaries, trustees have the obligation to obtain an authorization from the Federal Money Laundering Control Authority or to be affiliated to an SRO (self-regulatory organization)
Turks and Caicos	No	No	No	No	The Trusts Ordinance 1998, Ch. 124, Paras. 3, 7, 9, 12
United Kingdom	Not registered unless charity	No	No	No	
Uruguay	If holding land, must be registered	No	No	Settlor can also be the beneficiary of the trust	Uruguayan Trust Law, §17.703
Wyoming, United States	No (only statutory trust must be registered)	Trustee may not be settlor and must be resident of Wyoming	No	Settlor retains power to add or remove trustees and to amend trust	Wyoming Uniform Trust Code, §§4-10-401, -403, -103, -510, -602

Source: Authors' compilation.
Note: TCSP = trust and company service providers.
a. International Trusts Act, 1999, s.19.

TABLE E.7	Foundations			
Country	Entity registered?	Is there a residency requirement?	Corporate council members permitted?	References
Anguilla	Declaration of Establishment with Registrar	Local licensed secretary and registered agent	✓	Anguilla Private Foundation Act, 13 June 2008
Antigua and Barbuda				
Bahamas, The	✓	No	–	Foundations Act 2004
Belize				
Bermuda				Foundations are typically formed as companies limited by guarantee under the Companies Act
British Virgin Islands (BVI)				Foundations are typically formed as companies limited by guarantee (with shares–Hybrid) under the Companies Act
Cayman Islands				Foundations are typically formed as companies limited by guarantee or nonprofit companies under the Companies Law
Cook Islands				Foundations may be formed as companies limited by guarantee (with shares–Hybrid) under the Companies Act
Cyprus				Foundations are typically formed as companies limited by guarantee under the Companies Act

Jurisdiction				Notes
Czech Republic	✓	For public purposes only	No	Act on Foundations and Endowment Funds and on changes and supplements of certain related acts, Act No. 227/1997, Coll. Of September 3, 1997, §§1, 5, 11, 27
Delaware, United States				Public foundation and nonprofit company tax status applied for through the Internal Revenue Service
Dubai, United Arab Emirates		No	No	
Florida, United States				Public foundation and nonprofit (must be registered[a]) tax status applied for through the Internal Revenue Service
Gibraltar				Foundations may be formed as companies limited by guarantee under the Companies Act (Gibraltar Private Foundation Ordinance 1999)
Guernsey				Foundations are typically formed as companies limited by guarantee under the Companies Law; Guernsey is currently working on new Private Interest Foundation Law
Hong Kong SAR, China				Foundations are typically formed as companies limited by guarantee under the Companies Ordinance
Isle of Man				Foundations are typically formed as companies limited by guarantee (with shares–Hybrid) under the Companies Act

(continued next page)

Country	Entity registered?	Is there a residency requirement?	Corporate council members permitted?	References
Jersey	✓ Must be registered by a Jersey TCSP	Council may consist of one or more members, and must include one Jersey TCSP	✓	*Foundations may be formed as companies limited by guarantee under the Companies Law* Companies (Jersey) Law 1991, Art. 3G; Foundations (Jersey) Law 2009, Art. 18, 21; Foundations (Continuance) (Jersey) Regulations 2009 (the Continuance Regulations)
Liechtenstein (1) *Anstalt*	✓ *Must be registered using a Liechtenstein TCSP*	At least 1 member of the Board, authorized to represent and conduct business on its behalf must have a registered office in Liechtenstein. This member must also be authorized to practice as a lawyer, trustee, or auditor, or have other qualifications recognized by the government.	✓	Law on Persons and Companies (PGR), Articles 534, 537, 541
Liechtenstein (2) *Stiftungen*	✓	—	—	Foundation (Art. 552–570 PGR); PGR §§552, 1926; 2009 Amendment to Foundation Act
Luxembourg				
Mauritius				*Foundations may also be formed as companies limited by guarantee under the Companies Act*

Jurisdiction			
Netherlands Antilles (Stichting)			Must be registered; must have at least one resident director; may not be formed for commercial business, but may be used for asset management
Nevada, United States			Public foundation and nonprofit tax status applied for through the Internal Revenue Service
Nevis	No	✓	Nevis Multiform Foundation Ordinance 2004, ss. 3, 10, 11, 17, 62
Ontario, Canada			
Panama	Charter must be filed with the Public Registry Office	✓	Law No. 25 of 1995
Seychelles	–	✓	Foundation Act 2009, ss. 3, 2, 7, 21, 27, 32, 83; International Business Companies (Amendment) Act 2009
Singapore			Foundations may be formed as companies limited by guarantee under the Companies Act (Companies Act, Ch. 50, s.17).
South Africa			
St. Kitts	No	✓	Foundations Act 2003, ss. 3, 12, 20, 64
St. Lucia			

(continued next page)

TABLE E.7	Foundations (continued)			
Country	Entity registered?	Is there a residency requirement?	Corporate council members permitted?	References
St. Vincent and the Grenadines				Foundations may also be formed as companies limited by guarantee (with shares – Hybrid) under the International Business Companies (Amendment and Consolidation) Act 2007 (International Business Companies [Amendment and Consolidation] Act 2007)
Switzerland	✓	–	–	
Turks and Caicos				Foundations may be formed as companies limited by guarantee (with shares – Hybrid) under the Companies Ordinance (Turks and Caicos, Companies Ordinance 1998, Ch.122, para. 7)
United Kingdom				Foundations may be formed as companies limited by guarantee under the Companies Act (Companies Act 2006, Part 1)
Uruguay				
Wyoming, United States				Public foundation and nonprofit company tax status applied for through the Internal Revenue Service

Source: Authors' compilation.
Note: TCSP = trust and company service providers.
a. Florida Not For Profit Corporation Act, s. 617.0203.

Glossary

Beneficial owner. The natural person who ultimately owns or controls the corporate vehicle or benefits from its assets, the person on whose behalf a transaction is being conducted, or both. Beneficial owners also include those persons who exercise ultimate effective control over a legal person or arrangement.

Chain of corporate vehicles. This term generally refers to groups of two or more corporate vehicles connected through legal ownership.

Corporate vehicles. A broad concept that refers to all forms of legal entities and legal arrangements through which a wide variety of commercial activities are conducted and assets are held (for example, corporations, trusts, partnerships, foundations, and others).[1]

Designated Non-Financial Businesses and Professions (DNFBPs). This term encompasses casinos (including Internet-based casinos), real estate agents, dealers in precious metals, dealers in precious stones, lawyers, notaries, other independent legal professionals and accountants, and trust and company service providers.

Financial Intelligence Unit (FIU). "A central, national agency responsible for receiving (and as permitted, requesting), analyzing and disseminating to the competent authorities, disclosures of financial information: (i) concerning suspected proceeds of crime and potential financing of terrorism, or (ii) required by national legislation or regulation, in order to combat money laundering and terrorism financing."[2]

Foundation. A foundation is a legal entity that consists of a property that has been transferred into it to serve a particular purpose and has no owners or shareholders. Foundations are ordinarily managed by a board of directors, according to the terms of a foundation document or constitution. Some jurisdictions restrict foundations to public purposes (public foundations); other jurisdictions allow foundations to be established to fulfill private purposes (private foundations).

Gatekeeper. Includes accountants, lawyers, financial consultants, or other professionals holding accounts at a financial institution and acting on behalf of their clients, either knowingly or unwittingly, to move or conceal the proceeds of illegal activity. A criminal

---

1. For detailed discussion of the term "corporate vehicles" and selected forms of corporate vehicles, please see appendix C of this report.
2. Definition adopted at the plenary meeting of the Egmont Group, Rome, Italy, November 1996; as amended at the Egmont plenary meeting, Guernsey, June 2004.

may seek to use the gatekeeper to access the financial system, while remaining anonymous themselves.[3]

Grand corruption. A broad range of offenses, including bribery, embezzlement, trading in influence, misappropriation of state funds, illicit enrichment, and abuse of office committed by high-level public officials or senior officers of state-owned entities.

Hybrid company. Limited by a guarantee (similar to a foundation) but issues shares like a company.

International Business Corporation (IBC). This corporate vehicle, sometimes called an exempt company, is the primary corporate form employed by nonresidents in offshore financial centers. An IBC has the features of a corporation, but it is not permitted to conduct business within the incorporating jurisdiction and is generally exempt from local income taxes. In most jurisdictions, an IBC is not permitted to engage in banking, insurance, and other financial services.

Know your customer. The due diligence and bank regulation that financial institutions and other regulated entities must perform to identify their clients and ascertain relevant information (including source and destination of the funds) pertinent to doing financial business with them.[4]

Legal arrangements. Express trusts or other similar legal arrangements.[5]

Legal persons. Bodies corporate, foundations, *anstalts*, partnerships, or associations, or any similar bodies that can establish a permanent customer relationship with a financial institution or otherwise own property.[6]

Letters rogatory. A formal request from a court to a foreign court for some type of judicial assistance. It permits formal communication between the judiciary, a prosecutor, or law enforcement official of one jurisdiction, and his or her counterpart in another jurisdiction. A particular form of mutual legal assistance.[7]

Limited liability company (LLC). This is a business entity that provides limited liability to its owners (known as members). An LLC may be managed either by members or by one or more separate managers engaged by the LLC under the terms contained within its articles of organization.

---

3. Financial Action Task Force (FATF), "Guidance on the Risk-Based approach to Combating Money Laundering and Terrorist Financing: High Level Principles and Procedures" (June 2007), available at http:www.fatf-gafi.org/dataoecd/43/46/3896-576.pdf; and FATF, "Report on Money Laundering Typologies, 2000–2001" (February 2001), available at http://www.fatf-gafi.org/dataoecd/29/36/34038090.pdf.
4. Stolen Asset Recovery (StAR) Initiative, *Asset Recovery Handbook: A Guide for Practitioners* (Washington, DC: International Bank for Reconstruction and Development/World Bank, 2011), p. 195.
5. FATF, "Glossary to the 40 Recommendations," available at http://www.fatf-gafi.org/glossary/0,3414,en_32250379_32236930_35433764_1_1_1_1,00.html.
6. FATF, "Glossary to the 40 Recommendations," available at http://www.fatf-gafi.org/glossary/0,3414,en_32250379_32236930_35433764_1_1_1_1,00.html.
7. StAR Initiative, *Asset Recovery Handbook: A Guide for Practitioners* (Washington, DC: International Bank for Reconstruction and Development/World Bank, 2011), p. 251.

Mutual legal assistance (MLA). The process by which jurisdictions seek and provide assistance in gathering information, intelligence, and evidence for investigations; in implementing provisional measures; and in enforcing foreign orders and judgments.[8]

Partnership. A partnership is an association or two or more individuals or entities formed for the purpose of carrying out business activity. In contrast to corporations, traditional partnerships are entities in which at least one (in the case of limited partnerships) or all (in the case of general partnerships) of the partners have unlimited liability for the obligations of the partnership. In a limited partnership, the limited partners enjoy limited liability, provided that they do not participate actively in management decisions or bind the partnership.

Politically Exposed Persons (PEPs). "Individuals who are, or have been, entrusted with prominent public functions, their family members, and close associates."[9]

Trust. Also referred to as an "express trust,"[10] this corporate vehicle provides for the separation of legal ownership from beneficial ownership. It is an arrangement whereby property (including real, tangible, and intangible) is managed by one person for the benefit of others. A trust is created by one or more settlors who entrust property to the trustee or trustees. The trustees hold legal title to the trust property but are obliged to hold the property for the benefit of the beneficiaries (usually specified by the settlers who hold what is termed equitable title). The trustees owe a fiduciary duty to the beneficiaries, who are the beneficial owners of the trust property.

Trust and Company Service Providers (TCSPs). Any person or business that provides any of the following services to third parties: acting as a formation agent of legal persons; acting as (or arranging for another person to act as) a director or secretary of a company, a partner of a partnership, or a similar position in relation to other legal persons; providing a registered office, business address or accommodation, or correspondence or administrative address for a company, a partnership, or any other legal person or arrangements; acting as (or arranging for another person to act as) a trustee of an express trust; or acting as (or arranging for another person to act as) a nominee shareholder for another person.

---

8. StAR Initiative, *Asset Recovery Handbook: A Guide for Practitioners* (Washington, DC: International Bank for Reconstruction and Development/World Bank, 2011), p. 251.

9. Theodore S. Greenberg, Larissa Gray, Delphine Schantz, Carolin Gardner, and Michael Lathem, *Politically Exposed Persons: Preventive Measures for the Banking Sector* (Washington, DC: World Bank, 2010), p. 3, available at http://www.worldbank.org/star; and StAR Initiative, *Asset Recovery Handbook: A Guide for Practitioners* (Washington, DC: International Bank for Reconstruction and Development/World Bank, 2011), p. 251.

10. For more detailed discussion of trusts, please see appendix C of this report. See also the definition of "Express Trust," in "FATF Recommendations, Glossary: FATF Methodology," available at http://www.fatf-gafi.org/glossary/0,3414,en_32250379_32236920_34295666_1_1_1_1,00.html (accessed August 13, 2011).

Lightning Source UK Ltd.
Milton Keynes UK
UKOW020256100312

188681UK00001B/21/P